"What can I say? Ellie Kay's the Coupon Queen of the world! Actually, Ellie's ministry is one of the great services to families across our nation. I applaud her work in helping all of us be better stewards."

Dennis Rainey—Executive Director, Family Life

"Reading Ellie's book is like sitting down with a bright, hilarious friend over gourmet coffee and dark chocolate (purchased at bargain prices, of course). Her stories—both poignant and humorous—have an uncanny way of making concepts like 'budgeting' and 'saving' seem doable and fun."

Becky Freeman—Author & Speaker

"Ellie Kay has done it again! As she helps people save so they can share, she underscores Christ's teaching: 'It is more blessed to give than to receive.'"

James Robison—President, LIFE Outreach International

"They say money talks—and most of the time it just says goodbye! Want to know how to get your money to speak a different language? Get a copy of *How to Save Money Every Day* and put it into practice."

Dr. Karen J. Hayter—Producer, Family Net Television

"Ellie Kay's latest, *How to Save Money Every Day,* is just like her—practical, informative, and downright fun!"

Sandra P. Aldrich—Author & President/CEO, Bold Words

"With real-life stories, practical how-tos, and state-of-the-art shopping tips, Ellie Kay will have you laughing one minute and implementing her money-saving tips the next."

Carol Kent—Author & President, Speak Up Speaker Services

Books by Ellie Kay

How to Save Money Every Day

Shop, Save, and Share

HOW TO $ave Money Every Day

ELLIE KAY

BETHANY HOUSE
Minneapolis, Minnesota

Published by Bethany House Publishers
A Ministry of Bethany Fellowship International
11400 Hampshire Avenue South
Bloomington, Minnesota 55438
www.bethanyhouse.com

Printed in the United States of America by
Bethany Press International, Bloomington, Minnesota 55438

Library of Congress Cataloging-in-Publication Data

Kay, Ellie.
    How to save money every day : amaze your friends without embarrassing your family / by Ellie Kay.
        p. cm.
    ISBN 0-7642-2446-8 (pbk.)
    1. Consumer education. 2. Shopping. 3. Saving and investment. I. Title.
TX335 .K38697 2001
640'.73—dc21
                                                                    00-011426

This book is dedicated to Becky Freeman,

my mentor and friend. Thank you for your

selfless devotion to your friends—I want to be

just like you when I grow up!

And to the memory of my abuelita,

Basilisa Macias Gilabert.

ELLIE KAY is founder and author of *Shop, Save, and Share* Seminars and a gifted speaker and writer. She is a graduate of Colorado Christian University with a degree in management of human resources. She and her husband, Bob, a Stealth fighter pilot with the U.S. Air Force, have five children and make their home in New Mexico.

Ellie's first book, *Shop, Save, and Share,* presents a streamlined program to help families save hundreds of dollars a month on groceries and household supplies—and have an abundance to share with people in need. Filled with her signature humor and real-life stories, it contains easy-to-apply principles that allow most households to lower their food budgets 50 to 85 percent under national norms.

A wise and witty communicator, Ellie has appeared on over three hundred radio stations and numerous national TV shows.

If you wish to contact Ellie Kay for speaking engagements or to conduct a seminar, she can be reached at:

Ellie Kay
P.O. Box 202
Alamogordo, NM 88310
e-mail: ellie@elliekay.com
Web site: *www.elliekay.com*

Acknowledgments

I'd like to thank the people who have made this book possible. While there are scores of people who have enriched my life, I'd like to reserve this section for those who helped make this book a reality.

I'd like to thank God, who takes the simple things of this world and uses them to confound the wise. I'm simply amazed by His plans. Next, I'd like to thank my Beloved, the love-o'-my-life, the keeper-of-children-so-I-can-write-this-book-even-though-I-know-it-isn't-your-forte kind of a guy. You may miss exits on the highway, but you never miss an opportunity to encourage your ditzy wife. This book would not be possible without your support (and your taking our five children out of the house to go to McDonald's, swimming, Putt-Putt, and the park).

If we didn't have such pliable, great children, I couldn't write either. So I thank our oldest, Daniel, for the times he made dinner, cleaned the kitchen, and baby-sat his siblings—you're one special guy. I cherish Philip for his constant prayers and sensitivity when I just needed a hug—you are a treasure. I am so grateful to Bethany for allowing me to use the sometimes embarrassing stories from her little-girl years and for rubbing my shoulders when I'm tense. No wonder you're called our bunny, hopping from heart to heart. Thanks to Jonathan for faithfully mentioning his mama during prayer request time in Mrs. Guiterrez's first grade class—you're my precious buddy. Finally, I thank little Joshua, who brings levity to life and provides me with little-boy hugs and great one-liners like "I may *wike* my friend, Michele, but I *wuv* you, Mama."

I also owe a debt of gratitude to my mentor and friend, Becky Freeman, for her continual encouragement and for looking out for the best interests of her protégée. Thanks for putting me in touch with Chip MacGregor of Alive Communications. Thanks to Chip for helping me develop as an author and for keeping me laughing on a regular basis. I'm going to make you a split pea tie for all your trouble.

I want to thank Steve Laube, senior editor, for being my coach and cheerleader. And to the rest of my publishing family at Bethany House Publishers, especially Jeanne Mikkelson and Melissa Smith, I'm glad we share the common vision of sharing with others both home and abroad. Thanks also go to Rachel St. John-Gilbert for her free-lance editing expertise and for her love of pink boas and leopard-skin skirts. (This story is for another book and another time.) Also to Julie Klassen and Jeff Braun for adding so much to this project.

Thanks also to the "Fabulous Fifty" members of my prayer team and to the people who contributed their stories and tips for this book, especially my mom, Paquita Rawleigh, for the story of the four-year-old future Coupon Queen.

Last, but not least, I'd like to thank my Royal Court of Coupon Princesses (in alphabetical order): Madeline Brazell, Suzanne Chandler, Deb Flores, Cindy Kreiner, Jessica Nichols, Brenda Taylor, and Wendy Wendler. You are helping to bring the message of saving and sharing to the world.

To the readers of *Shop, Save, and Share*, I'd like to thank you for your scores of letters, e-mail messages, and stories of hope and encouragement.

And to *you*, thank you for buying this book. May God bless you as you seek to honor Him through saving money every day and sharing your newfound abundance with others.

Contents

Foreword

It is with great pleasure and honor that I (aka Ellie's husband) am writing this foreword. Basically, I'm doing it for two reasons: to let you know that everything in this book is true (you'll see what I mean when you read the first chapter; I've actually seen Ellie do this stuff) and because…well…I asked Ellie if I could.

Ellie was mulling over who would write the foreword for this labor of love (trust me on this one). Seeing an opportunity to save big bucks on phone calls and time on the Internet, I suggested that I could offer my services in exchange for home-cooked meals. So here I am…and I gotta tell you that writing doesn't come easy for me. I leave that to my Beloved, who is quite gifted, as you have already seen if you read *Shop, Save, and Share* or are about to discover with this gem. But enough drivel about me. (By the way…how do you know that a date with a fighter pilot is half over? He says: "Enough about flying, let's talk about me.")

Seriously, folks, please understand that Almighty God's grace and abundance are clearly at work within these pages. It has been through His divine intervention that Ellie has put this book together. She has sought His guidance every step of the way, not only with her writing, but with how she lives her life and how she encourages us to live ours as a family. These tips and techniques work if you're willing to let them. And it doesn't matter how much money your family takes in every month. The Lord has clearly shown us that the more we make, the more we can give to His kingdom and to further His work. It seems that He shows us every day how we can be happy and grateful with what we have, save as much as possible through commonsense living, and give to others.

So what's my point? You can not only save money every day, but you can have fun doing it and get the inexplicable satisfaction of knowing that you're making a difference in the lives of others as well. Please keep that in mind as you read. I know you'll enjoy the true stories, and I believe that you'll see your finances take a significant turn for the better as you follow Ellie's tips. She tells me that the best way to read this is with coffee and chocolate, so grab some and get ready to have some fun. May the Lord bless you as you seek to honor Him and bless others.

—Bob Kay

Introduction

Welcome to my wacky, wonderful world of saving money every day! If you missed my debut book, *Shop, Save, and Share*, then I should probably warn you about me. If you can handle a lady who finds herself at the podium of a major conference and looks down to realize she has her pants on backward, then I'm your gal.

My friends like to say that I'm "distracted" by the fact that I have five active school-aged children. They say that I'm preoccupied because I often play the single-mom role due to the fact that my husband's military career sends him on the road quite a bit. But they're just being nice. I'm a real ditz at times. I admit it. Regrettably, these half-witticisms aren't just a shtick that makes for a good radio interview. No, they aren't just fodder for writing. For me, this is a way of life. What my friends call "distracted," I prefer to call "multitasking."

I will forget the name of the town we lived in last year (we've lived in eleven places in the last thirteen years), but I can remember the price of every item in my grocery cart. At times, I can't even remember how old I am or how many years I've been married. I walk into a room and forget why I'm there, so I have to walk into the room again to remember.

Despite my obvious shortcomings, God has graciously decided to take those deficiencies in my life and do some fairly incredible things. When it comes to saving money, I am an idiot savant, in that my calculator-like brain can find the cheapest way to do or have just about anything. That is what this book is about—how you, too, can learn to save money every day.

Yet I don't believe that we should save money just so our family can live better or have more stuff. I truly feel my call in life is to show people how to save in one area so they can share more freely in other areas. Near the end of this book, in chapter 19, you'll read some inspiring true-life stories of people who have been able to do this very thing.

Sharing from our material abundance, whether it's groceries or money, unlocks a new world of opportunity and personal growth. There is no substitute for the feeling of meeting a specific need in an individual life. This sharing can be as simple as giving the ingredients for a cake to the family that needs to make a cake and can't afford it. Or it can be as far-reaching as feeding a family in Asia who will live because you give.

As you read, remember that God loves to use the simple things of this world to confound the wise. I also believe that God uses the simple *people* in this world, and it doesn't get much simpler than a woman like me.

One day I was sitting at a luncheon table with a group of ladies who were talking about one lady's profession. I heard only snippets of the chit-chat and then commented, "Oh, so you're a gynecologist?"

"No," replied the lady sitting next to me, as the rest of the ladies giggled, "I said I'm an *audiologist*."

If you can learn from a woman like that, then I'm your gal indeed.

How to Save Money at Home

CHAPTER ONE

A Day in the Life of a Savings Queen

Savings from Sunrise to Sunset

At 5:50 A.M. the clock radio ($3 at a yard sale) alarm sounds. The Savings Queen jumps out of bed and goes to the desk (won on *The Price Is Right*), where her clothing lies. She pulls on her warm-up suit (free, from a friend). She wakes her running partner, her oldest son (six-and-a-half hours of active labor), to hit the streets for their four-mile loop.

After pulling on her running shoes (half-price sale plus 20 percent off for opening a new charge card—which she later canceled), she and her son enjoy their run in the cool Southwest morning (free, courtesy of the Creator). After her workout, she takes a quick shower, washes her hair, and shaves her legs (soap, razor blades, shampoo, and conditioner all free with coupons).

She then makes her own special blend of gourmet coffee (wholesale—see *www.elliekay.com* for order form), because life is too short to drink bad coffee. She sets the table for breakfast as her son Jonathan comes into the room with a quick "Morning, Mama."

As he sits at the table, he picks up a box. "We only have six kinds of cereal this morning? Can I open a new box from the fifty boxes that are in the storage closet?"

The Savings Queen answers, "No, Jonathan, six boxes are more than enough. Remember Kabuli Alezo in Zaire? He'd be thrilled to choose from six boxes of cereal" (9¢ per box with coupons combined with sales).

She packs the five children's lunches with apples (from their tree), homemade chocolate chip cookies (49¢/dozen), meat and cheese sandwiches (bologna 49¢, cheese 19¢ with store card and double coupons) on homemade whole wheat bread (39¢/loaf).

Packing the lunch bags in the kids' backpacks (75 percent off at Staples' after-season clearance), she rushes them out the door and into the Suburban (purchased when two years old at 15 percent above wholesale).

"Do you have your jacket, Daniel?" ($6 at a yard sale).

Daniel shrugs, "No, but I have on my sweatshirt" ($5.50 at a thrift store, with the tags still on it).

"That will do, Daniel. Now, children, remember that as soon as you finish your homework this afternoon we're going out to eat dinner."

The car fills with screams of "Yea!" and "All right!"

"Where are we going?" asks Philip as he holds his violin ($12/month).

The Queen adjusts her crown a bit. "Well, today is Tuesday; what does that tell you?"

"Denny's!" sings the kids' chorus.

The Queen turns the corner and slows the car. "That's right. Today children eat free with two kid's meals per adult entrée. Because I have a coupon for 'buy one adult meal/get one free' and because they will accept both offers together, we'll feed our family of seven for $6 plus a $4 tip!"

The children kiss their mom (priceless) and bound out of the car to start their day at Community Christian School (first child—full price, second child—20 percent off, third child—30 percent off, children four and five—free). On the way home, Mom stops to fill up the car with gas

(15 percent less for cash plus $2 off eight gallons with a coupon) and grabs a quick coffee (refill mug free with an 8-gallon gas purchase).

She stops by the bookstore to grab a couple of videos for family night (two free children's videos daily) and buys a birthday gift for her friend Jessica (note cards at half off). She gets a refill of hazelnut coffee (25¢ donation to a literacy fund) and jumps into the car. She stops by the library to research some money-saving Internet sites for her upcoming book (free computer use) and downloads a "Web bucks" sheet for use at the grocery store (15¢ per printed page).

At the store, our Savings Queen does her usual shopping by buying a cart full of groceries ($230 before coupons) for $75 (20 bags of groceries). Running by for her free oil change (certificate from volunteer-of-the-month award), she writes thank-you notes (25¢ box at a rummage sale) in the waiting room of the service center and mails them (free postage from an Internet site).

At home, she sorts the items she purchased and gathers three bags of groceries for a family in the church that is out of work ($45 non-cash charitable donation on income tax). She vacuums with her Kirby (free from Grandma, rebuilt by Kirby's guarantee for $75) and washes clothes (50 pounds of soap for $9 at the wholesale club).

Making a quick change into a professional suit ($25 wash-and-wear), she adds her gold tone earrings, gold collar necklace with slide, and a lovely gold tone watch (all free from hosting a Premiere jewelry party for her girlfriend Brenda). On her way to the luncheon at which she's speaking (free lunch for speaker—plus honorarium), she stops by the florist to pick up her free floral bouquet (certificate earned by a son for a Mother's Day writing contest) for her desk at home.

Back at home she has a package waiting of free puzzles, toy cars, and T-shirts that she received from refunding (save for Christmas stocking stuffers). As she takes the package into the house (2,600-square-foot Southwestern style complete with hot tub—acquired through a VA loan assumption), her eyes fall on the lovely G. Harvey print in the formal den (free with donation to *Focus on the Family*). She thanks God for her many blessings and changes into a blue-jean romper (free from a friend who lost weight).

Back in the kitchen, she makes eight loaves of pumpkin bread in coffee cans to distribute as gifts to her Webmaster (does Web page for cost), her newspaper distributor (gives her rejected coupons), and letter carrier (lets her know when the post office has their food drive, so she can donate food). Then, she keeps one loaf for her kids' afternoon snack and freezes the other four to have on hand for last-minute hospitality and thank-you gifts (38¢ each).

She answers the phone (bought on sale using a credit card to earn bonus points) and speaks with her Beloved husband (does home repairs,

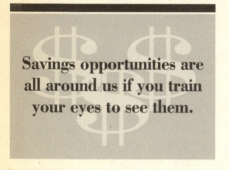

Savings opportunities are all around us if you train your eyes to see them.

bathes the children, and mops the kitchen floor—he works for food). Her Beloved informs her that they will have unexpected company arriving in town tomorrow night for dinner. Gracious as ever, the Savings Queen accepts the challenge with a nod of her crown (vintage-costume-jewelry-fashioned crown—retail $300, she paid $85). As she bids farewell to her Beloved, she gets a call on her business line for a live radio interview (free advertising for her books) and talks for an hour.

By now, it is late in the afternoon, but she has thirty minutes before she needs to pick up the children. For some strange reason, she feels a bit tired after her busy day. She sits down on her newly reupholstered couch (original fabric $38/yard, bought for $3/yard at a wholesaler) and rests with a book by her favorite author, Becky Freeman (sends Ellie a courtesy copy from the publisher for plugging the new book).

After picking up the children and getting homework done, Papa comes home (free flight suits courtesy of Uncle Sam) to take the family to Denny's. After dinner, back at home, Bob bathes the children (see above—hey, he works for food no matter who makes it), they all brush teeth (free toothpaste from a store coupon combined with a manufacturer's coupon, free toothbrushes from the dentist). The Kays put the kids to bed and say their prayers (always yields great dividends).

After she mops the kitchen floor (29¢ floor cleaner), she changes into her silk nightshirt and wrapper (a guilt gift from Bob when he went to flight training school in Florida for two months and left her in New York with 100 inches of snow). After a lengthy catch-up conversation with her Beloved, she reads her Bible (eternal value) and drops into bed to rest up for another day of savings.

Believe it or not, everything in the above story is true. It is amazing how anyone can save money every day. Savings opportunities are all around us if you train your eyes to see them.

After you read this book, you will be able to save money in all these different ways and many more.

✓ Know how to combine savings opportunities—like combining a store coupon with a manufacturer's coupon, or a new-credit discount with a half-price sale.
✓ Learn how to navigate your way around the World Wide Web to find some great opportunities to save money.
✓ Safeguard your primary e-mail account from junk mail while you sign up for freebies on the Internet.
✓ Distinguish the difference between a genuine savings opportunity and a pseudo savings gimmick.
✓ Begin a plan to pay down your mortgage and get out from under the load of consumer debt.
✓ Eat well and without deprivation while still sharing your abundance with others.

"You spend a billion here, you spend a billion there. Sooner or later it adds up to real money."

—SENATOR EVERETT DIRKSON

†

Don't Sweat the Big Stuff

Saving Big on Furniture and Appliances

It's not every day that you get to meet a legend—a real hero. Now Bob would say, "I live with a legend," but that's another story…. I *will* say that life as a fighter pilot's wife is never boring. Occasionally, we get to meet other fighter pilots who flew in World War II, Korea, or Vietnam. We can sit for hours and listen to their war stories. Who would have thought that having one of these heroes in our home for dinner one evening would give *me* another "war story" to tell?

When Bethany was four, Philip was six, Daniel was eight, and Jonathan and Joshua were babies, we had the honor of hosting a celebrity author/photographer in our home. Fighter pilot Brian was known in Air Force and flying circles for his books on the Thunderbirds and the SR-71. He's a true warrior who was badly burned when his jet was shot down in Vietnam. In fact, he was told that he would never walk again. Well, not only did he learn to walk—he got back on flying status! Brian went on to become the A-10 West Coast demo pilot and then fly the SR-71, making the finals to the Thunderbirds in the process.

Eventually, Brian began giving motivational speeches as a form of personal therapy after the war and his accident. In talking about his experience, he found healing and eventually became a much-in-demand public speaker. On a volunteer basis, Brian has shared his story with scores of boys' clubs, scouting organizations, and other children's groups.

My husband, Bob, had the privilege of being in on an aerial photo shoot as a featured AT-38 pilot for a book Brian was writing on fighter pilots. After the shoot, Bob invited this heroic man over for dinner. Brian has lived with severe facial scars for the past twenty years and was used to children's natural reactions. Nonetheless, we decided it would be a good idea to brief the children before he arrived.

We gathered the children in the living room. I took Bethany in my lap and told her, "Papa's friend has an owie on his face from being burned when his jet was shot down." Turning to the older boys, I continued, "He got burned while serving his country in Vietnam; he's a real hero—one who put service before self. You don't need to stare at his scars or ask him a bunch of questions; that would not be polite."

We were immediately besieged with questions like "Who shot him down?" and "Can we look at him when we talk to him?" We answered the children's questions and thought we were well prepared for Brian's arrival. We were wrong.

The doorbell rang. Bethany allowed Brian exactly two steps into the house before she announced in a characteristically loud voice, "I know why your face looks like that. It's because you got burned in an airplane." Brian, saint that he is, calmly smiled down at our four-year-old girl as Bob and I quickly tried to think of something to say to cover the embarrassment.

Unfortunately, *Philip* was the one who came to our rescue. "*Bethany!*" he sternly chastised his sister in front of all of us, "Papa told you *not* to talk about the man's face in front of him!" Then our six-year-old turned to Bob and exclaimed, "Papa! Bethany's talking about the hero's face!"

Have you ever walked in the presence of greatness? Do you know how to recognize a genuine hero? Have you ever seen grace in action?

Kenneth O. Gangel said in *Thus Spake Qoheleth,* "Success…is a matter of adjusting one's efforts to overcome obstacles and one's abilities to give the service needed by others." That is exactly what Brian did. In the middle of our profound embarrassment, we saw the characteristic that made this man a genuine hero. He adjusted his efforts to give us the service of grace by smiling and simply asking, "What's for dinner? I'm starved!"

We spent the rest of the evening listening to a man who overcame many obstacles to serve God and country. For one evening, we sat at the feet of a legend.

There's nothing quite like looking at the life of someone who's endured hardship, pain, and sacrifice to realize how good we have it. I mean, we may not like our nose, our job, or our house, but at least we have these things.

Many of us in the world today have a great need to get back to the basics—back to the things that matter most. This basic need explains the amazing success of the book *Don't Sweat the Small Stuff—And It's All Small Stuff,* by Richard Carlson. In the larger scheme of life, possessions are very much "small stuff." Yet money and our stewardship of money can quickly become "big stuff" if we are not vigilant in our efforts to protect our family's assets. One area where it's really easy to blow a lot of money before you realize it is in the area of major furniture and appliance purchases.

We don't have to sweat the small stuff—or the big stuff, for that matter—if we prepare in advance. Here are some ways to prepare for those high-priced purchases.

FURNITURE

In my book *Shop, Save, and Share,* I gave some great tips on how to buy both new and used furniture. Those tips are still very valuable advice and you may want to refer to them before making any major furniture purchase, but in this section we're going to explore a few new areas.

Taking Inventory

There are three questions that you need to ask yourself when you are considering major purchases:

✓ "Do I need it?"
✓ "Can I afford it?"
✓ "How am I going to pay for it?"

It's a good idea to write down your dream list and then take it to a furniture store. The "sticker shock," or the price of the furniture you just can't live without, may force you to reassess your furniture needs.

Even if your fantasy furniture is marked down 50 percent or more, if you have to finance it, you may be forced to reconsider. You should never buy furniture on credit without taking a look at the total price you'll end up paying for the purchase. The "steal" of a love seat that costs only $500 will end up costing you an amazing $1,200 after several years on a low-payment, high-interest-rate schedule. If you're buying several pieces of furniture, you could accumulate $10,000 in credit card debt for furniture alone. By making only the minimum payment on that loan, at 18 to 22 percent interest, it will take you more than 33 years and $26,000 to pay it off! Count the cost before you buy to avoid the endless cycle of debt.

All right, you've assessed the amount of cash you have available and the maximum amount you can pay for the furniture you need. Now what?

Exploring the Internet

Before you explore the Internet, be sure to read the tips and warnings in chapter 13. In general, though, first visit your local furniture store, sit on real furniture in the showroom, and write down the model and brand name of the furniture you like. Now you're set up to do some profitable searches on the Internet. Often the brochures offered at the furniture store will have a Web site for the manufacturer. If they don't, you can either use a search engine to find the Web address or try typing *www.(manufacturer's name).com*. For example, *www.broyhillfurniture.com*. Once you have located the manufacturer's site, look for an outlet store link. Search for the price (including shipping and handling), availability, and delivery time of the furniture you want. Then print out those prices and take them back to your local store to give them an opportunity to match the competition's price.

Another option is to explore the site and request a list of all the distributors of the brand name furniture in a 100-mile radius. Printing the price list and making a few calls to the stores in your area could save you as much as 50 percent on your choices. Be sure to show your sales resistance (see chapter 9) when you call the local stores for a price check, and don't forget to ask them if they can beat the deal you have by throwing in free delivery, a free fabric guard treatment, or any other freebie. So often these items are yours for the asking.

Furniture Craftsmen

It may surprise you to find out that *some* craftsmen can build a custom-made dining room set for less than the best sale price of a comparable quality set at a traditional store. (We're talking quality furniture here—not sale items from the local Stuff Mart.) It certainly can't hurt to inquire of the craftsmen in your area.

When we lived in Columbus, Mississippi, we traded our "early garage sale" motif for five thousand pounds of custom-made primitive country furniture. The furniture we bought has that "distressed" look typical of the style, and it moves well (we've already moved it three times in five years!). Amazingly, because we bought directly from the manufacturer (a dear old man who just loved to make furniture), we paid 30 percent less than *wholesale*! The fact that it was my dream furniture made the bargain all the sweeter.

To locate a craftsman in your area, call the local lumberyard, antique store, or furniture repair shop for recommendations. Or look in the Yellow Pages under Furniture Designers and Custom Builders.

Don't waste their time or yours when you call for an estimate. Decide the following before you call: (1) the style of furniture and how many pieces, (2) the kind and quality of wood, (3) whether you want paint, varnish, or bare wood, (4) the fabric design and/or pattern, and (5) your price range. Be flexible in exploring "wants" versus "needs" in the pieces you would like to order. Ask the right questions, such as:

"Can I see samples of your work and references?"

"Do you guarantee the pieces?"

"What is the estimated delivery time on the work?"

"If I order several rooms' worth of furniture, what percentage discount could you give me?"

"How long have you been building furniture?"

You may even consider asking, "Is there a less expensive style or way to build this piece that will make it more affordable for our family?"

A reputable craftsman will not be offended by these practical questions and should be willing to stand behind his or her work. The end result could be lovely, custom-made furniture that can be passed on to the next generation.

Model Homes

This is a creative approach that works best in larger towns or cities that are experiencing a boom in business for new homes. Call the local builders, especially those that have model homes, and ask the design manager how they liquidate the furniture in their model homes when they've sold the last home in the tract.

Rather than going to the expense of using a liquidation firm to rid themselves of this excess, they are often willing to sell to individuals. Granted, it would be easier to sell the contents to a wholesaler, but oftentimes you can pick up some beautiful pieces if your timing is right. You will need to pay cash or check (versus credit) for these items, so be prepared before you make an offer.

Keep in mind that the furniture in model homes is usually much smaller than the furniture you normally buy. Designers will place a double bed in the master bedroom rather than a queen in order to create the appearance of more space. The daybeds in these homes will usually accommodate a child rather than an adult, and the dining room sets may only have two to four chairs. Nonetheless, while these pieces are officially "used," they have only been used for demonstration and have not experienced the usual wear and tear of most furniture.

This is also a good way to pick up some appliances, although the color and size of those appliances will be limited.

Vintage Furniture

This is furniture built several decades ago that isn't old enough to qualify as antique. These pieces make for remarkable values because the craftsmanship is often superior to furniture built today. If you adopt the mind-set of a visionary when you go to an estate sale, garage sale, or secondhand furniture store, you could find some lasting values. Before you buy, turn the item over and look at the joints to see if they're in solid shape.

If you're looking for a couch, research in advance the cost of fabric and labor for reupholstering. For example, we found fabric at an outlet store for only $3/yard. The same fabric at the furniture store was $38/yard. We also knew in advance how much it would cost for labor to reupholster our couch and love seat. In the end, we saved 40 percent for the style of our choice using this approach. You can even find some great upholstery fabric values on the Internet by searching the manufacturer as outlined at the beginning of this section. The advantage of this kind of furniture is that you have quality for less that will last.

APPLIANCES

Secondhand Stores, Garage Sales, and Classifieds

The virtues and how-to's of finding great appliances at secondhand stores, garage sales, and through the newspaper were well covered in *Shop, Save, and Share*. I will say that if you're serious about buying appliances, and you don't already own this book, then check it out from the library. After twelve thousand loads of laundry, we *still* have the Maytag washer and dryer we bought used twelve years ago. We've only replaced a timing chain and another part damaged in a move—but the five hundred dollars we invested in them was money well spent.

Store Displays

Appliances that are removed from the box and used as store displays usually sell at discounted rates. By buying a store display and taking advantage of the reduced price and/or a rebate, you can save major dollars. The guarantee is usually the same as any other new appliance in a box. Call around to your local dealers and ask for these values.

Manufacturer's Extended Warranty

Don't waste precious dollars on these extended warranties; instead, use a credit card that will automatically double the manufacturer's warranty and then pay off the balance the next month. Some gold cards offer this double warranty option, so call your credit card company to make sure your card has this benefit.

Search the Internet

Refer to chapter 13 before buying anything on the Internet. Also, the techniques described in the "Exploring the Internet" section on page 26 work for appliances as well as furniture. Remember that shipping and handling add up on larger appliances. Still, this method is highly effective in getting a better price from your local dealer.

Bulletin Boards

A rather unconventional, yet highly effective way to find serviceable merchandise is to advertise what you need on a bulletin board—or check out the posted items to find out what is available. There are boards like these in grocery stores, churches, military family support centers, break rooms in places of employment, libraries, and many other places. Sometimes the perfect provision can be found by spending a few minutes looking in the local newspaper or any other public posting. Happy shopping!

"Sometimes it's the smallest things that can make the biggest difference."

—MICHAEL SHINABERY,
ALAMOGORDO DAILY NEWS,
AS QUOTED IN AN INTERVIEW
WITH THE COUPON QUEEN

CHAPTER THREE

Blown Away

Lengthening the Life of Cars, Clothing, and Careers

About six months after the release of my first book, it was time for another military move—our eleventh in thirteen years. We knew Bob was going to fly the snazziest jet on the block—the F-117A "Nighthawk" Stealth Fighter. We were excited for this opportunity for him, and we looked forward to seeing our old friends in New Mexico.

One Sunday a few weeks before the move, I opened the Sunday paper to search for the coupon inserts and found a startling headline: "Stealth Shot Down in Kosovo." The photo showed a charred heap of twisted metal—all that remained of the jet my husband was to fly.

I took the paper to Bob, stuffed it under his nose, and asked, "Is this supposed to inspire confidence? I thought they couldn't see you in a Stealth."

Bob shrugged his shoulders. "Well, the pilot was all right."

It just goes to show that even a fifty-five million dollar jet can have a bad day. As a matter of fact, when Bob went on to train in that weapon system, he was landing the jet one day and the parachute came out just fine, when suddenly a gust of wind wrapped the chute around the jet—a little weather accident that caused almost forty-five thousand dollars worth of damage.

Whether we fly jets, drive cars, or just live in a house full of kids, spills, scrapes, and stains happen. I think the Kays have had more than their fair share of these events. Even though I have hundreds of examples of Kay Family Mishaps, let me share just a couple.

Ever since lipstick was invented in Cleopatra's time, there have been little King Tuts and princesses who insist on exploring the various uses of makeup. When Bethany was 18 months old, I found her in front of my bathroom mirror, sitting on the sink, experimenting with my red lipstick. She'd taken a new tube and smeared it all over her entire face. Her cheeks, forehead, nose, and chin were covered with big globs of lipstick. When I discovered her, she was trying to wipe it off her face—with my white cashmere sweater!

> **Remove stains as quickly as possible, because once a stain gets through a wash and dry cycle, it's almost impossible to remove.**

Then there was the time I took the five children on a homeschool field trip to the donut factory. Joshua was a newborn, sleeping in the stroller. Jonathan was strapped on my back in a pack, and the other three children were within arm's reach. Jonathan fussed and grumped because he wanted to be in on the action on the floor, but he soon quieted down. About thirty minutes into the tour, I discovered the reason Jonathan was so quiet. His perch on my back was just the right height to have his pick of chocolate-filled donuts on the cooling rack. He'd grabbed several and stuffed them in his lap and then ate them as needed. He was such a thoughtful baby that he decided to share (it runs in the family). He found a fellow toddler who was also perched on his mother's backpack, and soon the two were exchanging donuts (behind their moms' backs). By the time I felt something wet and sticky on my neck, it was too late. Both moms ended up with chocolate-covered hair—and happy, but *very* hyperactive toddlers.

LITTLE TIPS FOR BIG SAVINGS

You can save hundreds of dollars each year by lengthening the life of clothing, cars—even careers, with the following tips. Another benefit is that when you're on your way to that important interview and the baby smears mustard on your suit, your home remedy could save the day. You save your jacket *and* your career—it's a two-for-one special!

Clothing and Other Fabrics

Here are some inexpensive tips to remove the most common stains. Be sure to test them first on a hidden area of the fabric. Remove stains as quickly as possible, because once a stain gets through a wash and dry cycle, it's almost impossible to remove.

✓ **Antiperspirant:** Mix 1 tablespoon of baking soda with 2 tablespoons of vinegar and soak a paper towel in the solution. Blot the stained area with the paper towel. Wash in the hottest temperature safe for the garment.

✓ **Ball-point pen ink:** Spray with hair spray and blot with a clean cloth. Nail polish remover (if safe for the fabric) and prewash sprays will work on some ink stains.

✓ **Blood:** The key is to get it while it's fresh. Rinse well with cold water, then use liquid detergent. Or dampen the stain and sprinkle with unflavored meat tenderizer. Or soak it in lukewarm ammonia water (3 tablespoons per gallon) and rinse.

✓ **Candle wax or crayon:** Scrape off as much as possible. Place a paper towel both under and on top of the stain and iron it on a low to medium setting. Go over any remaining stain with liquid detergent and water, then rinse and wash as usual.

✓ **Catsup:** Blot as much as possible. Do not rub, because rubbing solidifies the stain. Rinse or soak in cold water, spray with prewash, and wash as usual.

✓ **Chewing gum:** Rub with ice, then scrape off. Or put the garment in the freezer to harden the gum and then scrape it off. Dab with prewash and wash as usual.

✓ **Chocolate:** Use prewash or ammonia (3 tablespoons per gallon). Work well into the fabric and let it set. Rinse with cold water. (I usually eat a little more chocolate while I wait—it helps soothe my nerves as I wonder if I've ruined yet another jacket with this chocolate habit of mine.)

✓ **Coffee:** Sponge or soak in cold water as soon as possible. Use regular bleach or nonchlorine bleach, depending on the fabric, and wash in the hottest water possible for the fabric. (I like to make another cup of coffee and have it along with my chocolate while the garment is in the washer…hey, why cry over spilt coffee?)

✓ **Glue:** Loosen by saturating with a cloth soaked in white vinegar.

✓ **Grass:** Bleach according to fabric directions. Or presoak in hydrogen peroxide and launder as usual.

✓ **Grease:** Use powder or chalk to absorb as much grease as possible, or place the stain facedown on paper towels and stroke the back with dry-cleaning solvent on a clean white cloth. Then dampen with water and go over the stain with bar soap or shampoo.

✓ **Lipstick/cosmetics:** You could choose to never wear lipstick and have everyone think you're ill. Or, if you insist on wearing it and your little precious one makes a mess, then spray with prewash and rub with a white cloth or paper towel. Repeat, using a fresh towel each time. Then dampen, rub with bar soap, and rinse. If the stain remains (and it did on my cashmere sweater), work undiluted liquid detergent into the spot and then wash as usual.

✓ **Mildew:** Use lemon juice and salt, or white vinegar and salt. Place the garment out in the sun. Wash as usual, but wash separately.

✓ **Milk:** Soak in warm water and prewash.

- ✓ **Mustard:** Use white vinegar or hydrogen peroxide (never ammonia). Wash as usual.
- ✓ **Nail polish:** Sponge with polish remover or banana oil, then wash. Wash again. Don't use polish remover on acetate or triacetate fabrics.
- ✓ **Scorch:** Wash with detergent and the appropriate bleach. On heavily scorched areas, cover the stain with a cloth dampened with hydrogen peroxide. Cover with a dry cloth and press with a hot iron. Rinse well.
- ✓ **Soft drinks:** Sponge right away with cold water and rubbing alcohol.
- ✓ **Urine:** Blot with a solution of white vinegar and water.

Some of this material is taken from "800 Household Hints and Tips," by Globe Communications Corporation, 1995.

According to *Consumer Reports*, the best spot remover on the market for carpet and upholstery is a product called Spot Shot. My friend Rachel St. John-Gilbert turned me on to this product, and it is as good as any home remedy and far more versatile.

Cars

- ✓ **No smoking, please:** Never allow any smoking in your car. Not only is the tobacco smell hard to remove, cigarette fumes get into the glue in your vehicle and loosen the upholstery at the seams as well as any components—like the rearview mirror—that are glued on, thereby depreciating the value of your car.

> According to *Consumer Reports*, the best spot remover on the market for carpet and upholstery is a product called Spot Shot.

- ✓ **Stains:** Keep a bottle of Spot Shot (see Clothing and Other Fabrics section) or a bottle of club soda and a few paper towels in your trunk—these work wonderfully on new stains. See the previous section for specific stains, and remove them immediately. For older carpet stains, try 2 tablespoons of detergent, 3 tablespoons of vinegar, and 1 quart of warm water. Work into the stain, but don't soak. Blot as dry as possible. Sprinkle mud spots with cornstarch and let sit for 15 minutes, then vacuum.

✓ **Freshen:** Sprinkle the carpets of your car with baking soda or a commercial carpet freshener before vacuuming.

✓ **Tire care:** Common sense says to check your tire pressure frequently, but sometimes we forget. Too much or too little tire pressure costs precious gas mileage dollars and can lead to costlier accidents. Tires should be checked weekly. Rotate tires every five thousand miles to keep them wearing evenly and extend the life of your tires.

✓ **Maintenance checklist:** Proper maintenance will extend the life of your car by two or three years. How many of us know people who blew out the engine of a perfectly good car by ignoring the red light or forgetting to add oil? These kinds of mistakes are just too costly.

Weekly: Check the radiator fluid.

Every other refueling: Check the engine oil level.

Monthly: Check the battery's power indicator and cable connections for tightness and corrosion.

Check transmission and brake fluids, the air filter, belts, and hoses. Replace if these are worn, brittle, or soft.

As needed: Pay attention to warning lights.

✓ **Quick-Stop Oil Changes**

Coupons and other discounts: Go to my Web site at *www.elliekay.com* and click on *www.valpak.com* or *www.hotcoupons.com* for a list of local garages that offer discounts and coupons.

Frequent buyer program: Some shops offer one free oil change when you buy ten. Often you can even use coupons on the oil changes you purchase.

Reputation: You might want to call the shop and ask for customer references, because you could get a shop with inexperienced mechanics that could cost you more in the long run. Personal references for a shop are so very important.

✓ **Mom-and-pop savings:**

Drive and save: If you live in a larger city, driving thirty minutes to find a mom-and-pop repair shop could save you mega bucks. My friend Rachel has always done this wherever she has wandered. In Virginia Beach she found a shop like this that would work for peanuts (or almonds or walnuts). She saved a lot of money over the years.

> **Go to my Web site at *www.elliekay.com* and click on *www.valpak.com* or *www.hotcoupons.com* for a list of local garages that offer discounts and coupons.**

Locating a mechanic: To find an above-average mechanic in your area, go to *www.cartalk.com*, then select "Search the Site" and go to the alphabetical listing under "Mechanic Database." You can enter your zip code to start looking for a good mechanic in your area. Personal references are still (and probably always will be) the best way to find a reliable, honest, and less expensive mechanic.

Career

Do what you like. Like what you do. You might be asking yourself, "Why did she throw in a section on careers?" The answer is very simple: It doesn't matter how much money you save if you're unhappy in your work.

It only makes sense that if you dislike your job, you are more likely to:

✓ Overspend or live outside your budget in order to compensate with "feel good" items
✓ Try to fill the void with material things—this is oftentimes spelled D-E-B-T
✓ Fall prey to "get rich quick" schemes
✓ Accumulate mass amounts of debt for consumable items
✓ Have this dissatisfaction spill over into other areas of your life

On the other hand, if you are operating in your area of giftedness, then you will work with ease and effectiveness. Let's look at some strategies that can help increase contentment in your work and possibly save your career.

> **It doesn't matter how much money you save if you're unhappy in your work.**

Integrity. Sometimes the answer to your lousy job lies in a change of your attitude. Before changing jobs, ask yourself the questions below that I've taken and revised from *Tale of the Tardy Oxcart*, edited by Chuck Swindoll.

If you cannot answer yes to the following questions about your chosen career, then you may *never* be satisfied in your work—even if you land that dream job making a gazillion dollars a year!

Ask yourself, "Do I…"

✓ Respect my boss?
✓ Watch my words?

✓ Value my people?
✓ Know my limitations?
✓ Do my best?

Advice from a millionaire. Back when it meant something to be a millionaire, Andrew Carnegie said, "The average person puts only 25% of his energy and ability into his work. The world takes off its hat to those who put in more than 50% of their capacity, and stands on its head for those few and far between souls who devote 100%." This is true for all walks of life, no matter what your career calling is. We learn the following from Mr. Carnegie:

✓ *It takes so little to be above average.* Determine to devote your all to your call.
✓ *Your season is coming.* What you're doing now is preparing you for your next area of responsibility. Try to be content in today's season. Ten years of helping women's conversation stay focused and on track in small group Bible studies helped me gracefully host a talk show interviewing authors under the hot lights in front of the studio cameras.
✓ *Do it well.* It's not enough to be content in today's season if you want to be above average. More opportunities will come your way if you do your very best in the job you have now.
✓ *Setbacks are inevitable.* Getting laid off or fired can be the very best thing that ever happened to you. When my husband was passed over for a commander's job, we were devastated. But as we look back, we can see very clearly that the commander's job he eventually received was far better for our family and his career than the job he lost.

Bum Phillips, one of the winningest coaches of all times, said, "There are only two kinds of coaches: those who have been fired and those who are gonna be."

> **It takes so little to be above average. Determine to devote your all to your call.**

Motherhood as a career. Some of you work in the home, raising your precious children because you believe that is your calling. You are your own boss on long and busy days. Ask yourself the questions in the previous section entitled Integrity. When you can begin to answer them in the affirmative, you will find:

✓ Contentment in your circumstances
✓ Value despite society's devaluation of your chosen career
✓ Satisfaction in your chosen work
✓ Joy in the journey
✓ Confidence that this is a wonderful season
✓ Assurance that *your* season is coming

"Life is either a daring experience or nothing at all."

—HELEN KELLER

CHAPTER FOUR

Birth of a Baby Barbarian

Saving on Baby Items

I was pregnant ten months with our last child. You're thinking "This is more of that literary license stuff, right?" Well, kind of. The doctors said I was two weeks further along than I really was, and then I went more than two weeks past my due date. In my book, that adds up to being pregnant an extra month!

He may have been the last Kay baby, but oh, what a way to go out!

At seven o'clock on the morning of September 7, I woke up to get the children ready for an eight o'clock departure for a scheduled doctor's appointment. Induction paper work had to be filled out since the baby was so past due. My friend, Beth, was scheduled to watch the children. Bob left at seven-fifteen and I was having a few mild contractions, but they were just like the false labor pains I'd had for the last two months.

At seven-thirty my friend Pauline called from Colorado, and I told her of my discouragement at having to be induced. (All my other children were born with no drugs and no IVs—in the hospital, they were all natural births.) I asked her to pray that these contractions would get stronger and turn into the real thing on their own.

At 7:33, right after I hung up the phone, the first hard contraction hit, followed by another strong one *three* minutes later. I remember thinking, "Wow! When Pauline prays, things happen!" The third contraction hit two minutes later, with a hard one followed by two milder ones. Then the strangest thing happened—I felt the need to drive myself to pick up Bob rather than call someone to get me. Seven-year-old Daniel helped his younger siblings get into the van, and I drove them to Beth's house. We arrived at her curb with the horn honking.

She ran out of her house as I yelled, "I'm in labor, and I'm going to go pick up Bob!"

Beth grabbed Jonathan out of his car seat, while the other children piled out. "Don't you think I should drive you, Ellie?" Her eyes showed great concern.

I put the van into gear. "No! I'm going to get Bob—don't call him or he'll panic!"

At the squadron, Bob was about to go fly, and he happened to be looking out the window when I drove into the parking lot.

He met my van outside. "Hi, Beloved, are you dropping off some bread for the guys?"

I put the van in park. "Yeah, honey, I'm dropping something—but it ain't bread!"

I was in between contractions and announced, "This is it; I'm in labor!"

Even though we had many children, Bob still panicked every time we had a baby. He stood there in his little flight suit, just staring at me.

I called, "Come on, let's go!"

He turned pale. "Are you kidding?"

Another contraction was coming. "No, let's go NOW!"

Bob ran back into the squadron while I slowly moved to the passenger side of the van. In the squadron, Bob dropped his parachute on the floor and shouted to the operations officer, "I'm having a baby!" Then he ran out.

As Bob took the steering wheel to drive to the hospital, I concentrated on breathing. The contractions were now one minute apart and very intense. Bob, panicked as usual, drove like a maniac to get to the hospital.

We stopped at yet another red light and in between contractions I issued reminders, "Beloved, please get the video camera out of the van, and don't forget my bag, either."

As the light turned green, he took off faster than a dragster on the block and declared, "Oh my goodness, the contractions are less than a minute apart! Don't worry about the camera! Just concentrate on your breathing!"

Our van screamed into the hospital parking lot as Bob pulled into a No Parking slot in front of the ER doors. With the engine running, Bob dashed into the Emergency Room and shouted, "My wife is having a baby, NOW!"

The staff looked up at the crazed father-to-be in a flight suit. Bob allowed them exactly two seconds to move and then grabbed a wheel-chair, slammed it through the ER doors, and brought it outside, where I was standing by the van.

He helped me into the chair, mumbling, "We've got a bunch of rocket scientists in there."

Once inside, he ran down the hall, ramming me into an occasional wall when he turned a tight corner. I couldn't talk because there were only a few seconds between contractions. My mouth couldn't speak, but my mind was saying, "Bob, I am in labor here, would you please stop using me as a missile?!"

Just then I saw the double doors at the end of the hall to Labor and Delivery. I was relieved we were almost there. Rapidly my relief turned into concern because the wheelchair was not losing speed, it was gain-ing momentum as Bob sought to accomplish his mission.

My mind shouted, *The door! The door! It's an automatic door with a button on the side of the wall! It's not designed to be opened by the feet of women in wheelchairs! You'd better slow down, or this is the last child you'll ever have!*

Bob slammed the chair through the double doors, much to the sur-prise of the nursing staff at their nearby desk. I heard him mumble,

"Some automatic doors!"

The LDR nurses were shocked at our ill-mannered arrival.

"Wait a minute! Who are you?" They asked the overzealous pilot and his human battering ram.

"I'm Bob, and she," he pointed to me, "is going to have that baby right now!" His eyes were wild as he tried to convince the veteran nurses of my advanced condition.

I couldn't respond because I was focusing on a screw in the door hinge while breathing my way through another intense contraction.

Apparently, Bob thought the nurses were hearing-impaired because he kept shouting answers to their questions with high-pitched responses such as:

"Ellie Kay!"

"43 weeks!"

"Fifth child!"

"Dr. Holzhauer!"

"Of course I'm the father! Who else do you think the father is? What are you, a rocket scientist?"

Then, as a drowning man will come up one more time for air, he bellowed, "Oh, my goodness, the van engine is still running and it's parked in the ER zone!"

Then…he was gone.

With the Red Baron out of the room, the nurses relaxed as they gave me a robe and helped me to the bathroom to change. No sooner had I gotten the robe on than the baby slammed down the birth canal. Simultaneously, my water broke, revealing meconium in the fluid; if the baby breathed in that fluid, he would almost surely get pneumonia.

I held on to the metal rail for support and called to the nurses, "Whoa! Something's happening here; I need your help!"

The nurses helped me to the bed, and I laid back on the pillows, exclaiming again, "Something's happening!"

The nurse took one look and said, "Lady, you're about to have a baby!"

The meaning of her words sunk in as she shouted, "She's complete! Emergency delivery! Labor room two! Get Dr. Holzhauer—STAT!"

The other nurse asked, "Where's her husband?"

I answered in my mind, *He's parking the car!*

Thankfully, the doctor was in the hospital making rounds and arrived in seconds, out of breath from running. He knelt by my side and whispered, "You can push, Ellie. I'm right here."

At 8:05 A.M., with one intense effort, Joshua Steven was born. The doctor suctioned the meconium, and they put him on the warming tray to finish that crucial job.

About that time, Bob raced backed in the room shouting, "How is she?"

"Mistah," said the nurse who looked like Mammy from *Gone With the Wind*, "You done had yo'self a fine man-child!"

He looked to the warming tray and saw his son, a ten-pound-eight-ounce Baby Huey. Joshua earned the nickname Conan, the baby barbarian, because he always does things in a big way. He was delivered just twenty-five minutes after I picked Bob up from work.

"A baby!" Bob yelled. "I was just parking the car!"

SUPPLIES FOR THE BABY BARBARIAN

We can all see who Joshua takes after in our family. You may not have a baby barbarian; you may not *want* a baby barbarian. You may just have a very civilized, sweet child, but either way, each baby needs all the paraphernalia common to little rug runners. Whether you're providing for one baby or triplets, here are some tips to make those dollars go further.

Baby Wipes

You'll go through a ton of these babies in the course of a month. If you can't find them on sale or if they're still too expensive with a coupon, a Web buck, or a store coupon, then why not just make your own? Here's the recipe I used for wipes for my last three babies:

1 round plastic container with a lid (about 6 inches tall and wide enough to accommodate 1/2 roll of paper towels)
1 roll of heavy duty paper towels (no cheap store brands)

1/4 cup baby oil
1/4 cup baby shampoo
1/4 cup baby bath soap
1 to 2 cups water (depending on the absorbency of the towels)

Cut a small X (about an inch long) in the plastic lid of the container. Cut the paper towels in half to make two short rolls of towels. Use one and save one. (I use Bob's hacksaw. He usually discovers it, dull and covered with paper, when he tries to cut something else. Then he reacts with his usual quiet dignity and grace.) Put the baby oil, baby shampoo, and baby bath in the plastic container and add 1 cup of water. Stir well. Place the paper towel, cut side up, in the water for a few minutes. Then turn it over, cut side down, to let the other side absorb the liquid. Let sit for five minutes. If the roll of paper towel still has dry portions on it, then keep adding water, 1/4 cup at a time, at five minute intervals, until the towels are completely damp (not dripping, just damp). After the center of the paper towel tube is wet, gently pull it out of the center of the towels. Pull the towels from the center, and thread through the X in the lid of the container. Seal. Will keep fresh for up to a month.

Diapers

If you are considering going with cloth diapers to save money, then think this through again because you won't save money after laundering and the initial investment of cloth diapers. However, if you choose cloth for ecological purposes, then knock yourself out ("You go, girl!").

If you choose to go with disposable diapers, try to only buy diapers that are on sale and with a coupon. Also check out *www.valupage.com* for Web bucks, which can give you cash back on the diapers you purchase, good on your next shopping trip. You could get Web bucks for diapers you would purchase anyway; every dollar adds up on this costly expense for babies.

To get your favorite manufacturers' coupons, sign up at the doctor's office for diaper promotions from the leading brands. They should start sending you coupons, usually with an informative booklet or magazine, every one or two months.

For more coupons, go to your favorite brand's Web site by typing *www.(brandname).com*. For example, *www.pampers.com* or *www.huggies.com* or *www.luvs.com*. Many of these sites will even have gift certificates available for purchase, which is a practical, money-saving gift to request for your baby shower.

Once I got ten bags of diapers for free because one store had a buy one/get one free store coupon. That coupon, when taken to my favorite store, was then considered a competitor's coupon. So I'm getting the diapers for half price because of that competitor's coupon. I got ten of those coupons from my friends and family. My favorite store (that honored competitors' coupons) had an advertised special on their brand of diapers that was also buy one/get one free. So the competitor's coupon (funded by the advertising department) combined with the store special (funded by the store) let me get the diapers for free. All I paid was the tax. OOOOH, baby!

For more coupons, go to your favorite brand's Web site by typing *www.(brandname).com*. For example, *www.pampers.com* or *www.huggies.com* or *www.luvs.com*.

Clothing

Get over the idea that Junior has to be dressed in brand-new clothing that he'll grow out of in a month! You can buy used clothing and not deprive your child. Babies' and younger children's clothing is worn, on the average, for only *six weeks*! Do you think a baby could wear out his clothes in that amount of time?

One mom asked me, "Oooh, what about the germs that come from wearing used clothing?"

I responded, "So you wash it in hot water and kill any germs. Tell me, do you take sheets with you when you go stay at the Marriott? Don't you sleep on used sheets there?"

What's the difference? The difference is about a 50 to 85 percent savings on children's clothing. Here are some very practical tips to stretch those clothing dollars.

✓ **Garage sales:** See *Shop, Save, and Share* to strategize and shop effectively at yard sales; these are going to be your best bargains.

✓ **Baby showers:** If you are blessed to have more than one baby shower, like a church shower and a neighborhood shower, then ask each group for different size clothing, starting with ages 3 to 6 months. Your baby might not even fit in the tiny 0 to 3 month clothes (Conan started out in 6 to 9 month clothing), and you'll probably get a lot of these in the mail from people who couldn't come to a shower. Pick up a few of these tiny clothes from garage sales so you'll have a supply on hand. Ask one group for size 6 to 12 months and another for 12 months or older.

✓ **Make a list:** It's not self-serving to ask for specific baby things at a shower. A good hostess will ask you for a list, so if you're expecting, start compiling one now. The hostess will include this in the invitations. Most people appreciate specifics, and it's fairly easy to exchange duplicates.

✓ **Returns:** After the baby gets here, people will probably ask you how they can help. If you didn't have a chance to return and exchange baby clothes or if your baby is a different gender than you expected, ask a friend to run this errand for you. She can get you a gift certificate, and you can save it to purchase exactly the size and style clothing your child needs. This one tip can clothe your baby for six months! (I got two baby outfits that were too small and they cost $45 each! I shopped the sales on the return and bought twelve outfits!)

✓ **Barter:** Don't be afraid to ask your sister or a friend for her baby clothes, especially if you know they just had their last child. If it makes you (and them) feel better, then offer to barter for the trade. I traded a tan leather easy chair, which was only 18 months old, for $250 worth of services and merchandise. I would have only gotten about $200 at a yard sale or consignment store for the chair, and I figured Conan's Native-American name means "He Who Runs With Ink Pen," so why should I keep a tan leather chair? (Dennis Rainey told me at a radio taping, "I don't think I'd like a teenager who answers to 'Conan,'" so we changed Joshua's nickname to 'Mighty Man of God'!)

Baby Furniture

See chapter 2 and ask yourself the following questions to get the right value for your family:

- ✓ *"Is this for our first child, and do we plan on having more?"* You may do well to buy new and consider it an investment if this is your first child. If this is a late-in-your-life baby, then all you need is a nice-looking used crib to make it through one baby.
- ✓ *"How long will we need this crib?"* If you plan on three or more years between children, then you may want to consider a crib that will convert to a youth bed. Otherwise, you'll need the crib for the next baby before his older sibling is out of it. Most children outgrow a youth bed by about age six.
- ✓ *"What is the quality and construction of this used furniture?"* If the construction is solid and you are handy with some putty and paint (non-toxic), then buy used.

> **If you have to go into debt to buy the furniture you feel your child is entitled to, then you need to reevaluate your priorities. Materialism makes paupers of us all.**

✓ *"Could I purchase a display model?"* Most merchandisers sell their display models at a considerable discount.

✓ *"Will this possibly be someone's gift to us?"* Don't buy baby furniture until you are reasonably certain that this will not be a gift from Mom and Dad or Grandma and Grandpa.

✓ *"Is this furniture functional, practical, and reasonable?"* If you have to go into debt to buy the furniture you feel your child is entitled to (your baby, by the way, will not care what he sleeps in), then you need to reevaluate your priorities. Materialism makes paupers of us all.

Food

I got thirty boxes of baby juice free today and I don't have a baby! I'll donate them to a crisis pregnancy center, or perhaps I'll pour the apple juice into Bob's breakfast glass and see if he'll notice. Here are some great ways to save on baby food.

✓ **Freebies:** Remember to sign up for formula samples through your doctor's office (you may need to ask for this) and take advantage of any special offers included with the free formula samples you receive during your hospital stay. Keep checking my Web site for the latest toll-free numbers, free samples, and money-saving links.

✓ **Commercial baby food:** You can go to your favorite brand name site (the way we showed you in the Diapers section) to check out available coupons and savings. For starters, try *www.similac.com* or 1-800-222-9546 and *www.gerber.com* or 1-800-443-7237. You could also call the toll-free operator at 1-800-555-1212 and ask for the toll-free number of your favorite brand. Then call and ask them to send you coupons. You will then get on their regular mailing list and receive other promotional offers.

✓ **Grind your own:** Invest in a small grinder with removable plastic parts. This is a minimal investment with maximum savings.

Fresh: Grind several portions of freshly prepared vegetables before you add salt and other seasonings. You may have to add a little water as you grind. Place portions in airtight plastic containers and refrigerate immediately if you are not going to serve them right away. They will be good for about four days.

Canned: If you don't have time to steam or boil fresh vegetables, buy cans of no-salt-added vegetables and get the equivalent of four jars of baby food for a quarter of the price. Keep in mind that canned veggies lose some of their nutritional value, so fresh is better—but canned is a good second choice.

> **If you don't have time to steam or boil fresh vegetables, buy cans of no-salt-added vegetables and get the equivalent of four jars of baby food for a quarter of the price.**

Leftovers: "Better safe than sorry" is the old saying. Don't feed your baby leftovers. If you've already reheated a portion from the initial cooking, don't serve it again.

"You know, Mama, snuggling you is the faborite part of my day. You've got the bestest kissies in de whole world!"

—FOUR-YEAR-OLD CONAN
TO THE COUPON QUEEN

CHAPTER FIVE

Eggplant Extravaganza

Minimal Effort/Maximum Yield Gardens

I hate eggplant. I always have. I always will. My earliest recollection of this detestable vegetable was when it appeared on my plate when I was seven years old. As my thoughts wander back to that fateful night, I can still see the slimy chunks looking like bits of squid with little seeds all over it—no doubt the remnants of tentacles. Never mind the fact that I'd never even *seen* squid, much less tasted it. I was convinced that this eggplant stuff *had* to be an invertebrate, like the ones we studied in Mrs. Brewer's third grade class. My young mind turned to the memory of Bruce Miller leaning over my school desk and whispering in my ear, "I bet your abuela used to eat squid in Spain." The thought made me sick.

My mother interrupted these thoughts, rescuing me from the mental taunts of Bruce and squid with an announcement, "You have to eat at least half of your eggplant, Ellie. It came from Abuelita's garden, and it's very good for you."

I looked over at my Spanish grandmother as she narrowed her eyes, daring me to discredit her glorious eggplant. Of all the veggies in Abuela's expansive garden, we had to draw the eggplant card at this meal, right on the heels (or should I say tentacles) of squid day at school. This woman had a green thumb that could grow grapefruit-sized lemons out of a tree she planted in a clay pot. Much to my chagrin, I discovered that she had grown three acres of eggplant. Oh, what I would have given to eat a gigantic lemon on that particular occasion when faced with a giant squid instead.

Slowly, I took a bite of the dreaded dish and discovered that it tasted *worse* than it looked. Quickly, I washed down the mouthful with a gulp of milk. Pretending to chew, I proceeded to eat exactly half of the eggplant "pill style," swallowing each bite with more milk. Holding my breath helped. After each bite, I'd smile dutifully at Abuela, in an effort to silently praise her prized Old-World plant. This proved to be a critical mistake.

Abuelita smiled back and said, "Quieres mas, niña?"

I couldn't believe it. *Did I want more?*

Before I could say, "Not on your vida, Grandma," Abuela gave me another large helping of the slimy stuff.

Then and there I came up with a plan—a wonderful, marvelous plan to rid my poor family of the cultural eggplant curse. I decided I'd sell Abuela's vegetables door-to-door. The next morning proved to be a bright summer day in Texas, and I told Abuela about the plan to provide fresh vegetables at a reasonable cost for all our wonderful neighbors and friends. She could raise a little eggplant money of her own too.

Even as a seven-year-old, I had a keen sense of marketing strategy. I decided to refrain from calling these vegetables by their real name. After all, who in their right mind would buy something called an *eggplant*? It reminded me of some kind of hybrid of poultry and plants—some weird experiment gone terribly wrong.

So I looked up eggplant in the dictionary and found the scientific name for it. Abuela and I agreed on a profit-sharing plan, and I took out down the road with four dozen vegetables in my red wagon. I went to Mrs. Cooperman's house first and touted the value of the purple *Solanum melongena* plant. I told her, "It's a tropical Old-World plant, grown from seed that my Spanish grandma brought over from Jerez de la Frontera. Its ovoid fruit is considered a delicacy."

Mrs. Cooperman looked in my wagon, "Why, Ellie, it just looks like plain old eggplant to me!" My hopes sank until she continued.

"But my husband just *loves* my eggplant casserole. I've been making it ever since we first got married thirty years ago. Sometimes I have a hard time finding a real pretty purple plant. I'll take four."

I bagged her purchase and collected the money. As she took the bag she smiled, "Did you know eggplant can make you thirsty? Why, my husband always drinks gallons of tea when he eats my casserole."

"I drink milk with mine," I told her with my best Shirley Temple smile.

I felt a little sorry for poor Mr. Cooperman.

I spent all morning peddling my wares, and by day's end I'd sold all those veggies at quite a nice return. I even bought a few myself (after all, I got half of the profits) and gave them away as gifts. Yes, even as a child, I loved to give things away—especially eggplant. Mrs. Brewer got a couple; my Sunday School teacher, Mrs. Farrar, got a few; and I even took some down to Bruce Miller's house. Besides whispering squid stories in my ear at school, he also pulled my braids on the bus and made fun of my missing teeth.

I gave his mother five.

Despite the eggplant dilemma, I liked working in my abuela's garden. There was nothing like sitting in between the rows of vegetables and digging my toes into the soil. The dirt on top was hot, but the soil underneath was cool and moist. I'd pull a carrot right out of the ground, wipe the dirt off on my shirt, and take a big bite.

As an adult, I wanted to carry on this tradition with my children. But each time we'd take the kids out to our patch of soil, carefully plant the seeds and water them, we'd find ourselves moving before the crop could be harvested. Each time, I'd think about the tender shoots we left behind, wondering if someone was putting their toes in our dirt and having a horticultural treat on us.

That Kay family tradition continued until this past year. We finally stayed in one place long enough to harvest our own veggies. We had stir-fry several times a week with an assortment of beans, tomatoes, carrots, peppers, squash, and zucchini. The kids didn't care for the zucchini, so I made a great chocolate cake out of it that they ate without knowing it was a vegetable in disguise. There was no eggplant in my garden.

We even hated to go to California for two weeks because we didn't want to leave our fresh produce behind! When we did come back from our vacation, the kids immediately ran into the backyard. They pulled fat carrots from the ground and picked big peppers and scores of beans from the vine. But Daniel found the grand prize—an *enormous* zucchini that weighed in at nine pounds!

> **Besides providing an opportunity for a family bonding experience, growing your own vegetables is also a wonderful way of saving money.**

You know, my kids are as giving as I was as a youngster; sometimes their generosity amazes me. They insisted that Mr. Ben King, their children's church teacher, have the prize zucchini.

Rumor has it he washed it down with milk.

———

Besides providing an opportunity for a family bonding experience, growing your own vegetables is also a wonderful way of saving money. While I don't claim to be an expert in this area, I have compiled a few tips that can help everyone from the novice eggplanter to the veteran gardener.

HELP! I HAVE NO PLACE TO PLANT!
Container Gardening

You don't need an outdoor area to plant, and you don't have to have a green thumb to grow a few vegetables in the space you have allotted. Recently, when I was on one of my favorite radio shows, *Midday Connection*, a caller named Lori from Nicetown, Indiana, addressed this point when she talked about the special-needs adults she works with.

"I help these adults learn to plant practically anything in a pot in their rooms. It doesn't take much to plant a bean or grow a tomato plant. Even if you live in an apartment and don't have a yard, you can still grow vegetables!" Lori is right!

The new rage for city dwellers and others without the space or dirt to grow a conventional garden is "container gardening." Basically, with some ingenuity and a little know-how, you can grow plants in window boxes, barrels and tubs, urns—even pots and hanging baskets! Spots that are currently barren brick or wood can be turned into a miniature garden. You can turn a terrace, rooftop, or other unusual spot into an area to grow fresh vegetables.

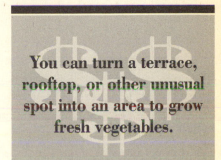

You can turn a terrace, rooftop, or other unusual spot into an area to grow fresh vegetables.

If you read the instructions on the seed package or the directions that come with the young plants from a nursery, you can determine which container works best for each kind of plant. Tell your nursery specialist that you are going to try container gardening, and he or she will direct you to the plant suited for your space and amount of sunlight. If you want to explore this area further, you may want to check out two books listed in the appendix that are excellent resources for master-gardeners-to-be.

You don't have to read another book to get started. Just follow the basics listed in the following sections, and with your choice of a container you'll soon be on your way to reaping a harvest.

Advantages of container gardening: One main plus is that containers can be moved to take advantage of sunlight—most plants need at least six hours of sunlight each day. You might want to consider keeping your containers on a moveable cart for this reason.

Grow any vegetable. Almost any vegetable can be grown in this way, but there are some varieties that have been developed especially for containers and are marked as such at your seed store.

Use inexpensive containers. There's no reason to buy expensive planters when garage sale or flea market finds make the best containers. Bushel baskets, apple boxes (fixed with wooden slats to prevent leaking), and five-gallon buckets obtained free from a health food store, donut factory, or restaurant make great containers. Be creative. Don't worry about a little rust or some chipped paint on an antique container—it will add personality and texture to your garden. Just remember that each container should be large enough to hold at least six to ten inches of soil.

Drainage. Container gardens need a lot more drainage than regular gardens because of the nature of the small system. You could drill holes on the sides near the base of your container, in pairs one above the other every three inches. If you have drainage holes in the bottom already, set your container on wooden blocks off the ground.

The bottom of the container should have at least one inch of drainage material such as tiny gravel. The lowest drainage holes should be a half inch below the drainage material.

Watering. Water early in the morning or late in the day to avoid evaporation. Be sure to soak the soil, rather than sprinkling the foliage. Regularly water each plant according to the seed packet or nursery plant instructions.

How to Get Started With a Garden
Gardening Basics

Decide what to plant. Select your seeds or plants depending on the type of garden (container or traditional), your climate, planting season, space available, and what your family likes to eat.

Prepare the soil. The old-fashioned way of preparing the soil in my home country of Texas is still the best way to prepare it today. For a basic garden, use potting soil and composted manure (no, I'm not going to make manure jokes; that would be tasteless). The key to a healthy plant is healthy, vitamin-rich soil.

Grow more than you need. As a general rule you should grow 20 percent more than you think you'll need in a given year, because any seed may fail. You can share your surplus with those in need.

Start seeds indoors. Many plants grow better if started from seed indoors or in a homemade cold frame (see Season Extenders). This is especially important in colder climates with shorter growing seasons, since some plants, such as Brussels sprouts and peppers, take four months or more to mature. (The instructions printed on the seed packet will give you germination time and number of days to maturity to help you determine how early to start the seeds as well as how deep to plant that specific variety of seed.)

Styrofoam cups, egg cartons, shallow wooden boxes, and nursery flats are a few good containers in which to start seeds.

Water regularly so the soil doesn't dry out, but avoid over-watering, which may cause the seeds to rot. Another way to keep the soil moist is to cover your planting cups with plastic wrap (use a rubber band to keep the wrap taut) or small squares of recycled glass. This will keep the moisture even and keep the soil from drying out if you can't water every day. Be sure to remove the cover as soon as the sprouts appear.

> **Grow 20 percent more than you think you'll need in a given year, because any seed may fail. You can share your surplus with those in need.**

Place the plant containers directly under a strong light (fluorescent and/or regular incandescent light bulbs will do, or you can purchase a special grow light from a nursery). Raise the plants as close to the light as possible when they are small to keep them from growing too leggy as they reach for the light. Or place the plants next to a light-filled south window—but rotate the containers regularly as they bend toward the sun.

When the greenery is two to four inches above the soil, you're ready to transplant the plants into tilled ground or a larger container.

Tear off the Styrofoam and soak the plants in a shallow, cool bucket of water while you are preparing the soil. Once they are in their permanent home, water lightly. It is so important to water each plant according to the directions—too much water is as bad as too little.

Plant your garden at the right time. There's a different time to plant those seeds in New York than in California. That's why seed packages and catalogs have wonderful guidelines called *directions*. This "tip" may sound fairly lame to veteran gardeners, but you wouldn't believe how many people plant when they feel like it rather than when the package says is a good time for their climate and location. These guidelines, also available from state cooperative extension offices and the United States Department of Agriculture (*www.gardening.usda.gov/region.html*), are there for a reason— follow them.

Save those seeds. One of the dilemmas gardeners face every year is whether to take a chance and use leftover seeds purchased last year or to buy fresh ones every year. Pam West of Batavia, Illinois, worked for one of the largest seed companies in the nation. She said in Amy Dacyczyn's *Tightwad Gazette II* (Villard Books) that one of her jobs was to relabel seed packages from the year before with the current germination information after the seeds were tested in the lab. She wrote: "I was amazed to find out that in most cases, the germination percentage actually went *up* from the previous year, sometimes as much as 10 to 15 percent. So use those seeds you bought last year and save your new seeds for next year."

The average storage limitations for seeds are:

✓ One to two years: corn, lettuce, parsley, parsnips
✓ Three to five years: asparagus, beans, cabbage, carrots, celery, chicory, endive, okra, peas, peppers, radishes, and spinach
✓ Five or more years: beets, cucumbers, and tomatoes

Store seeds in an airtight container in the refrigerator or in a cool, dry place. You can even test your own seeds for germination a few weeks before planting by sandwiching ten seeds in a moist paper towel and keeping the towel moist for a week or so. If at least seven seeds sprout, then your seeds are about as viable as new ones!

Tomato Plants

These are the most common vegetable grown in the home garden and usually the easiest to grow. If you are going to buy tomato plants, never buy a tomato plant that already has tomatoes on it, as the plants won't grow as well and the total yield will be diminished.

To root a tomato plant firmly in the ground, dig a trench about 18 inches long and 12 inches deep, depending on the height of each tomato plant. Take the healthy tomato plant and cut off almost all of the lower branches with gardening sheers. Lay the plant in the trench with one branch above the ground. If you live in an area with late spring winds, the deeper trench will also protect the young plants from being damaged. Your tomato plant will root off of the entire stem and you will have solid roots for an incredible yield.

Bonus Tip: When your tomato plant begins to grow so much that it needs to be supported with a plant stand, use old sections of panty hose to tie the vines. They are pliable, soft, and perfect for this task. Strips of cut-up plastic bags (like the newspaper comes in) work great too.

Fertilizer and Mulch

There are many products on the market that will fertilize and mulch your vegetables and help them grow faster and better. When we were kids, my abuela would take us around the neighborhood in our pickup truck to look for fresh grass clippings set out by the lawns. When we found said bags, she'd stop the truck and we would grab the bags of grass and throw them into the back of the truck. (Today, when I see a bag of grass clippings on the edge of a lawn, I'm *still* mortified at the thought that someone is going to come along and make me take it.) When we had fifteen to twenty bags, we'd go home and help her unload these into her compost pile for mulch. I do things differently than Abuela did.

For fertilizer, I use Miracle-Gro or Peter's commercial fertilizer. I save and clean empty milk jugs, fill them with water and fertilizer, and have enough for a couple weeks at a time. I fertilize our seeds or plantings three times a week for the first four weeks and twice a week thereafter.

HOW TO KEEP COSTS LOW
Tips for Frugal Gardening

Buy used. We've already talked about finding inexpensive containers, but you'll also find other gardening supplies at garage sales, or you may be able to borrow them from friends and family. Don't invest in an expensive Rototiller that you only need once or twice a season. Instead, go in on a daily rental with a friend: You can till your plot in the morning and she can till hers in the afternoon (in the hot, blazing sun, of course). Or, if you have a large garden and plan to work it for many years, look for a used tiller.

Use seeds. Whenever possible, grow your vegetables from seeds, since this costs about one-tenth the price of nursery seedlings. If you live in a colder climate with a short growing season, start your seeds indoors using the method described earlier.

> Whenever possible, grow your vegetables from seeds, since this costs about one-tenth the price of nursery seedlings.

To find the best price on seeds, visit Fedco Seeds, a co-op for seed packers, at their Internet address: *www.fedcoseeds.com*.

Or to get on their mailing list, send two dollars to:

Fedco Seeds
P.O. Box 520-A
Waterville, ME 04903

Avoid pricey season extenders. There are products on the market such as row covers, hoop houses, Wall-o'-Water protectors, and cold frames that will extend the growing season somewhat. Unless you can make your own cold frame (for areas that get little snow) with scavenged lumber and an old window, avoid these devices, as they will drive up the cost of gardening considerably.

Alternative supplies. Avoid garden paraphernalia, especially the pricey accessories sold in gardening catalogs. As mentioned earlier, Styrofoam cups and egg cartons make great seed starters. Plastic milk jugs can become mini-greenhouses, and old wire fencing can be cut and shaped into tomato cages. Reuse nursery plant containers and take advantage of your community compost site if available.

Swap seedlings. Share seeds or swap seedlings with a gardening partner to save on seed costs and cut down on the variety of seedlings each of you has to start.

Weed out weeds. Control weeds by pulling them once a week. If you hoe or till between rows once a week, the freshly disturbed soil won't allow new weeds to take root. If you can't hoe all season, then pay special attention to weeding for the first few weeks your garden is planted. This is the critical time period because weeds can choke out tender new shoots. Once the plants are taller than the weeds, they will do fine.

Choose carefully. As we said, it is important to choose the right vegetables for your climate. If you have limited time or space to garden, it is also important to choose produce that costs the most at the grocery store. Strawberries and lettuce, for example, are more expensive than carrots and potatoes. You'll save more in the store by growing the more expensive produce.

> If you have limited time or space to garden, choose produce that costs the most at the grocery store, like strawberries and lettuce.

Also consider the space and effort required for the vegetables you choose. A sprawling Brussels sprout plant may yield enough for just one meal. Bush beans and lettuce, on the other hand, require little space for a relatively high yield.

Seek advice. When you move to a new area, talk with successful gardeners or farmers at the farmers' market. Ask which crops tend to need the most pesticides and avoid those crops, because these treatments can be very expensive. Ask which vegetables do well in that climate and for other tips on gardening in that part of the country.

County extension offices. Take advantage of your county extension office. Some local offices will test your soil for free, so you'll know what kind and how much fertilizer to use. Also, some have Master Gardener programs in which experts teach you every aspect of gardening—for free.

Be patient. Even the best of gardeners have bad years. Be patient with your level of experience, knowing that every season that goes by will teach you something new.

**"Though old in years,
I am but a young gardener."**

—THOMAS JEFFERSON

**"Neither the one who plants
nor the one who waters is anything,
but God who causes the growth."**

—1 CORINTHIANS 3:7 NASB

CHAPTER SIX

The Coupon Kids

Teaching Kids About Money

While we were in the grocery store, Bethany was sorting her coupons to find the one for a free Russell Stover's candy bar.

"Mama, am I a Coupon Princess?" she suddenly asked as she looked up from her work.

"Yes," I replied as I searched for a Post coupon to get free cereal. "Yes, you are a Coupon Princess."

"Mama?" she asked again, "Then why don't I have a crown?"

I stopped my coupon search as I looked into her eyes. I knew she really liked the crown that I wear for publicity photos and on television shows. Because it was made with stones from vintage costume jewelry, I don't let her play with it. Still, I knew she admired the lovely tiara.

"Why, you don't really *need* a crown to prove you're a princess, do you?"

With pleading eyes she tugged at her braid. "But I really *want* a crown. Do you suppose I could have one when I'm twenty-one?"

Suddenly, I wasn't looking at my eight-year-old daughter. In my mind, I envisioned a much older, beautiful young lady with Bethany's face, her fawn-colored hair and her crystal-blue eyes. The thought of my little princess all grown up brought an unexpected wave of sadness over me—my children seemed to be growing up so fast. Wasn't it just yesterday that she made little old ladies giggle with her infant smiles?

Bethany's voice broke into my melancholy thoughts, "Mama?"

Brought back to the present, I reached down to stroke her cheek tenderly and answered, "Yes, my precious girl, what do you want to know?"

"Can I have your crown when you die?"

So often, parents feel they should shield their children from the cold, cruel world of financial responsibilities. After all, kids will have to learn that harsh reality all too soon anyway, won't they?

I agree that we don't want to burden our children with financial problems: That isn't fair to them. On the other hand, there are honest (and age-appropriate) methods that will teach our children about money. Even small children can learn financial concepts. If we teach them while they're young and in our home, they'll be prepared for fiscal responsibilities as a young adult. As a matter of fact, if we train them well, they may view finances as a blessing, not a burden.

TIPS TO TEACH MONEY TIPS
Modeling

There's a saying I've heard about instructors: "Those who can't do—teach." Well, I have a teaching background and I have to disagree. Sure, most of us have seen people in training or instructional positions and wondered, "What in the world are they doing *teaching*?" Poor instructors provide an inconsistent example. We want to be positive role models for our children as we demonstrate good financial stewardship before them. We can't truly teach our children when we don't model that life-style.

How can we teach them to budget if we don't have a budget? Isn't it a bit hypocritical to tell them to tithe 10 percent when we tithe nothing or to save 10 percent when we save nothing? How much credibility do we hold with them if we don't allow them to owe us money and yet *we* are charged to the limit on credit cards?

Purpose to practice what you preach—that's the first step in teaching kids about money.

Delayed Gratification

We live in an "add water and stir" world. We can get things when we want them, how we want them, and without waiting. Ron Blue, in his book *Master Your Money,* said the best definition of worldly financial success he has heard came from one of his oldest daughter's friends: "To have whatever you want whenever you want it."

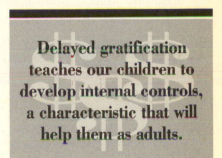

Delayed gratification teaches our children to develop internal controls, a characteristic that will help them as adults.

Waiting provides opportunities for character growth and refinement; we miss so much when we won't wait. There are some wonderful advantages to delayed gratification, especially in finances.

When your child wants the latest toy advertised in a commercial, you don't have to run out and buy it. If the neighbors buy their child a new bike, you don't have to buy one for Junior. When you're in the store and your little precious sees some cool candy, you don't have to instantly fulfill his every whim! Delayed gratification teaches our children to develop internal controls, a characteristic that will help them as adults.

Personally, Bob and I let our children earn a portion of their big purchases and have no qualms about denying many of their little demands to buy impulse items. Bethany spent eight months earning half of the amount needed for an American Girl doll. We paid for the other half, and she got it for her birthday. Do you think she values that doll? You bet she does! She's very careful when playing with it and puts it away when she's finished. Do you think she would value it as much if we gave her several of these dolls just to keep up with the latest trend? She might, but I don't think so.

Currently, the three oldest children are saving money for new bikes in the spring. They'll be less likely to leave these valued bikes out in the rain when they've earned a portion of their purchase. The other day, when they were helping me cut coupons, they found a coupon for bikes ordered through Huffy. They paid a third less than at a discount store, and the purchase price included delivery. Yes, delayed gratification teaches the value of a dollar.

Allowance

In his book *Making Your Children Mind Without Losing Yours*, best-selling author Dr. Kevin Leman said: "The allowance is a practical and effective way to give children the opportunity to begin to manage money, and at the same time it gives them the feeling of positive self-worth." Some families choose to give their children an allowance and use it as a teaching tool. Here are some basic guidelines for the use of an allowance.

✓ Tie in the allowance with responsibility.
✓ Teach the child she is responsible for spending her
   allowance wisely.
✓ Try basing the amount on the child's age. An older child
   would get more allowance than his younger siblings.
✓ Give allowance on the same day each week—it gives the
   child something to look forward to.
✓ Budget the children's allowance as a part of your monthly
   expenses.
✓ Give the child the freedom to make foolish decisions—it's
   a great way to educate. It is also called "learning the
   hard way."
✓ An allowance is *not* a payment for chores. It *is* awarded
   along with a certain number of responsibilities—and
   both are age-appropriate.
✓ If a child fails to live up to his responsibilities (or chores),
   then he will *choose* to forfeit a portion of his allowance
   to pay someone else to do his chores. For example: If I

pay Daniel, from Bethany's allowance, to make
Bethany's bed, then guess who is going to start making
Bethany's bed? You've got it—Bethany is! Try it, it
works!

Banking

We have a plastic bank for each child with three separate compartments: a store, a church, and a bank. Each compartment has a place to
deposit money for that specific area. The children are learning to save
10 percent, give 10 percent to the
local church (and more to another
charity if they choose), and use the
remaining amount as they like. If
they're saving for a special purchase, such as the bikes, they set
up a new savings account (kept
separate from the 10 percent in
their plastic bank). We do this
because the money they are saving for a bike will not be kept per-
manently in a savings account, but
will eventually be spent on the special purchase item.

> **If I pay Daniel, from Bethany's allowance, to make Bethany's bed, then guess who is going to start making Bethany's bed? You've got it—Bethany is! Try it, it works!**

When our children have about twenty-five dollars saved in their
plastic bank, we open a savings account for them at a real bank. They
usually open this savings account by the age of seven. Our oldest,
Daniel, at the age of thirteen, also has his first mutual fund in addition
to his savings account, to which he contributes $50/month from his
newspaper route earnings.

When they hit their teens, we will open a checking account for them.
They will learn to write checks, balance the checkbook, and pay for special items. They will do all these things while in our household so we
can model, coach, and mentor them.

Budget

Even young children can learn how to budget their money. The banking system we just discussed helps children to save and give—we also need to teach them how to spend wisely. One of the ways we teach the value of spending wisely is at garage sales.

I'll give my five-year-old $2 to spend at the yard sales. I tell him that we'll be going to many sales and once the money is gone, he won't get any more. There is a requirement that they consult me on purchases that cost more than 25¢. This way, I am available to coach them on the value of the desired item. For example, Bethany wanted to buy a bunny for her collection that cost $1.50. It meant she would spend the majority of her money on this one item. I reminded her that she bought a cuter bunny the previous weekend for only 25¢. The choice was hers to make. She decided to wait and found a newer bunny for only 50¢ later in the day, and we applauded her business savvy.

We do the same thing with our children at carnivals, book sales, on vacations, at the zoo, and at grocery stores. They have a set amount of money, or their allowance, and they must choose how to spend it. This is one way to tie in responsibility with accountability.

COACHING AND MENTORING

When it comes to money, we can act authoritative and demand that our children comply. Or we can come alongside them, cheer their good decisions, and help them see the results of their bad choices. Coaches stay on the sidelines while providing direction and guidance. Our kids are the players, and they've got to learn to make the wise calls on their own. We want to encourage them to win the game.

From a mentoring perspective, we share our financial history. We share the good as well as bad decisions we've made—and their natural consequences. Sometimes the fact that our children are currently living the consequences of bad decisions is the best teaching tool.

YOUNG ENTREPRENEURS

Productive children grow into productive adults—and (usually) lead happier lives. In my book *Shop, Save, and Share*, I outlined some of my business endeavors that began when I was a second-grader and continued into adulthood. I appreciate my parents' encouragement in those endeavors. Likewise, Daniel and Philip have successfully managed garage sale lemonade stands as well as a lawn-raking business called Rakes R Us. They printed handouts and delivered them to friends and neighbors. In these jobs, I knew the people they worked for, and therefore felt comfortable with their safety. The money my children earn is theirs to save, spend, or give—and they do all three with gusto.

Even though earning money helps build self-esteem and encourages responsibility, children need supervision and accountability in their business endeavors. Teach your children to finish the job, do it well, and do it in a timely manner. Baby-sitters who will do their work well can command higher fees than the run-of-the-mill sitter. Who wouldn't pay more to have the sitter wash the children's dinner dishes and have the house as tidy as they left it?

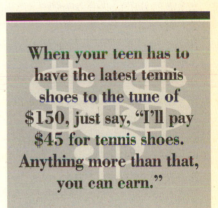

When your teen has to have the latest tennis shoes to the tune of $150, just say, "I'll pay $45 for tennis shoes. Anything more than that, you can earn."

TEENS DO W-2

When your teenager is old enough to have a part-time job, you may want to encourage them to file their own taxes. Because they're making only a small amount of money, the tax structure is still very simple. Many colleges offer courses, available to high school students, that teach basic tax preparation skills. You and your teenager can decide if that is the best option for your family.

NO TICKKI, NO BUYEE—ANSWERS FOR PARENTS OF TEENS

Bob had to fly a jet to the Philippines several years ago and had an eye-opening experience. The majority of people in this country had little and worked very hard to meet life's basic needs. He purchased a ticket ahead of time for what was supposed to be a wonderful dinner.

When he got to the banquet room, he couldn't find his ticket.

The lady at the door who was taking tickets was emphatic: "No tickki, no buyee." Meaning that if he didn't buy a ticket, he couldn't eat their food. He tried to explain that he had a ticket, but couldn't find it. The answer was the same as she shook her head and dug in her heels. "No, Mistah. No *tickki*, no *buyee*."

We could learn something from that culture—hard work, for one thing. When your teen has to have the latest tennis shoes to the tune of $150, just say, "I'll pay $45 for tennis shoes. Anything more than that, you can earn." This teaches teens the value of a dollar. If they want to go to Six Flags and hold out their no-longer-pudgy hands, let them earn the price of the ticket and give them some spending money if you wish.

If they grumble over the fact that they must buy their own ticket when "all the other parents are buying *their* kids' tickets," the answer is simple. Just say, "No buyee, no tickki."

LONG-TERM BENEFITS

Let's face it, most of us didn't learn financial responsibility in our teens. Just imagine where you would be today if you'd started working on the miracle of compounding interest in your twenties. There are other benefits to teaching our children financial responsibility while they are in our home. Here are just a few of them.

- ✓ Fewer arguments over what they want and what you can afford.
- ✓ They are less likely to become "boomerang kids" who return to your home in their adult years due to poor financial management.
- ✓ They will learn to spend less than they earn and be a financial success.
- ✓ They will not be in bondage to debt.
- ✓ They are far more likely to be content or satisfied with their situation and thereby live a more productive and healthy life.

✓ The lives they positively impact with their financial resources will last for all eternity.

✓ They will realize that money is never the goal, but a resource used to accomplish worthy goals and obligations.

✓ Your grandchildren are less likely to be brought up in a broken home, since more than 50 percent of divorced couples cite finances as the number one reason for the divorce.

✓ Your children will be in a position to take care of you in your old age.

"Happiness is not based on money. And the best proof of that is our family."

—CHRISTINA ONASSIS

How to
Save Money
in Your
Neighborhood

CHAPTER SEVEN

Coupon Criminals vs. Coupon Champions

Bringing Double Coupons to Your Community

I became the Coupon Queen when I hosted a weekly television spot in New York. "Her majesty" was frequently recognized in public as grocery store checkers screamed and ran for the break room when they saw me coming. One day when I was in line with my coupons, I politely warned the middle-aged man in line behind me, "You may want to move to another line because I have a lot of coupons."

The big man with a beard replied cheerfully, "Oh, that's all right; my wife and I use coupons too."

About *fifteen minutes* later, the checker was finally finished with the Coupon Queen's coupons.

The checker looked at the good-natured man and informed him, "This lady just saved $112 in coupons and only paid $30 for that cart of groceries."

Amazed, the man's jaw dropped open as he turned to me and simply asked, "Will you marry me?"

By the way, that man was not my husband, Bob. I want a man who will love me for who I am—not for my coupons. Getting marriage proposals is only one of the many things that can happen to a Coupon Queen in the grocery store. One of my princesses, Wendy, had an interesting experience after a recent local seminar. During this presentation I introduced my "royal court" to the audience, and each princess shared a savings tip from her experience.

The following Saturday when Wendy was in the grocery store, she was stopped by several customers. Each one asked, "Aren't you a coupon princess?"

Wendy would roll her lovely violet eyes, fluff her black hair with one hand, and bat her eyelashes as she humbly answered, "Well, yes, dahling. As a matter of fact, I *am* a member of the royal court."

To which the coupon pauper would quickly ask, "Then could you please answer a question?"

Wendy wasn't used to all the local attention as she held court in the grocery store, and she certainly wasn't prepared for what happened next. About two-thirds of the way through the store, she realized that someone was following her. Sure enough, this woman was mimicking each of her actions.

When Wendy looked at Glad garbage bags that were on sale for $1.50, she'd take out her 65¢ coupon (which would be doubled at the checkout) and put the item in her cart. Then she proceeded down the aisle. When Wendy looked back, the lady who was following her slowly crept up to the Glad bags, looked through her coupons, located the desired one, and smiled with delight as she threw her bounty of 20¢ garbage bags into her own cart.

This was repeated for the next several aisles. Wendy found the good deals and the coupon-princess-in-training bagged the bargains in her wake.

The moral of this story is: Yes, you too can be Coupon Royalty, but be prepared to be stalked by paparazzi in the grocery store.

Not everyone you find in the coupon business is a legitimate and noble royal heir. Take Coupon Connie, for example. This woman was featured in the *Dallas Morning News* a number of years ago. Just to show you how compulsive couponing and rebating can be when taken to extreme, Connie was brought up on twenty-three federal fraud and racketeering charges and found guilty on several counts.

Connie drove a BMW, wore a mink coat, and scrounged through dumpsters to get the UPC codes off of empty product boxes. In turn, she sold these completed rebates to the highest bidder—an illegal practice. Rebates are very specific in that they usually allow only one rebate per household. Buying, selling, or trading these rebates is against the law—so watch out for rebate clubs that deal in completed rebates!

Connie also had another business on the side—she manufactured coupons in her basement.

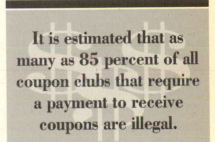

You can save money without becoming a coupon criminal. It is estimated that as many as 85 percent of all coupon clubs that require a payment to receive coupons are illegal. These organizations also offer the "opportunity" to make money at home by selling coupon books or clipping coupons. Some even offer money for coupons by the pound.

In order to keep your integrity intact, the Federal Trade Commission (*www.federaltradecommission.com*) brochure entitled "Costly Coupon Scams" suggests that consumers tempted to buy into a coupon clipping business ask:

- ✓ for details of the company's refund policy;
- ✓ for the total cost of the work-at-home program, including supplies, equipment, and membership fees;
- ✓ who will pay you, whether you'll be paid on salary or commission, and when you will get your first paycheck;
- ✓ the Better Business Bureau and the local consumer protection agency in their own area and in the area where the promoter is based, whether consumers have complained about the promoter;

✓ about the postage costs and processing fees associated with
    getting the coupons.

In addition to these questions, the Coupon Information Corporation (*www.cents-off.com*), a nonprofit organization dedicated to fighting coupon fraud, says you should also ask the following:

✓ Where do you get the coupons?
✓ How do you prevent stolen or counterfeit coupons from
    entering your inventory?
✓ Has any manufacturer endorsed the organization? (If yes,
    ask for the name and phone number.)
✓ How many of your distributors are making a profit? Ask
    for the overall average.

After the success of *Shop, Save, and Share,* many readers wanted to know how to bring double coupons to their area since they did not have this opportunity available to them. I developed the following guidelines that may prove successful for those of you who live in coupon-deprived areas.

COUPON PROFESSIONALS

When approaching a store manager about the possibility of introducing double coupons to the store, conduct yourself as a professional; remember that you never get a second chance to make a first impression. Dress well, find a baby-sitter for Junior, and make an appointment to speak with the store manager regarding consumer feedback. Stress that you are not trying to sell anything; you just would like ten minutes to discuss a couple of positive suggestions that could enhance customer relations. If you want, you can ask an upbeat, positive friend to go along.

Strategies

The supermarket industry is an extremely competitive market (sorry for the pun), and customer feedback is critical. You might want to get a few friends to sign a petition that reads something like "I would shop more often at Big G food stores if they would periodically offer double coupons." (But don't gather signatures on store property.)

With the support of a petition, you won't be standing alone in your appeal. You might even want to take the manager cookies as a "thank you for meeting with me" gift. (I recommend homemade chocolate chip cookies.)

Be positive. When you meet with the manager of your local store and ask him or her to consider offering double coupons, start with a positive statement, like "When I shop at your store, I'm always impressed with how friendly your staff is." Not many customers go to the trouble of scheduling an appointment, and the manager needs to feel comfortable that you are not complaining or selling, but offering positive suggestions.

Suggest alternatives. The manager may tell you that regional headquarters sets the coupon policy. If so, ask if he could possibly get permission from regional to try double coupons on a trial basis— maybe the slowest day of the week (usually a Tuesday or Thursday) or even just one day a month to begin with (it's better than nothing at all). The store could monitor their sales and see how double couponing is working. They may even find an increase in sales as they gain customers who have never shopped at their store.

> When you meet with the manager of your local store and ask him or her to consider offering double coupons, start with a positive statement, like "When I shop at your store, I'm always impressed with how friendly your staff is."

Follow up. After you've made your appeal to the store manager, follow up on the contact. If you aren't satisfied that your request has been heard, get the name and address of corporate headquarters. Be sure that you make copies of your petition, so you can send a copy to headquarters if necessary.

Be thankful. Be sure to thank the store manager for her time, and if she does try double coupons, write letters to her supervisors at the regional office expressing your gratitude.

Be prayerful. Ray Hilbert, the founder and president of the Legacy Group, makes it his business to coach and mentor corporate professionals in both secular and Christian environments. He also writes a daily devotional that you can access through *www.thelegacycoach.com.* The following is his devotional entitled "You Are Favored." It is an excellent perspective to keep in mind before you make your appeal.

Nehemiah 1:11

"O Lord, let your ear be attentive to the prayer of this your servant and to the prayer of your servants who delight in revering your name. Give your servant success today by granting him favor in the presence of this man."

These words were written by the Old Testament prophet, Nehemiah, re-telling the prayer of Moses as Moses was about to go before Pharaoh to ask for the release of the Israelite people from slavery.

> Ask God to grant you favor and success in what you are doing. Ask Him for the right words to say. Ask Him for the right attitude in which to say those words. Ask the Lord to grant you success, and then as His servant, you will give the Lord all the Glory!
>
> —Ray Hilbert

Do you have any important meetings today? Will you be making a presentation to a key (or potential) client/customer? Do you need to ask someone for something that is big or important to you? Is there a conflict in a relationship that needs to be resolved? If you are serving the Lord, ask Him to be attentive to your prayer. Ask God to grant you favor and success in what you are doing. Ask Him for the right words to say. Ask Him for the right attitude in which to say those words. Ask the Lord to grant you success, and then as His servant, you will give the Lord all the Glory!

Used with permission, Ray Hilbert (©2000)

Ask God for the right timing, for favor with the manager, for an attitude of gratefulness and humility, and for His will to be done in the situation. You may not get double coupons in your area, but you will know that you were obedient in the attempt. May God grant you success in the areas in which He leads.

———

"The trouble with success is that the formula is the same as the one for a nervous breakdown."

—*EXECUTIVE DIGEST*, QUOTED IN LLOYD CORY, *QUOTE UNQUOTE*

CHAPTER EIGHT

The Coupon Queen Reigns

Saving Money in the Grocery Store

I made my national television debut (besides being on *The Price Is Right*) on James and Betty Robison's *Life Today* show. We made a video product to raise money for needy children in Third World countries based on the book and did a lot of on-location filming. Naturally, one of those locations was the grocery store.

James Robison's lovely daughter, Rhonda, helped with the taping as I took her around the grocery store, giving her instructions on how to shop wisely and save lots of money. She has four children and found our approach to groceries to be effective in cutting costs for her family. She is a self-admitted "grocery nomad," so we filmed her wandering around the store with a blank look on her face, muttering, "Now where is the peanut butter?"

We also talked the store manager into delivering a line at the checkout stand. It was also his national television debut. Rhonda asked me, "What do the checkers say when you go through their line?"

I answered, "Well, Rhonda, some of them scream and run for the break room, but most of them say…"

Then the camera panned to the store manager, who was still standing by the register, and he said (drum roll, please), "Wow! *I* need to use coupons!"

By this time, there were a lot of customers at the checkouts, watching the commotion and wondering what in the world was going on with the woman wearing a crown and being followed by cameramen and a production crew.

There was one final shot of us pushing the cart out of the store. As I walked by the crowds of people waiting at the checkout stand, I gave my best Elizabethan royal wave. I felt as if I were in the scene from *The Sound of Music* where the guests at the ball wave good-bye to the von Trapp children.

The camera panned to the customers and checkers, most of whom gave us the royal wave in return, while some of them just stared. You can imagine what you'd do if you just wanted to go to the store and grab some milk and then saw the Coupon Queen with her entourage—it would make for interesting dinner conversation.

We taped sixteen hours for the four-hour video product, and by the day's end, we were exhausted, even though everything had gone well. That is, until we taped the final segment.

I was giving my trademark "Coupon Seminar" that I've given almost a thousand times. I began talking about a woman I met in the grocery store known as Yenta (the matchmaker from *Fiddler on the Roof*). I started telling her story, imitating a thick New York accent.

I reached the point in the tale where she shouts at the bag boy to push her cart of groceries. She screams, "If you don't push these groceries, then this woman is going to put her back out! She'll sue your store and do you know where you'll end up? I'll tell you where you'll end up! In the poorhouse—that's what! In the *poorhouse*!"

That is when disaster struck. God has a way of keeping us humble in front of the bright lights and cameras.

I don't know what happened to my last line about the poorhouse. I *do* know it was the end of a long day of taping and I was incredibly tired.

I also know that I have a speech impediment that can occur when I'm tired. Nonetheless, I still can't believe I said this, but right there in the studio, with five cameras rolling, fifteen crew members watching, and a live studio audience listening to my every word, I said: "Do you know where you'll end up? In the whorehouse—that's what!"

No, I didn't say poorhouse.

The fact that a variation of this word is also found in some translations of 1 Samuel 20:30 was of no comfort to me.

The audience burst into uncontrollable laughter while I stood at the podium in shock.

When Bob, who was in the studio audience, fell out of his chair, I could safely say they were rolling in the aisles. The only redeeming aspect of my terrible blunder was that they got some great tape of the audience members laughing.

I turned five shades of red as my humility bucket was filled. Then I looked at the director and said: "I suppose you'll want a retake on that line, huh?"

Well, there's nothing like our daily routine and regular chores to keep us humble when we think we're becoming a hotshot. I thought I had covered every element of grocery shopping in my last book, but I was wrong.

You may think that there is no more comprehensive book on grocery shopping than *Shop, Save, and Share*, and you're right! It is a master's course on how to find, swap, organize, use, combine, and double every type of coupon (store, manufacturer's, instant, competitor's, etc.) for maximum savings. However, this area is always changing, and there are constantly new ways of saving money every day at the grocery store. Here are some favorite new tips:

MENUS

One of the most common questions I have asked of me is: "Do you plan menus for the week?"

My answer is: "I plan my menus according to what I have in my pantry."

Since the majority of things I buy are purchased on sale and with a coupon, I know I've paid the lowest price possible for those products in my pantry. This saves more money than the menu plan approach.

In the menu approach, you decide what you will eat for the week and then you're committed to buying those items whether you have a coupon or not and whether they are on sale or not.

Using the *Shop, Save, and Share* method, I may have to supplement a few items like cottage cheese or fresh tomatoes. But I usually have the vast majority of the items I will need already in stock. Therefore I will save more money than with the menu approach to grocery shopping.

> **Prioritize and maximize your freezer space by packing items in freezer bags or freezer containers. Then you'll have room for chicken breasts when they go on sale for 79¢ a pound.**

MILK, MEAT, AND PRODUCE

Another commonly asked question is: "What do you do about meat, milk, and produce? I rarely find coupons for these items."

Look further into this chapter for tips on buying produce at a better price.

For meat, buy when it's on sale and stock up. Even if you don't have a terribly large freezer, you can still prioritize and maximize your freezer space by packing items in freezer bags or freezer containers. Then you'll have room for chicken breasts when they go on sale for 79¢ a pound.

I usually buy milk wherever it is on sale. Since most people buy this staple every week, it is oftentimes on sale *somewhere* in your town. If you don't want to make a trip to the store just for the sale-priced milk, then check and see if the store you are going to has a policy to honor competitors' ads.

Many Wal-Marts will honor all competitors' ads. All you have to do is take in the competitor's ad with the sale price on any of the items you want. Check with the store manager, but they usually substitute other store brands with their own brand. For example, I had an ad for 12-packs of IGA brand soda in the sale circular I brought to Wal-Mart. They substituted their Sam's brand for that soda, and I got it for the sale price.

Most stores that honor competitors' ads do have some restrictions. They will usually not honor advertised store coupons, percentage discounts, or buy one/get one free pricing. But it is still worth your time and money to ask the right questions at your local store.

E-MAIL CLUBS

I've heard from thousands of people who have already started their own legal and profitable coupon swapboxes using the method I recommended in *Shop, Save, and Share*. For those of you who haven't discovered this resource, I've included a copy of the instructions that you can photocopy and use to start your own box in your neighborhood, workplace, or church (see page 101).

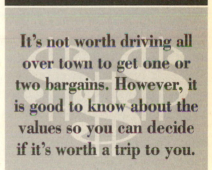

It's not worth driving all over town to get one or two bargains. However, it is good to know about the values so you can decide if it's worth a trip to you.

An easy and highly productive addition to your swapbox club is an e-mail club. These are designed to help you find the best values within your own community. I was a member of a highly successful e-mail club in northern New York that passes on not only the local news, but information on freebies that are found on the Internet as well. I've heard about free coffee, postage, baby shoes, and more through the e-mail club's news. This has been one of my greatest resources for the links that are posted on my Web site.

In addition to Internet offers, this club can alert its members to local manager specials, clearance sales, and even regular weekly sales. Hey, even the Coupon Queen misses a good deal in the store once in a while! When someone goes to Wal-Mart and discovers that they have a cart of Vaseline lotion marked down to a dollar, they would alert the contact person and she would spread the word. If you're going to that store anyway, and you have a dollar coupon off any size of Vaseline, then you can look for the steal of a deal.

Of course, you'll want to keep things in balance; it's not worth driving all over town to get one or two bargains. However, it is good to know about the values so you can decide if it's worth a trip to you (especially if you're going to the store anyway).

One word of caution: There is no need to exchange any money in this type of club. The e-mail account is free, and everything about this club should be free of charge to its members.

Here are the steps to get a club started in your area:

✓ Establish a person who will serve as the point of contact (POC) for your local club; everyone will forward their information to this person. It should be someone who is familiar with the Internet, enjoys it, and will be on the Internet anyway on a regular basis.

✓ The POC will set up a free e-mail account for your club through a service such as Juno. Just call 1-800-654-JUNO or write: New Members Dept., 120 W. 45th St., NY, NY 10036. (See chapter 13 for additional free e-mail services.)

✓ Make sure that this account is served through a personal home computer and not a business account. The POC needs to do this on their own time and not their employer's.

✓ Members will e-mail their good deals to the POC as they find them. The POC will, in turn, send out a mass mailing once a day as the information becomes available. (Some clubs only mail every other day or once a week, depending upon participation and the weekly values.)

✓ Make sure that the POC sends out the mass e-mails using blind carbon copies to protect the privacy of club members.

✓ The POC should check out any Internet site before she forwards this information to the members. The local

values (grocery stores, discount department stores, etc.)
do not require a time-consuming personal visit.

✓ Send your POC a thank-you note every now and then for
her valuable volunteer service to your family and the
community.

✓ Have fun! If it isn't fun and enjoyable to save money and
help others do the same, it's really not worth it.

LOCAL COUPON BOOKS

While the rule of thumb remains that you should never pay money
for coupons, the local coupon book is an exception. These books, commonly known as Entertainment or Happenings books, are used primarily as fund raisers for organizations. They include coupons for free
or reduced-price meals, services, admissions, and other values. They are
usually worth the price you pay for them (anywhere from twenty-five
to thirty-five dollars per book) and usually last for about a year. The fact
that you are helping the nonprofit organization raise funds is a bonus.

If you visit a certain area often or you are about to move, you can
check the availability of these books in that new area by visiting my
Web site at *www.elliekay.com* and linking to *www.entertainment.com*.
Or write to Entertainment Books at 605 E. Robinson St., Suite 135,
Orlando, Florida 32801. Phone 1-407-425-0057 or e-mail them at
askus@entertainment.com.

These books are also a good way to raise money for your school or
organization.

FRUITS AND VEGETABLES

Whether you live in New York City or Alamogordo, New Mexico,
you can save money on fruits and vegetables the way your grandma did.
Cathy Zuidema from Wallaceburg, Ontario, sent me this time-honored
tip: "Make friends with the veggie/fruit man at your grocery store or produce market. I get tomatoes, carrots, bananas, and fruit of all different
kinds for less than half price. Say, would you like my carrot cake jam
recipe?" (I told her yes, and the recipe is great! You can e-mail me for
it.)

The vegetables that Cathy's veggie/fruit man throws out often only have a slight bruise or other minor defect. Look at the rejects as they are sorting vegetables and ask to buy them at a substantially lower price. It's so easy to cut a bad spot out of a green pepper when you're making a salad or to discard the bruise in an apple when you're making a pie.

If you live near a wholesale produce supplier, you can ask to go through their rejected vegetables, which are probably in better shape than the discards in the grocery store because a wholesaler has to consider additional distribution time and handling when sorting their vegetables. One lady got enough strawberries from a wholesaler to make jam for her entire Christmas list—the regular price in a grocery store would have been over a hundred dollars!

> **Make friends with the veggie/fruit man at your grocery store or produce market and get tomatoes, carrots, bananas, and fruit of all different kinds for less than half price.**

FOOD CO-OPS

There are a wide assortment of food co-ops that range from a few friends going in on produce together to highly organized groups that keep track of hours, dues, and surcharges. Here are some guidelines to profitable buying through a food co-op.

Locating a Club Near You

Look in your local Yellow Pages under Cooperatives or Grocers, Retail. If you don't find any co-ops listed, try one of these:

- ✓ Call your local homeschool group. Homeschoolers are typically value-minded and enjoy eating healthy, fresh foods.
- ✓ I order my whole-wheat kernels from a co-op I found by looking under Bakery Supplies in the Yellow Pages.
- ✓ Look under Wholesale Distributors in the Yellow Pages to

locate a wholesaler in your area. Even if they don't sell to individuals, they can probably give you the name of a local co-op or buying club they sell to.

✓ Call your city's Chamber of Commerce and ask for a point of contact for any food co-ops in the city.

✓ The County Cooperative Extension Service can probably give you the name of any local co-ops (plus information on home economics classes they might offer).

✓ If all of these options fail (unlikely, but possible), then send a self-addressed stamped envelope to:

Co-op Directory Services
1254 Etna St.
St. Paul, MN 55106-2120

Start Your Own Produce Co-op

This is feasible for people who live near a produce wholesaler, which are usually in or near urban areas. With as little as thirty dollars per person per month, you could cut your food budget significantly by getting wholesale prices on produce.

To set up a small, successful produce co-op:

✓ Limit your group to about ten members (otherwise it will get very complicated in a hurry and become very burdensome for the members).

✓ Have each member list their personal produce likes and dislikes.

✓ Evaluate these lists and eliminate any item that appears three or more times on the "dislike" list and add any item that appears three or more times on the "like" list.

✓ Call the local wholesale vendors to find one who will work with you. Tell him you will be buying $150 worth of produce every two weeks in a mini co-op you're starting.

✓ Schedule ten buying dates and pick-up dates (pick-up

dates will be the day after the buying dates) for the next five months, so every member can sign up for a date.

✓ Collect the initial $15 for each member as they fill out the information form (see page 95). They cannot turn in a form without the $15 deposit.

✓ On the first buying date, the first member will take the group's $150 to the wholesaler to buy the produce. I recommend you call the wholesaler in advance, tell him the kinds of produce you want, and ask him to gather $150 worth of those items. Call around until you find a wholesaler who will work with you on this.

✓ The designated member will then take the produce home and divide it in ten equal portions (this is a great family bonding experience).

✓ The day after the buying date is the pick-up date, when co-op members will go to the designated member's home and pick up their groceries.

✓ If they are not picked up within 48 hours of the designated pick-up date, the member forfeits their produce and their $15 (talk about an incentive to pick them up when you're supposed to!). The buyer will then donate the produce to a needy family or organization (the Kay family always needs produce!).

✓ The members will pay their $15 at the time of the produce pick-up so the next member will have the money for the next buying session.

✓ The designated member will then give the $150 they've collected to the next buyer on the list.

✓ If a member is going out of town, it is their responsibility to find a substitute with $15 for that time (otherwise the co-op fund will be left short).

✓ If a member cannot be the buyer on the date they signed up for, they are responsible to switch with someone else or find another person who will accept their responsibility.

These guidelines have proven to be effective for successful co-op groups. You can modify these to meet your group's unique needs. Feel free to photocopy these guidelines and pass them out at your first group meeting. The same photocopy permission applies to the co-op application that follows. However, the copyright rules still apply to the rest of the information in this book. Your group may decide to increase the individual amount to $20 every two weeks or even decrease it to $10 and do it weekly. You'll discover what works best for your group.

On the application form below, I went ahead and filled in the first item in the "dislike" category. (See chapter 5 if you don't get it and tell the other people in your co-op to get a copy of this book from the library or bookstore so they can get it too.)

Produce Co-op
Information Application

Name: _____

Address: _____

Home Phone:_____ Work: _____

E-mail: _____

Deposit of $_____ Paid on the date of _____

Produce Likes: _____

_____

Produce Dislikes: _eggplant_ _____

_____

Produce Co-op Buyer
Dates and Delivery Dates

Name	*Buy Dates*	*Pick-Up Dates*
You are signing up to be the designated buyer from the wholesaler on this date.	These are the dates your group has determined will be the dates to buy produce.	These are the days after the Buy Dates when all members are required to pick up produce.

A Note on Other Food Co-ops

As you can see from our "simple" produce co-op, these organizations, while profitable for the value-minded family, can lead to a serious time commitment. Before you join an existing co-op, be sure to obtain a list of the co-op rules and guidelines. Here are some of the questions that handout should answer so you can decide whether this is a good option for your family:

✓ Is there a joining fee?
✓ How long has this co-op been in existence?
✓ Is there a governing board for this co-op?
✓ What kind of time commitment is involved?
✓ Are there surcharges? How much are the surcharges?
✓ Are there processing fees?
✓ Do you have to be a member to make an occasional purchase?
✓ Can I have the names and phone numbers of a couple of other members to ask their opinions?
✓ Do we have a voice in the items we receive?
✓ Do we order the specific things we want?

> Co-ops can be a wonderful way to extend your food budget, but if you are a busy person with limited time, it is imperative that you know the specifics of what you're committing to when you join.

Co-ops can be a wonderful way to extend your food budget, but if you are a busy person with limited time, it is imperative that you know the specifics of what you're committing to when you join.

SHARE

SHARE is an acronym for the Self-Help and Resource Exchange. This national food distribution program is sponsored by a network of churches, unions, community centers, and other volunteer-oriented organizations. There probably already is one in your neighborhood.

SHARE is a viable alternative to the previously mentioned co-ops and does not require a regular commitment, membership dues, or time commitments. Basically, the way this program works is that you donate two hours of community service a month and sign up for the program the month in advance. Sign-ups are conducted by a host organization that will give you a form to have signed to validate your volunteer community service (teaching Sunday school, leading Girl Scouts, cleaning a widow's garage, etc.).

You will buy a package of groceries worth anywhere from $40 to $45 (amounts vary) for $15 (this price could have gone up, too, so check with your local SHARE). They will usually accept this $15 in food stamps or cash. This is not a government program, so participants do not have to meet income requirements in order to participate. The SHARE program buys their food from wholesalers or from growers. You will then pick up your food at a specific time and place or forfeit your prepaid investment.

The SHARE package includes fifteen items, including 6 to 10 pounds of meat, 4 to 7 pounds of fresh vegetables, and 2 to 4 pounds of fruits. SHARE buys only nutritious food and ensures that people with poor food-buying habits are getting at least some healthy food.

With my Coupon Queen approach to buying groceries, I can get these prices or even better values with the methods I use. However, this is a great program for those who do not aspire to coupon royalty status and still want to get some better values on fresh foods.

For information on the SHARE program nearest you, go to *www.worldshare.com,* or to start one, contact:

SHARE
1250 Delevan Dr.
San Diego, CA 92102
(619) 525-2200

ASSORTED TIPS

✓ **Dial for dollars.** If you like a particular item, check the package to see if the company has a toll-free customer number. By calling, you can often get coupons for that item. I've received coupons for free items and many cents-off ones too.

✓ **Just buy a handful.** If your recipe only calls for a few pieces of cauliflower or broccoli, don't waste money on an entire head—especially if your family is not inclined to eat those items. Pick up what you need from the salad bar and avoid the waste.

✓ **No substitutes, please.** Don't waste money on egg substitutes; make your own by just using egg whites. Most of these pricey items are made primarily with egg whites, along with dyes and thickeners.

✓ **Mix your own.** If plain yogurt is less expensive than fruit flavors in your grocery store, make your own flavored yogurt by mixing plain yogurt with fresh fruits or preserves.

✓ **Don't opt for convenience.** Quick-cooking rice can cost twice as much. Buy the regular rice, cook more than you need, and freeze the leftovers to use as needed. You can also add your own seasonings to noodles, rice, vegetables, and pasta to save on the prepackaged variety. (You'll also use less salt by doing this.)

✓ **Weigh your produce.** Not all five-pound bags of apples are created equally—they can vary by as much as half a pound—so weigh before you buy.

✓ **Be a latecomer.** Ask your grocer about late-day markdowns in the bakery, meat, dairy, and floral departments. Meats that are near the expiration date can easily be frozen and then used immediately after they are thawed.

✓ **Rain checks always.** Sometimes I'm grateful when they

> **If your recipe only calls for a few pieces of cauliflower or broccoli, don't waste money on an entire head. Pick up what you need from the salad bar and avoid the waste.**

are out of an item, especially if my coupon has some time on it before it expires. I can usually request a higher quantity on my rain check and have time to collect more coupons for that item while I wait for it to be restocked. I get free items all the time this way.

✓ **Save and share.** Just a friendly reminder that you don't shop for what you need in the store, you shop for what is a good value. Buy the items that are on sale that you have coupons for so you pay the lowest price possible; that way you'll have the items on hand when you need them. You'll also have extra to share with those in need.

**"She is like the merchant ships,
She brings her food from afar."**

—PROVERBS 31:14 NKJV

Coupon Swapbox Instructions

1. Coupons are in zipping plastic bags and contain a name card in the front of each bag. A name card is an index-card-sized piece of paper with names signed on it.

2. Please take a bag and remove the coupons you want from that bag. Sign your name on the name card. **Do not add new coupons to an existing bag.**

3. Put the coupons you're donating in a new bag with your name signed on a new name card. Place the new bag in the swapbox.

4. In the future, only pick those bags without your name on the name card. (You've already gone through the coupons in the bags with your name on them.)

5. Place all your expired coupons in the bag marked "Expired Coupons." We will send these to a military family overseas who can use them in a military commissary up to six months past the expiration date.

6. Have fun! If you have any questions, please call the coupon coordinator _____ at _____.

CHAPTER NINE

Trapping Mice and Killing Rats

Developing Sales Resistance

I was hosting my first coffee for the spouses of my husband's new unit. I wanted to keep the evening simple and decided to forego the traditional crystal, silver, and china. Since we were new to the area, I creatively tried to center the coffee around a common military theme; thus, we had a "moving coffee." The invitations were printed on packing paper glued to small pieces of moving boxes. We thought the entertainment could be assessing the damage of our household goods.

Everything had to be nice—but not so nice that the coffee would be a hard act to follow the next month. Believe me when I say there would be *no problem* to follow this coffee—a trip to Burger King would have provided more ambiance. Several days were spent in preparing the food, house, and agenda. The table was decorated with boxes, packing paper, and claim forms. The cake arrived from the baker, my friend Diane. It depicted the Kays (in stick figures) in front of our new house. There was a moving van in the background. The evening of the coffee, I put the finishing touches on the table while Bob watched Jonathan and

Joshua, aka Señor Mischief and his protégé.

Then their apprentice, Courtney, arrived. She was a two-year-old bit of feminine fluff who lived across the street. She was also the self-proclaimed president of the tricycle gang on Fort Drum Circle. Her petite frame, blue eyes, and blond curls belied the fact that she could hold her own against my then three- and four-year-old boys. Joshua couldn't say her name very well so he called her Corky.

Have you ever heard of synergy? That's where $1 + 1 + 1 = 6$! Well, synergy took over while Bob "watched" the little ones and chatted with Courtney's father in our garage. They were discussing the finer points of artillery warfare when they were interrupted by a series of piercing screams. The shrieks, coming from inside the house, sounded like those of a woman who had just seen a mouse. The fact was, she hadn't seen *a* mouse, she had seen three. Their names were Joshua, Jonathan, and Corky.

As Bob ran toward the house, the front door burst open, and he was run over by three blind mice scrambling out of the house. Their paws were covered with a gooey mess; their eyes shut tightly in fear. Behind them ran the farmer's wife, carrying a broom and shouting incoherently (thankfully, she left her carving knife on the kitchen counter). Inside, Bob saw the reason for his wife's wrath. While he was supposed to be watching the mice, they had added another item to the Kays' list of damaged household goods: the cake.

It might surprise you, then, that I decided to take the three blind mice to the grocery store while I was baby-sitting Courtney one afternoon.

My reasoning was fairly basic: (1) Bethany was playing with a friend; (2) The two older boys were at the youth center; (3) There were only three children left.

I usually take five kids to the store. How difficult could it be to take three kids?

I had forgotten about mice—and synergy.

Jonathan wanted to sit by Courtney. "Because I love her, Mama."

Joshua screamed, "I wuv her too!"

Courtney tossed her blond curls and smiled demurely.

As I strapped all three preschoolers into the back seat of the Suburban, the boys continued to fight over who loved Courtney more.

This should have been the first indication that traveling with mice would not be easy. But I wasn't thinking about mice, I was thinking about coupons and the grocery store. I popped in an *Adventures in Odyssey* cassette tape, and the boys stopped yelling so they could listen to Mr. Whittaker and the gang.

When we got to the parking lot, rain was coming down in a steady drizzle. We had only brought one umbrella, so Jonathan, Joshua, and Courtney used it. As they shared the large gray umbrella and walked across the parking lot, they looked like one large rat—with three sets of legs. The conspicuous rodent, with a little blond tail, stopped traffic as people let it pass. We finally maneuvered our way across the parking lot and reached the front door.

Once inside the store, the collective rat refused to get into the cart. Instead, they scattered from their open cage—wanting FREEDOM! You may be thinking *Who was in control here, anyway?*

I'll admit it, *they* were in control. I'm afraid of rodents.

Synergy continued. They fed off each other—*and* they fed off candy in the open bins by the produce department. At the end of the second aisle, each mouse grabbed a bag of Attends and threw them into the cart as they announced, "We got you diapers."

Throughout the store, I removed wayward products the mice threw into the cart, putting these items back on the shelf. After an hour of scolding, dirty looks, and bribes, it was time to give up. The mice helped me wheel the cart to the checkout. They continued to "help" as they threw bread, crackers, and *eggs* onto the moving belt so the clerk could begin scanning the groceries.

"This stuff works pretty well. My mom uses it," the young clerk said as he held up a package of Movana.

"Wait a minute! I didn't get that." As I took the box, the lettering caught my eye, "Advanced St. John's Wort to Safely and Naturally Balance Emotions and Promote a Feeling of Well-Being."

I looked behind me and saw a commotion with Courtney and Jonathan. He was begging and she was tossing her curls.

Come to think of it, I could stand to naturally balance my emotions, I thought to myself.

But now Joshua was missing. I searched the front of the store and found him doing a somersault in front of an irritated customer—blocking her exit.

Yep, I need a feeling of well-being here.

I placed a $2-off Movana coupon on the counter as I told the checker, "Here, I may need this after all."

Whether you're managing a group of mice at home or running the rat race, it would be nice to have that St. John's Wort feeling when we face daily challenges. Wouldn't it be especially great to remain calm, cool, and collected when you have to deal with those who would try and take away our time, money, and composure? I'm talking specifically about developing sales resistance.

IMPROVE YOUR SALES RESISTANCE

We all have to interact with telephone marketers (usually during the dinner hour) and high-pressure salesmen when shopping for a car, buying a home, or even selecting an outfit at the mall. These usually well-meaning people can talk us into buying things that we don't need, with money we don't have, to impress people we don't like.

Here are some quick, yet effective, tips to help you develop sales resistance and in the process save thousands of dollars every year.

Keep Your Phone Number to Yourself!

Whenever possible, only give your address and do not include your phone number on catalog orders, promotions, and other offers. Be very judicious in giving out your phone number. Try to give an e-mail address instead, for any correspondence.

"Remove My Name from Telephone Solicitations, Please!"

If you do find your phone number on these marketing lists, you do have some recourse. Simply ask the caller to put your name on their "Do not call list." They're required by law to comply with your request. Or, if you prefer, to remove your name from many of these lists at one time, send your complete name, address, and phone number (with area code) to:

> Telephone Preference Service
> Direct Marketing Association
> P.O. Box 9014
> Farmingdale, NY 11735

Junk E-Mail

See chapter 13 for tips on how to avoid cyber junk mail.

Stop the Junk Snail Mail

To opt out of direct-mail marketing lists and curb the deluge of junk mail that flows into your home, write a letter giving your complete name, name variations, and mailing address to:

> Mail Preference Service
> Direct Marketing Association
> P.O. Box 9008
> Farmingdale, NY 11735

"Remove Me from Unsolicited Credit Card Applications, Please!"

The Fair Credit Reporting Act (FCRA) of 1996 gives you the right to opt out of direct marketing lists used by credit bureaus.

In accordance with the provisions of the FCRA, you can call one phone number (1-800-353-0809) to exercise your opt-out option. This is an automated system that will prompt you to answer questions that will identify you. It usually takes around three months for your instructions to reach the big three credit bureaus, but it will stop those unsolicited credit card applications you receive in the mail.

Time Is Money

Statistics indicate that the more time you spend on the phone with a telemarketer, the more likely he or she will get the sale. When another long-distance company or Uncle Joe's Newspaper calls, just say, "No, thank you, I'm not interested." Then promptly hang up the phone. This isn't rude; it's just good stewardship of your time. Some people just hang up with no comment, and that is impolite. But defining your family's time and financial boundaries and the fact that you don't want to waste the telemarketer's time is a very good thing. If you have to, write "No, thank you, I'm not interested" on an index card and tape it next to your phone to remind yourself of your commitment to good time (and financial) stewardship.

Stop Talking!

In the world of sales, marketers are trained to let people talk themselves into the sale. If you're negotiating for a car, a house, furniture, or practically anything that requires negotiations (even a yard sale) and you make an offer to the salesperson, you need to be quiet after you've made the offer. Statistics show that once an offer is made, the next person to talk will generally be the loser.

Be Armed and Dangerous

Before you face any salesperson you need to do your homework. Do your research, and find out what would be a good value for that particular item. Decide *ahead of time* what you will pay and stick to that budget! Don't be afraid to walk out and think about it for a week. More often than not, that outfit will still be in the store, that car will still be on the lot, and that house will still be for sale in a week's time, and you'll have the satisfaction of knowing that you didn't give in to impulse buying.

Most importantly, do your prayer homework. Bathe each purchase (no matter how big or seemingly small) in the power of prayer, and watch God give you the wisdom you need when you need it!

"You can do more than pray after you have prayed, but you cannot do more than pray until you have prayed."

—JOHN BUNYAN

CHAPTER TEN

Bunnies Just Want to Be Free

Finding Freebies

When our daughter, Bethany, was two years old, she was the delight of almost everyone she met. Her blond hair and bonny blue eyes were an irresistible combination, but it was her contagious smiles that made for many new friends. Our little "bunny" found that each face was just a territory to be conquered as she smiled, blew kisses, and performed upon command.

There was one thing that Bethany would *not* do, however, and that was to be left behind by her big brothers. If they got some cars, she had to have cars. If they went to Sunday school, she had to leave the nursery and find a Sunday school class to attend. If they got bikes, she had to have a bike. Actually, she didn't get a bike. She got a shoe.

Bethany's riding toy in the shape of a big pink tennis shoe got many miles on it. The shoe fit and she rode it! She loved to ride it round and round the circle in our housing area's driveway. The housing area consisted of a series of circular areas all connected in a horseshoe shaped main street. We let her ride the circle with supervision, but the main street was off-limits for all the children.

One day I was unloading groceries from our van and ran inside to answer the phone. I must have been inside for about five minutes when I went back out to check on the bunny, who had been strapped into her car seat. She wasn't in the van, she wasn't in the yard, she wasn't riding in the circle with the boys—she wasn't *anywhere*!

We were also missing one large pink shoe.

As I was running from house to house in our cluster of homes, asking if anyone had seen a little bunny, a neighbor drove into the circle with a smiling blond girl and a bright pink shoe in the front seat.

> There are many so-called free offers out there, but you need to evaluate each one because there are scams wrapped up in some of the "free" labels as well.

Apparently, as soon as I went in the house to answer the phone, she talked the boys into letting her out of her car seat, then she hopped on her shoe and made tracks. When the neighbor saw her, she was careening down the sidewalk, feet up in the air, blond curls trailing in the wind and having a joyride to newfound freedom.

Our neighbor recognized Bethany and brought her home to her panic-stricken mother. I thanked God for guardian angels and kind neighbors.

I guess that's just shoe business.

I think we're all a little bit like Bethany at times—we enjoy our freedom. There are many kinds of freedom besides the ability to ride a shoe down the street unencumbered. Financial freedom is something that this book is designed to help you achieve. Part of financial freedom, however, is the ability to differentiate a genuine freebie from a pseudo freebie.

There are many so-called free offers out there, but you need to evaluate each one because there are scams wrapped up in some of the "free" labels as well. Here are some questions to consider as you evaluate a free item on the Internet, in the store, or through the mail.

✓ Do I have to pay anything for this offer?

✓ What is the bottom line in dollars that following up on this
offer will cost me?

✓ Do I pay shipping and handling?

✓ What is the cost of shipping and handling?

✓ What is the total price per item when shipping and handling are added?

✓ Is this item truly worth the bottom line price after shipping
and handling?

✓ What is the long-term commitment to take advantage of
this free offer? (This is especially a consideration in
CD, tape, and book clubs.)

✓ Is this a reputable company?

✓ What is the average price per item for commitment
purchases?

✓ What will following up on this offer cost me in terms of
time?

✓ Could I get this item free and give it to someone who
needs it more than I do?

CURRENT FREEBIES

We research all the freebies that are posted at *www.elliekay.com* for
value and quality. Even though we don't officially endorse the products
or companies that these freebies represent, we have viewed the offers
individually. The determining factor we use before posting these offers
is: "Would I take advantage of this offer myself? Is it worth my time and
money?"

That's why we've posted freebie offers for Starbucks Coffee, free
coupons you can download legally, and free bath products that offer a
$10 gift certificate and end up costing me 24¢ for three bars of foo-foo
soap. Great offers like these are worth my time and money.

I'll give you two examples of offers I received today. The first was
an offer passed along by *www.coolsavings.com*, which included the
wording, "And, as a 1st-time eNutrition customer you will save $10 with
a minimum $35 purchase on any sports nutrition, weight management,

body & senses products, vitamins, supplements and more!"

Now, I've found some great deals through *www.coolsavings.com* (you can sign up through my Web site), but you have to evaluate every offer. The above offer requires that I spend a minimum of $25 after the discount in order to take advantage of the promotion. Forget it! I'm not spending $25! I would call that *spending* money, not *saving* money.

On the other hand, I got an offer from *www.drugstore.com* that offered a free gift worth $20 with any purchase. Since there was no minimum purchase and there was a photo of the gift package (complete with sizes and scents), I took advantage of this offer. I bought a $3 Garden Botanika buttermilk cleansing bar, paid $2.95 in shipping and handling, and got a six-piece gift set free. I look at it as getting a birthday gift, postpartum mom gift, or a hospitality gift for only $5.95. Which brings me to my next point.

> **When you consider getting a freebie, think outside the shoebox. Ask yourself, "Could I get this item free and give it to someone who needs it more than I do?"**

CONSIDER FREEBIES AS SHARIES

A recurrent theme in my writing and speaking is sharing. When you consider getting a freebie, think outside the shoebox. Ask yourself the questions outlined on page 111, paying special consideration to the one about sharing: "Could I get this item free and give it to someone who needs it more than I do?" If you can get three free packages of diapers just for making a phone call and they don't require you to have a baby to get the diapers, then take three minutes and get the free diapers to give to someone.

I hear about God's provision through freebies all the time. A single mom from Colorado gets free copies of the Sunday paper inserts by going through the recycled papers at her apartment complex. She secured permission from the manager and with an hour of elbow grease each week, she gets around fifty inserts that others discarded. Not only does she give away some of these inserts to other couponers, listen to what else she has to say: "I'm getting dozens of free items each week. Last week, I took eight bags of toiletries to a crisis pregnancy center. Here I thought that I was the needy one, and Ellie showed me through her helpful instruction that I can be the one to *give* help. I have a greater sense of self-esteem and worth as I've learned to manage on my limited income and still reach out to help others. This has been life-changing for me. Thank you, Ellie (and I like your cutesy stories!)" (posted at *www.amazon.com*).

LIBRARY RESOURCES ON FREEBIES

Not only does the library offer free access to the Internet, but it also offers books you should research as leads to other freebies. If they don't stock these titles, ask for an interlibrary loan.

- ✓ *Guide to Free Attractions, USA* (Cottage Publications)
- ✓ *Guide to Free Campgrounds, USA* (Cottage Publications)
- ✓ *The Student Guide: Financial Aid* (Federal Government)

OTHER FREEBIES

Airfare (see more in chapter 11)

If a flight is overbooked, you are usually offered a free round-trip ticket anywhere in the continental United States if you will give up your seat and take the next flight. Sometimes, the later flight will arrive only minutes behind your scheduled flight due to connections and delays.

I've even heard from people who book themselves on almost full flights with partially booked following flights. Then, when they check in, they check to see if the plane is full and offer their seat in exchange for a later flight and a round-trip pass.

You can check your airline's schedule by viewing the arrival and departure times on its Web site. (See chapter 11 for Web addresses for the major airlines.)

Toll-Free Numbers

Before you pay for a toll call to any large organization or company, start by calling toll-free directory assistance at 1-800-555-1212. It's rare that a large organization doesn't have a toll-free number.

Newspaper Ads

Many newspapers and "swap" publications have classified ad sections that list "free-for-the-taking" items. Sometimes you may need only slight repairs with minimal costs to get a serviceable appliance or other needed item.

Free Business Advice

There's an organization called SCORE, which is a consulting arm of the Small Business Administration. If you have a home-based business or any small business, they are available with free advice. Call 1-800-634-0245.

Free Government Publications

To request a complete catalog of dozens of free consumer booklets, write to the Consumer Information Center-2D, P.O. Box 100, Pueblo, CO 81002.

"Those of us who enjoy riding on two-wheel vehicles will tell you that the reason there is such a thrill in it is that you feel so free."

—CHUCK SWINDOLL,
TALE OF THE TARDY OXCART

CHAPTER ELEVEN

Dunkin' Donuts Duo

Cheap Dates/Cheap Travel

She had long red hair, liked to laugh, and wore a plastic Oreo cookie necklace. She played the clarinet and I played the "burping bedpost" (our nickname for the bassoon). From the first time I saw her sitting in Mr. Pitt's sixth grade band class, I knew she'd be my best friend. Donna Nicholson was not just an average friend; she was a kindred spirit—she still is. Now she's Donna Thomas, RN, wife of Rob, and mother of three precious girls.

Donna and I didn't do drugs, sex, or rock and roll. (Well, maybe just a teensy-weensy bit of rock and roll.) We were good girls. We got mostly A's, went to the church youth group together, and even played the piano for a senior center on Sundays.

While our peers went to parties to get rip-roaring drunk, Donna and I made our own fun. We'd go rip-roaring around in my Datsun B210—sans artificial stimulants. We often drove to one of our favorite places—Dunkin' Donuts. We liked to hit it around 10 P.M. Since not many folks eat donuts that late, we'd have the place to ourselves.

One night when we pulled into the parking lot, things looked a little strange. We could see the only worker, a donut guy, through the window—and boy, was he having fun. He was throwing donuts high in the air, watching them plop into a tub of glaze, and then laughing hysterically. He looked as if he were on a Bavarian cream sugar high.

We suddenly had an idea inspired by Starsky and Hutch, two guys who were partners on a popular cop show of the same name. Donna and I were partners too—in fun. I burst into the donut shop's front door and threw my back against the front wall, my hands held together as if I were pointing a gun. The donut guy held a tray of three dozen chocolate glazed donuts in his hands. Somehow, despite his obvious surprise, he managed to hold onto that tray.

"This is a bust! I'll cover you, Starsky!"

Then Donna ran in, her fingers drawn and legs bent in a low squat. "Stick 'em up, dude! This is a bust and you've been busted."

Mr. Donut carefully set down the tray of donuts. He may have been on a sugar high, but he knew the difference between a finger and a gun. He played along, as if he believed us. "What? Say, man, you can't bust me. I'm clean—except for this glaze." He licked his fingers. "Ah, chocolate."

He said the magic word—chocolate.

"Now, are you cops going to order some donuts, or what? I'm cool, now, you know I'm cool." He washed his hands as he laughed at our silly antics.

As we sat down and ate our chocolate-glazed donuts and drank our milk, we said, "You know, life doesn't get much better than this."

When we left the shop, we had to go through our exit routine.

Donna ran around the front display case and pushed her back against the wall. She shouted, "OK, I gotcha covered, Hutch. We'd better split this joint!" (which meant we were leaving).

I did a somersault out the doorway, "That's a big ten-four, Starsky."

We had strategically left the windows down on my Datsun. True to the form of entrance à la Starsky and Hutch, we jumped through the windows and into the car. As we backed out of the parking space, we looked through the window of the donut shop. A donut flew through the air—plop! It landed in the glaze. The silent laughter from within the donut shop matched our laughter back in the car.

———————————

In this chapter, we're going to learn how to save money on entertainment, vacations, and just plain fun. You may think these cheap thrills started for me during my high school years as a member of the Dunkin' Donuts Duo, but they began long before that. I'll let my mom, Paquita Rawleigh, tell you about the frugal beginnings of a future Coupon Queen:

> It was on one of our vacations to the coast of Galveston, Texas, that my four-year-old daughter, Ellie, got her first taste of being an entrepreneur. We were on our way to the beach, and at the time, there was only one very busy street that led vacationers to the warm sands. Traffic was heavy and we progressed slowly.
>
> The girls were getting tired and fidgeting, so I had the brainy idea of asking them, "Would you girls like to get out of the car and go on a scavenger hunt for bottles?"
>
> They weren't the least bit excited until I added, "I will give you three cents for every bottle you can get."
>
> Back in the mid-sixties, recycling meant fixing a tricycle. Most of our sodas came in glass bottles, since we didn't have the aluminum cans we use today. The grocery stores paid cash for our glass empties, and there were plenty of empties on the side of the road to the beach. As people drank the last of their cool soda, they cast their bottles into the empty fields, and they gently settled into the soft sand.
>
> When the car stopped once again, the girls and I got out to start our scavenger hunt. As we filled our bags with bottles, the girls got excited by the prospect of their three cents per bottle. By the time their dad caught up to us in his car, we were tired and sweaty and ready to cool off in the nearby ocean.
>
> After we got home, I went to the store with the bottles, and when I came back I called the girls into the kitchen. I put five

shining dimes on the table and watched Ellie's eyes get as big as saucers.

"Is it my money, Mama?" she asked.

"Well, the first dime is for you to put in the Sunday School plate for the Lord, OK?" I told her as she nodded. "Two dimes go into your piggy bank and these last two dimes…"

I was interrupted by Ellie as she exclaimed, "What about those two dimes, Mama, what about them?"

I smiled at my little girl, "Those two dimes are yours to do as you like."

"Oh, Mama," she shouted as she danced around the room, "I'm rich! I'm rich!"

I smiled as I watched my little girl and thought, "There goes my littlest entrepreneur!"

It was the first time she earned money due to her own efforts, and I knew it wouldn't be the last. I knew that she was a serious and responsible little girl who showed skill beyond her years. Little did I know that I was raising the future Coupon Queen.

Whether you are a born saver or you just want to learn how to do more with less, the following quick tips will help you save money on having fun.

ZOO MEMBERSHIPS

Most zoos are members of a reciprocal zoo association. This means you pay a fee with the zoo of your choice and you get reciprocal privileges in several hundred other zoos, aquariums, and wildlife parks across the country. Our local zoo in Alamogordo is a small facility and only charges $25 per year for a family membership. However, with our membership card we've gone to the El Paso Zoo free (it would have cost $18 for the family for the day), the Albuquerque Biological Park (saved $23 for the day), and the Los Angeles Zoo (saved $34). As a matter of fact, we maintained our zoo membership when we moved from New Mexico to New York and got free entrance to zoos in New

York for less than the annual membership of our local zoo.

Check out the American Zoo Association at *www.aza.org*, where you can view the several hundred zoos available in this reciprocal zoo program. After we visited our friends Mark and Diane Thomas in Albuquerque and they saw us get in free, they joined the Alameda Park Zoo in Alamogordo and had the membership tickets mailed to them in Albuquerque. Now they visit our zoo, their own zoo, and many others for a fraction of the price. These memberships often offer discounts at the bookstore and passes to special exhibits. For more information, you can contact our zoo at:

Alameda Park Zoo
P.O. Box 596
Alamogordo, NM 88310
(505) 439-4290

> **Pay a fee with the zoo of your choice and get reciprocal privileges in several hundred other zoos, aquariums, and wildlife parks across the country.**

MUSEUM MEMBERSHIPS

Museum memberships work the same way zoo memberships do, with a reciprocal list that can save you locally and when you travel. With our zoo and museum memberships we are never at a loss for fun, free, and new things to do in another city. We joined the New Mexico Museum of Natural History for only $40 a year and received an ASTC (Association of Science Trade Centers) passport. This passport allowed us access to hundreds of museums, even though we only visited a dozen other museums on our trips in the last year, *plus* our membership included passes to the Dynamax theater.

New Mexico Museum of Natural History
1801 Mountain Road NW
Albuquerque, NM 87122
(505) 841-2803

You can search just about every museum in the country by area if you go to *www.museum.ca.org.*

Something to remember: Museums participating in the ASTC

Travel Passport Program agree to waive general admission fees for one another's members, but fees for planetariums, theaters, and special exhibitions are not waived unless specified.

With this pass, we can visit our local space museum, where the kids love to operate the new space shuttle simulator. Our friends joined this museum and sent an additional card to their college student daughter in New York City, so she can also take advantage of the free entertainment. Check out the more than four hundred museums listed at *www.astc.org* for more information or write to the New Mexico Museum, listed above.

> *Go to your favorite restaurant's site on the Internet by entering www.(favorite restaurant's name).com. For example, go to www.bennigans.com and see what promotional offers they may have posted.*

PARKS AND OPEN SPACES

Few things are more romantic than a picnic in a park. If you have any suitable open space nearby, make up a picnic lunch and sit somewhere beautiful and enjoy the scenery.

Hiking is a great way to combine exercise with togetherness. Discover the countryside around you. You'll be amazed at what's on your doorstep. Search "hiking trails" on the Internet for a multitude of ideas. For a complete "what, when, where, and how" of hiking and walking, go to *www.trails.com*. Or for a full listing of national parks go to *www.nps.gov/parks.html*. If you are a member of AAA, then you must check out *www.aaa.com* for tried-and-true vacation sites. For state searches of hundreds of leisure activities on federal lands, go to *www.recreation.gov*.

DINNER

Don't forget that there are coupons available for many dinner places you enjoy. Look in the FSI (Free Standing Inserts) in your Sunday paper when you're collecting your grocery store coupons. Go to your favorite restaurant's site on the Internet by entering *www.(favorite restaurant's name).com*. For example, go to *www.bennigans.com* and see what promotional offers they may have posted. Go to *www.valpak.com* for local offers and *www.citysearch.com* to find bargain restaurants neighborhood by neighborhood.

TRAVEL
Maps

Whether you're taking a major cross-country trip, going to a nearby city, or just looking for that new restaurant across town, print out a free map from the Internet before you hit the road. Click on *www.mapquest.com* or *www.mapblast.com*, or for more specific road trips, try *www.mapsonus.com* and *www.interstate4U.com*.

The Travel Industry Association at *www.tia.org* lists state tourism offices with links and lots of pictures.

Weather

If you want to check out the weather where you're going, you can look at *www.weather.com*, *www.accuweather.com*, or *www.worldclimate.com*.

Travel Deals

If you're going to travel soon, it's worth your time to check out the fares available on the Internet at sites such as *www.bestfares.com, www.expedia.com* (or 1-800-397-3342), *www.smarterliving.com*, and *www.cheaptickets.com*.

For last-minute hotel rooms you could go to the very large TravelWeb site and look for Click-It! Weekends at *www.travelweb.com*. Each Monday they post the coming weekend's special offers.

Online Auctions

After you read the information in chapter 13 about Internet safety and auctions (for even more information, look at *www.safeshopping.org*), you may want to look at some of the auctions on the Internet. Online auction sites for airline tickets and other travel needs are mushrooming all over the Web. They are low on service but high on value. Look for established sites such as *www.ebay.com, www.boxlott.com, www.skyauction.com*, or *www.bidtripper.com* for some good values. Or call 1-888-538-0733 to be alerted when an auction item comes up matching your travel criteria. You could get half-price hotels, rental cars, plane tickets, entertainment tickets, etc. But you'll need to do your research on a number of the travel sites listed to know what a good value is. For example, even though airfare to Chicago can be cheap (they have two major airports, served by dozens of airlines), city hotel costs can be steep. Finding a cheaper hotel at an auction could be a better value.

> **Online auction sites for airline tickets and other travel needs are mushrooming all over the Web. Look for established sites such as *www.ebay.com, www.boxlott.com, www.skyauction.com*, or *www.bidtripper.com* for some good values.**

The best-known name in the online auction field is *www.priceline.com*, where no one bids against you, they just let you know if you can have the price you bid.

I've used sites like Priceline before, and the way it works is simple:

✓ Do your research on the lowest fare you can find and plan to bid on Priceline about 20 percent lower than that fare. If you don't get the bid, you've lost nothing.

✓ Have your credit card ready.

✓ Enter your destination, departing and arrival airports, and dates of departure and arrival.

✓ Enter your price bid.

Usually, within 24 hours you'll have an acceptance or rejection. If you are rejected, *you can't enter the same information with a higher price!* You will have to change one of the pieces of information, like departure or arrival airports or travel dates, and then make your bid again with a higher price. The key is to look at all the options of arrivals and departures and bid on the most popular airports and most convenient departure and arrival times first and save some other airports in the same vicinity as a backup in case they don't accept your price.

Once you make a bid and they accept it—there are no refunds or changes! So this system is only good if you have some flexibility in your schedule and know you won't need to make changes.

My friend, Brenda Taylor, had to drive fifty miles out of the way, leave on a date she didn't want to leave, and arrive later than expected just to save $50. Since she couldn't use the flight as a frequent flier benefit on her usual airline, she decided it wasn't worth it. You'll have to decide if the savings are worth the inconveniences.

On the other hand, a college student we know booked a flight from California to New York to see some friends for only $150. She booked it six months in advance, and it was truly worth the risk as there really was no inconvenience in her case.

If you're flying outside the United States, you may want to look at *www.state.gov* for global travel restrictions before you book a flight.

Airline Internet Specials

One final tip is to try the airlines directly for their Internet specials. Most major U.S. carriers offer these weekly specials. You can try American Airlines at *www.im.aa.com*, TWA's TransWorld Specials at *www.twa.com/dcspecials*, US Airways' E-Savers at *www.usairways.com*, United's E-Fares at *www.ual.com*, or Northwest Airlines' CyberSavers at *www.nwa.com*. I tried Southwest Airlines at *www.southwestairlines.com* for their Click'n Save Specials. I just booked two round-trip, nonstop tickets from El Paso to Dallas for a total of $220 (only $110 each). The catches are that you have to buy well in advance, they're nonrefundable, and no changes can be made. There are no reserved seats on this airline, but that is why they have some of the cheapest fares in the industry. If you get to the gate about an hour and fifteen minutes ahead of departure time, you can be one of the first people on the plane and get a comfortable seat in the bulkhead area (unless there are handicapped individuals flying, who have priority).

These flights are usually booked, which is why the industry sometimes refers to them as "cattle cars."

Happy flying!

Hotels

Besides some of the auction sites we've already mentioned, you can also check hotel sites for their weekly Internet specials. Try the following for e-mail alerts: Hyatt at *www.hyatt.com*, Radisson at *www.radisson.com/hotdeals*, Holiday Inn at *www.bass-hotels.com/holiday-inn*, Best Western at *www.bestwestern.com*, and the Hilton at *www.hilton.com*.

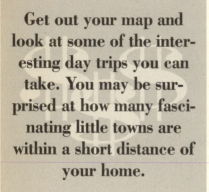

> **Get out your map and look at some of the interesting day trips you can take. You may be surprised at how many fascinating little towns are within a short distance of your home.**

Day Trips

A change is as good as rest, they say. So get out your map and look at some of the interesting day trips you can take. You may be surprised at how many fascinating little towns are within a short distance of your home. There will be lots of places you can take your family to look at historic buildings and interesting architecture, or just wander around markets or antique stores. If you go to *www.bestsmalltowns.com*, you will find sites that will help you decide.

HAVE FUN

Some of the best dates I've had with Bob have been the simplest ones. When we take time out of our hectic schedules, turn off the radio, television, and computer, and just enjoy one another's company, we find we don't need much.

Our family has discovered that we don't need a trip to Rio, an expensive meal at a posh restaurant, or a big day at a theme park to have genuine, guilt-free fun. Paying a big credit card bill or adding more debt to your family's already stretched debt load isn't fun.

Family fun is about being together before the kids are grown. It's learning to listen to those babies you had. It's about learning to laugh at a *situation*, not at another person. It's about learning to laugh with others and yourself over moments that are truly comical through the eyeglasses of time and distance.

It's great to have a family joke fest, trying to creatively wash away the stresses of life over coffee and brownies or soda and popcorn. God gave us creativity and humor to entertain ourselves. We don't need the trappings of things and activities to find genuine relaxation.

"Charles Haddon Spurgeon was criticized constantly by the press because of his humor. Do you know at times, in the middle of his sermon, he would lean back and laugh to the top of that great London Tabernacle? Shocked those people to death. The press would write it out: 'Look at that. Irreverent.' I think the best answer he ever gave was this,

'If my critics only knew how much I held back, they would commend me.'"

—J. OSWALD SANDERS,
SPIRITUAL LEADERSHIP

CHAPTER TWELVE

The Ghosts of Christmas Past

Holiday Savings

The creepy organ music rose to a crescendo as the eight-year-old girl huddled on the sofa, shaking with fright. She hated watching these scary movies that her parents enjoyed, but she hated being alone upstairs when they were watching a scary movie even more. So here she found herself, fighting those familiar feelings of panic when suddenly a blood-curdling "Aaaaghh!" filled the air. The little girl hid her eyes to shut out the image of a mummy attacking a woman.

At precisely the same moment the woman in the movie screamed, a pillow hit the little girl on the head as a deep voice bellowed, "Boogeda, boogeda, boo!" scaring the wee-wee out of the wee girl.

This was my dad's idea of a joke. Pretty lame, huh?

I didn't think it was funny then, and I don't think it's funny to get scared now. I vowed that when I was old enough to choose, I wouldn't watch any movie or TV program that was designed to entertain primarily by scaring the wits out of the viewer.

To this day, I haven't watched a horror film, slasher movie, or any similar genre. I never enjoyed the nightmares that followed my child-hood exposure to monsters, and my children don't have to contend with them.

Besides that, I get scared enough when I look in the mirror first thing in the morning! (When did my eyelids start to do that foldy-over thing, anyway?)

Do you have any ghosts in your past? Maybe they live in your present, or maybe you're creating them right now for your future. I'm not talking about Alfred Hitchcock or Vincent Price; I'm talking about poor financial choices you made in your past that are haunting you now.

> **In the long run, the finan-cial pressure your family experiences is simply not worth the temporary satisfaction of the item that robbed you of your financial freedom.**

One of the greatest times that the temptation to overspend can hit you is during a holiday. Buying on credit or blowing your budget on holiday "necessities" is the same thing as planting a horrific mental image in your mind that is scary and threatening. Planting extra debt into your already surmounting debt load is like watching *Friday the 13th* and then going for a midnight walk in the woods alone. It's inevitable that you and your family will feel the anxiety of amassed debt. In the long run, the financial pressure your family experiences is simply not worth the temporary satisfaction of the item that robbed you of your financial freedom.

Here are some tips to navigate your way through each of the major holidays and keep you from scaring yourself when you pay your credit card bills.

NEW YEAR'S DAY
New Ways for New Days

My business is the busiest at this time of year because people tend to make New Year's resolutions about two things: finances and health. This is a good day to take out the video camera and ask each family member to think of goals they have for the new year. These can be ways they want to grow physically, financially, spiritually, or intellectually. Then the next January first, pull out the old videos and evaluate the progress of your goals and make next year's tape.

Another good way to celebrate the new year is to take a gift basket or baked good to a friend you didn't get to see over the rush of the Christmas holidays. It's not too late to give a holiday greeting. Why, we get holiday cards and letters all the way up to June!

You might want to start an annual photo album or scrapbook as a family. We've been doing this for ten years and have more than twenty volumes. Periodically, but especially on New Year's Day, we like to look at the photos. It gives our family a sense of where we've been and a feeling of heritage. These memories also stir up hopes for the future and the destiny that God has for each of us as we see how quickly time passes.

VALENTINE'S DAY/MOTHER'S DAY/FATHER'S DAY
The Many Languages of Love

Bob and I used to give our children very nice presents on holidays other than Christmas, but then realized they were starting to think that the holidays were essentially all about them! Besides that, when you start multiplying a simple gift times five about five times a year, the spending can quickly get out of control!

We developed a creative way of handling many of these holidays and extended this idea to Mother's Day, Father's Day, and Grandparents' Day. We issue coupon books with homemade coupons for items the family members truly enjoy. This little booklet has about ten coupons in it and requires plenty of forethought. They are gifts of time and love. One Mother's Day, Daniel gave me coupons for five free baby-sitting hours, Philip gave me a coupon for doing one of my chores, and Bethany gave me a coupon for a back rub. Joshua and Jonathan gave me five free kisses that were worth ten on double coupon days!

We gave them each a coupon for a trip out with Mom or Dad for ice cream, one free bed-making day, a trip to the park, a candy bar of their choice, and their favorite breakfast for a day—I think you get the general idea. The key is individualizing the coupon book and taking the time to make it special.

> **Issue coupon books with homemade coupons for items the family members truly enjoy. They are gifts of time and love.**

EASTER
Eggciting Eggstravanganzas

I shop for Easter clothes months in advance, using my traditional methods of scouring garage sales, clearance racks, and consignment stores. This year, I found a lovely Jessica McClintock by Gunne Sax for only eight dollars at a consignment store for Bethany and saved it for Easter. The boys looked so nice in their suits from consignment stores that even Joshua (aka Conan) wanted to wear a tie like his older brothers. Of course, when the children's choir sang on the stage, his shirt was untucked, his tie was barely hanging on to his collar, and his hair was askew, despite loads of hair spray. Jonathan (aka Sweetpea) stood beside him looking dapper in his neatly pressed suit, perfectly placed hair, and sharp black bow tie.

For the last ten years, we've replaced the traditional Easter basket (which usually runs about twenty dollars per child, or a total of a hundred dollars for our family) with something worth far more—a special egg hunt. We have color-coded eggs—one color for each child—and hide equal numbers of each, so competition doesn't displace the eggcitement of the hunt.

In among the eggs, we have twelve very special eggs that are numbered. You can make your own or order these "Resurrection Eggs" from Family Life Today at 1-501-223-8663 or find them on the Web at *www.familylife.com*. We made ours ten years ago before these eggs were available on the market.

Once they are all found, we gather as a family and Bob asks for the eggs in order. As each child contributes his numbered egg, he has a part in the telling of the most wonderful story ever told. Here are the contents of the eggs and the story:

1. Contains a cracker, a remembrance of the Last Supper.
2. Holds a dime, representing the silver coins Judas received for betraying Jesus.
3. Contains a piece of rope like the soldiers used to bind Jesus' hands when they arrested him.
4. This egg is filled with purple cloth, symbolic of royalty and the taunting Jesus faced when He called himself King.
5. Carries a thorn for the prickly crown pressed onto Jesus' head.
6. Opens to a cross representing the one Jesus died on so we could be forgiven.
7. Holds a nail, as Christ was nailed to the cross.
8. Has a piece of sponge, reminding us of the vinegar given to Jesus when He asked for water.
9. Carries a toothpick with a foil tip, symbolic of the spear hurled into Jesus' side.
10. Contains a piece of gauze, symbolizing Jesus' burial wrapping.
11. Cradles a rock, symbolic of the tombstone rolled away by an angel.
12. Is empty! The tomb was empty because Jesus is no longer dead, but alive!

> We've replaced the traditional Easter basket (which usually runs about twenty dollars per child, or a hundred dollars for our family) with something worth far more—a special egg hunt.

INDEPENDENCE DAY, JULY 4TH
A Fun and Free Freedom Fest

I remember the first July 4th Bob and I were married. I went to a veterans' parade in a small community outside the Los Angeles area where Bob did a flyby at the end of the parade. As the mighty F-4 Phantoms thundered overhead and the afterburners kicked in, the crowd cheered. Young boys looked with longing at those jets, and one of them shouted, "I'm going to fly jets when I grow up!" I was so proud of my husband as I began to realize what being a military wife would involve.

This holiday celebrates the freedom our country enjoys and the heroes who protect that freedom. The best celebration we ever had on this holiday was when we were stationed with the Army at Fort Drum, New York. They didn't have Air Force flybys, but they had a festive party with food booths, events for the children, and the most sensational fireworks display we've ever witnessed as the Army Band played patriotic music.

Even if you live in a state where fireworks are legal, you don't have to spend lots of money on your own fireworks display. Check with the Chamber of Commerce or your state's Web site to find out where the best fireworks displays are. If you live near a military base, they will doubtless have quite a display, and many of these events are open to the community.

Some other fun and inexpensive ways to celebrate this holiday are to have a sidewalk chalk contest for children to draw patriotic pictures such as a flag, the Liberty Bell, or an eagle. Make a Jell-O flag by layering red and blue gelatin in a rectangular mold (remembering, of course, that the first layer needs to set up before the second layer is added). Once the gelatin is set, remove it to a flat serving tray and ice with whipped topping. Use strawberries for stripes and blueberries for stars, and you'll have a decoration you can really sink your teeth into!

THANKSGIVING
Let's Talk Turkey

By using my method of grocery shopping, this is the best time of the year to stock up on baking supplies, because the loss leaders (items grocery stores sell at less than cost to get you to come into their store) and coupon values are best at this time. The more items you can bake and give as holiday gifts, the more money you can save. Almost everyone enjoys homemade goodies, so stock up during this season and save money on the next!

The largest expenditure for this holiday tends to be the meat. If you watch the sales, frequent buyer deals, and store coupons, you can usually find an amazing deal. Last Thanksgiving, Albertson's had a buy one/get one free deal on their store brand turkeys. Their competitor, IGA, had a store coupon for a store brand 12- to 15-pound turkey for $6. Since Albertson's honors competitors' coupons, I was able to take the IGA coupon there and get the first turkey I bought for only $6. Since the buy one/get one free was a store special and not a coupon special, I got the second turkey free. So I got two 15-pound (always get the most meat in the weight range they offer) turkeys for only $6. I kept one and shared one with the Salvation Army, which was having a shortage of turkeys that year.

> **The more items you can bake and give as holiday gifts, the more money you can save. Almost everyone enjoys homemade goodies, so stock up during this season and save money on the next!**

Thankful Traditions

Not every "savings" can be measured in dollars and cents. One of the things we emphasize in our family is saving *memories*. Our "thankful tree" was featured in a *Woman's Day* magazine one year. It took two photographers eight rolls of film and four hours to get one photo for the magazine. (Joshua was missing for one roll of film, and we didn't notice until we saw him making faces from *behind* the photographers and we asked, "What are you doing back there?")

The tip we gave is how we stay in touch with family and friends during this holiday. On November first, we make a thankful tree on poster board and put it on our wall or front door. The tree is bare because the leaves that we make out of construction paper have not been gathered yet. The leaves have each person's name on them and say, "Grandma Rawleigh is thankful for _____." But we leave the tree bare at the beginning of the season to teach the children how barren our lives are without the giving of thanks.

We make and send the leaves to friends and family around the world along with a self-addressed envelope. When these envelopes begin to come back, the children get excited as they take turns opening them. At dinner each night, we read the leaf that arrived that day, give thanks along with those who are thankful, and put the leaf on our tree. By Thanksgiving Day, we have a tree full of thanks. We carefully save the leaves in an envelope marked by the year and keep all in our Thanksgiving decoration box. Each year we read the leaves from past years.

> **If three gifts was good enough for baby Jesus, then three gifts is good enough for them.**

We never know when this year's leaf might be someone's last, or which family might have a new leaf on next year's tree. So we give thanks.

CHRISTMAS
It's Not Crazy-mas, It's Christ-mas!

Since the publication of *Shop, Save, and Share*, I've heard back from other families who have started their own "Christmas Simplification Plan" by limiting their gifts to three per person. We told the Kay family babes years ago that if three gifts was good enough for baby Jesus, then three gifts is good enough for them. This tradition has kept the focus of the season where it belongs, and it's kept us out of debt too.

Listen to what Sandy from Colorado writes:

> I wanted to try your Christmas simplification plan with the

three gifts but didn't know how our family would take it. But our finances really needed it. It seems like it takes forever to pay off the credit card bills from Christmas. We explained the idea to the kids, and they seemed to understand. They even made a game of trying to pick three simple gifts they really wanted.

Well, it worked beautifully! We had told the kids they might not get everything on their list, and we found clearance items, like you said, that weren't on the list but the kids liked even better than the things that were on the list. For the first time in seven years, we don't have credit bills to pay off from Christmas. The emphasis was on the reason for the season, and we don't have the headaches of bills to pay. Why didn't we start this years ago? Thank you, Ellie Kay, for your work in this area.

> **Write down your purchases—and where you stashed them—on a piece of paper and tape it to next year's December calendar page.**

Sandy is so right when she says that it seems to take forever to pay credit card bills. The average American family spends until May of the following year paying off Christmas debt. That doesn't leave much time to save for vacations or to service other debt, does it?

Here are some tips to help your Christmas stay focused and on budget.

Document Your Purchases

There's nothing like buying Christmas paper to wrap those presents early, only to discover a month later that you have tons of paper you bought at the end-of-season clearance last year and forgot about it. Or you get a good deal on gifts for teachers and then realize you bought those earlier in the year and forgot where you put them. Write down your purchases—and where you stashed them—on a piece of paper and tape it to next year's December calendar page.

Kids Need to Save Too!

Part of teaching your children about money is helping them to plan ahead and, as they get older, pay for their gifts. We give our younger children a certain amount to spend, then when they are around eight years old, we match them dollar for dollar on what they've saved to spend. By the time they are twelve, they are buying their own gifts with their money. Encourage the children to get odd jobs in the summer to save for Christmas. At age thirteen, Daniel not only earned enough money to open a mutual fund over the course of a year, but he also pays for quality gifts, pays his tithe, and takes pride in his ability to manage money.

> **If you decorate the day after Thanksgiving, you not only avoid being out on the busiest shopping day of the year, but you'll save money too.**

Start Early

In February, make a tentative gift-shopping list so you can watch for sales during the year. If you decide on an entirely homemade holiday, make it a family project to begin those handcrafted decorations and gifts in the summer.

Jams and Jellies

By preparing your jams and jellies when the fruit is in season, you can save a lot of money. Present your homemade gifts in interesting baskets, boxes, tins, or other containers you've found at garage sales or on clearance shelves. For great ideas on presenting your gifts, go to *www.janejarrell.com.*

Decorate Early

If you decorate the day after Thanksgiving, you not only avoid being out on the busiest shopping day of the year, but you'll save money too. By organizing all the Christmas decorations, you'll discover which items you need and which ones you do not need. Then you can look for those lights that are on sale to replace the ones that didn't survive the year. You also won't duplicate items that you bought on clearance the previous year. With your home decorated so festively, you'll also be less inclined to impulse-buy holiday decorations.

Bartering Moms

Kathie Peel and Judie Byrd, in their book *A Mother's Manual for Holiday Survival* (Focus on the Family Publishing), advise planning a "mother's trade-out week." During the week before Christmas five moms will each plan an activity for all the kids that will last about four to five hours. So each mom gets four days off that week and entertains the kids one day. In Kathie and Judie's example, one mom had a kids' cooking day, another did holiday crafts, and another mom took the kids to the dollar theater. Sounds like a legitimate trade-off to me!

Wrap As You Buy

But don't forget to label whom each gift is for. You may want to keep a master list of the gifts, listing the contents and numbering them as you buy them.

Sharing Christmas

Sometimes the gift of time is the greatest gift of all during the holidays. There are a number of ways you can brighten the holidays of those around you and share the season. We like to visit nursing homes and just spend time with the residents, talking and sharing. If you know of an elderly neighbor or friend who rarely gets to decorate for the holidays, why not help them set up a tree and lights? Then after the season is over, help them put the decorations away.

Invite a single parent and his or her family over for the holiday dinner—these can be the hardest times of the year for people who go it alone, and the warmth of another family is usually welcomed.

One of the traditions on military bases is a holiday cookie drive. Last year, we collected 120,000 cookies and distributed them to police officers, fire fighters, and others who worked the holiday shift. Your family could take a basket of goodies to your local fire fighters or police officers on duty. I know they would enjoy those treats on

Christmas Eve! We even bake cookies for the mail carriers and sanitation workers. We place these in easy-to-carry plastic bags and include a can of soda.

Emergency Gift Closet

You may want to have extra gifts on hand in case an unexpected guest turns up with a present in hand. These can appeal to a broad range of tastes. Some ideas are holiday CDs, classic holiday videos such as *It's a Wonderful Life* or *White Christmas*, and holiday fashion accessories, including cuff links, earrings, socks, and scarves—most people love to wear their holiday duds.

Financial Help

One last idea is to give an anonymous gift of money to someone who desperately needs it. You could write a check to your local church and ask them to pass the money along to the family, or you could buy a money order to mail to the family. While you might include a card or message, don't sign it. Remember that the One who sees these acts of love done in secret will one day reward you openly.

Seize the day,
Seize whatever you can,
For time slips away
Just like hourglass sand.
Seize the day and pray
For grace from God's hand,
Then nothing will stand in your way,
Seize the day.

—CAROLYN ARENDS

How to
Save Money
in Your World

CHAPTER THIRTEEN

Savings in Cyberspace

Avoiding Tidal Waves While Surfing the Net

"Mama, you said you'd read me my book. Are you workin' on de 'pooter *again*?" Joshua asked as he came into our home office and crawled into my lap. I'd been working hard on my computer to finish two major deadlines as well as answering scores of daily e-mail messages. I knew he wanted some attention, and I began to feel guilty as I realized that "only twenty minutes" on the computer had mysteriously turned into two hours. I worked *out of the home* in order to be able to *stay home* with my children. How consistent was it to essentially tell my preschooler, "Go away and play; I've got work to do," when he was supposed to be the priority?

I looked at my little guy. At age five Joshua was the youngest of our five children. Don't get me wrong, I *love* babies and wouldn't mind having twins next, but I suppose you have to stop sometime. The last time I asked Bob for another baby, he brought home a ten-week-old cocker spaniel puppy—that chewed my new slippers, did nasty things on the carpet, and had dog breath. I'm *still* trying to forgive my Beloved!

Joshua tugged on my arm, bringing me back to reality.

"Yes, Joshua, I'm still working on the 'pooter. I have to get this last thing done; then I'll read your book." I put him down on the floor and went back to the keyboard.

All of the sudden, out of nowhere, a still, small voice in my mind said, "He won't ask you to read to him forever. One day he'll be bigger, and there will be no more time for reading books."

I turned from my desk and watched Joshua walk out of the room. His shoulders were stooped in disappointment as he carried his well-worn books in the Abeka Little Book Series. I thought of how quickly Daniel had jumped from the toddler years to the teen years. It was so much like the song from the musical *Fiddler on the Roof*: "I don't remember growing older, when did they? Sunrise, sunset, swiftly flow the days."

> **Put time with your family ahead of time surfing the Internet and you'll save more than you bargained for.**

Tears welled up in my eyes as I thought about how quickly the years were passing. "What really matters most?" I asked myself. I quickly wiped the tears with the back of my hand and called, "Joshua, little buddy, come back here!"

My adventurous, active little guy, who rarely sits still long enough for me to read to him, much less *requests* that I read, ran back into the room.

"Yes, Mama?" he inquired hopefully, still clutching his books.

I put out my arms, "Come here, little guy, I want to read to you. We'll practice your letters and sounds."

As he nestled into my ample lap, he turned around, his blue eyes looking into mine and asked, "But what about the work you have to do on the 'pooter, Mama?"

"The 'pooter can wait, son." I kissed the top of his head. "The 'pooter can wait."

You may wonder what the story you just read has to do with tips on saving money on the Internet. I'd like to answer that with the best tip you'll find in this chapter: Put time with your family ahead of time surfing the Internet and you'll save more than you bargained for. You'll save wonderful memories and essential communication, and the result will be treasured relationships.

You see, the Internet is to our generation what the television set was to our parents' generation or the radio was to our grandparents' generation. From 1900 to the 1930s, families gathered in the evenings on the porch or in the parlor and played board games, sang around the piano or guitar, or just talked. Families were strong in those days, too, because of the rich communication that existed in the family unit.

In the thirties and forties, households acquired their first radio, and they gathered around the huge box to listen to their favorite weekly programs. Imagine the Waltons listening to the show and laughing as they looked each other in the face and connected with this entertainment. After the show was over, they would sit back and talk and laugh again. Initially, there was limited radio programming, and this medium was not a significant interruption to family time.

In the fifties and sixties, families stopped looking at smiling faces around the radio and instead directed their attention toward a box called the television set. Each form of media has become more demanding of our time and attention. By the seventies and eighties, most televisions were on whenever families were home; we ate meals around the silly tube and gave it a place of priority in the home. Communication continued to diminish to the point that today's child will spend one hundred minutes watching television for every minute spent talking to a parent.

In the nineties and the new millennium, the Internet has isolated families even more as an activity that eats our time and requires little to no interaction with other family members. If we don't set firm boundaries for these intruders into family life, any money saved by surfing the Net could be considered a loss if it robs us of critical time spent on relationships. It's great to save money with the many opportunities that exist via our computers, but we can't use saving money as an excuse to ignore time with those people who matter most. Sometimes, you just have to shut off the 'pooter.

With the above exhortation as a caveat, let's look at some productive ways of successfully navigating the information highway.

BEFORE YOU EXPLORE

Before you explore the Internet, you should have the address for the Internet Fraud Information Center posted by your computer. Their Web address is *www.fraud.org*, and their toll-free number is 1-800-876-7060. You can also call your local Better Business Bureau or check *www.bbb.com*. You should always check out an Internet merchant before doing any online transactions.

Also, be sure to have a good antivirus protection program set up on your computer before you go surfing and before you download any files from the Internet or any files sent via e-mail. Antivirus programs from Norton, McAfee, etc. (as well as other computer accessories), can often be purchased at warehouse clubs for as little as 50 percent of what you might pay at a computer superstore. It's important to update your antivirus program regularly; these updates are typically available online for free during the first year, then for a nominal fee thereafter.

Bonus Tip: Find great deals on computers by looking at the Sunday newspaper advertising inserts and then pitting two computer superstores against each other in a match-price war on closeout models. Also, if after your purchase you see the store advertising a scanner or printer "free with purchase," take advantage of the store's one-month price guarantee by going back to get that item.

CYBER JUNK MAIL

I have discovered that it's a good idea to set up a junk e-mail address to use when you sign up for offers online. This keeps your work e-mail and personal e-mail free of the junk e-mail that invariably starts arriving once you sign up at a site. They'll sell your address to one site, and they'll sell it to another and so on and so on and so on...

The solution is very simple: Set up a junk mail address at a free e-mail site like hotmail.com, yahoo.com, angelfire.com, or Juno (call 1-800-654-JUNO or write: New Members Dept., 120 W. 45th St., NY, NY 10036). Give this address when you sign up for offers and save your primary e-mail account for your friends.

Bonus Tip: There are many Internet service providers (ISPs) that offer free Internet access as well as free e-mail, such as altavista.com, netzero.com, and freeinternet.com. Most free sites subject you to varying amounts of advertising, so view each service carefully before choosing.

KEEP YOUR INFORMATION TO YOURSELF!

This topic can't be emphasized too much. It's very wise to be prudent in dispersing demographic information (age, gender, income) on the Internet. It's even wiser to keep personal information (name, address, date of birth) to yourself. The wisest approach is to be extremely cautious in releasing any financial or legal information (social security information, credit card information, credit history). Each of these areas should be viewed with increasing levels of caution.

> It's a good idea to set up a junk e-mail address to use when you sign up for offers online. This keeps your work e-mail and personal e-mail free of the junk e-mail that invariably starts arriving once you sign up at a site.

Bidder Beware!

Beware of giving credit card information on sites such as *www.priceline.com*. Once you give this information, you are agreeing to purchase the item, and it WILL be charged to your credit card. Usually, you cannot get a price quote without a commitment on sites such as this one.

SECURE SITES

The final level of information we discussed above (credit card information, etc.) should only be released in a secure site or a site that will not allow third parties to view the information in transit. All secured sites are indicated by an *s* after the http address in the browser box, or a closed lock or unbroken key is listed as a symbol of a secure site. Before you give any vital information such as credit card numbers, make sure you're using a secure site. Some computers have software that will warn you of sending unsecured information. If you're not sure if the site is secure, you shouldn't buy the product.

The reason for all this prudence is the simple fact that the Internet has a dark side. Information is power, and you don't want the wrong people to get your information for the wrong purpose. Sometimes the Darth Mauls of the Internet will get this information through sweepstakes entries, newsletters, or even open e-mail accounts (where your e-mail address is displayed on an open copy rather than a blind carbon copy). They also gather data on you when you visit a site. Many Web sites deposit data called "cookies" on your hard drive. Retailers use those cookies to note your tastes and preferences. The next time you visit the site, there are ads that are tailor-made to your interests. The consequences of releasing information can be as innocuous as unwanted e-mail or as extreme as criminal acts such as credit card fraud and theft.

> **Before you give any vital information such as credit card numbers, make sure you're using a secure site. If you're not sure if the site is secure, you shouldn't buy the product.**

PRIVACY ON THE INTERNET

It is far more difficult than you might think to remain anonymous on the Internet. For an eye-opening demonstration of the way banner ads are used to gather information at the sites you visit, go to the Web site of privacy expert Russell Smith at *www.privacy.net*.

Many Web browsers, including the popular Netscape and Internet Explorer, allow you to block cookies that are being deposited on your computer and used to gather data about you for e-tailers (Internet retailers). Just consult the user manual or go to Online Help to learn the correct settings.

KEEPING KIDS PROTECTED

Children are especially vulnerable to Internet hoaxes and scams. We don't allow our children unsupervised access to the computer. It is imperative that we teach our children Internet safety and make sure they understand they shouldn't give personal information (such as their name, street address, age, the name of their school, etc.) when they are on the Internet at school or at the library.

I was aghast to find out that our thirteen-year-old had been giving his name, age, and street address to various sites in order to enter contests in the computer lab at his Christian school.

CHAT ROOMS AND FILTERS

We recommend that no child be allowed access to chat rooms without parental supervision. (Personally, we don't allow our children to visit *any* chat rooms, and we stay away from most of

> Never allow other people unsupervised access to your computer, and always have your computer set up to only run with a password.

them too.) It's a good idea to keep your computer in the family room or other high traffic area rather than a bedroom or secluded area. Another option to consider is installing a filter (software designed to keep inappropriate material off our computers) on your computer. For more information about filters and Christian chat rooms, visit *www.crosswalk.com.*

ACCESS TO ONE-CLICK BUYING

Another reason to be careful with people who have access to your computer is the fact that once you've purchased items from your favorite sites, the next time the site is accessed, it can automatically pull up all your personal information, including your credit card number. For example, if you purchase some books at amazon.com, then another user accesses that site from your computer, he or she could use the site's one-click buying system to place an order that would automatically be charged to your credit card.

Therefore, never allow other people (including your children's friends or your own) unsupervised access to your computer, and always have your computer set up to only run with a password. Speaking of passwords, it's a good idea *not* to use the same password at every site that requires one. For example, use a different password for your e-mail service than you use for purchases at amazon.com, which is yet again different from the password you use to buy airline tickets at expedia.com.

You may also want to consider disconnecting the modem from your phone line when your computer is not in use. This habit could prevent a hacker from accessing your computer through the phone line, turning it on and gathering credit card and other information.

POST OFFICE BOXES

You may even want to consider getting the smallest size box available at your local post office (about twenty dollars every six months) for the times you will need to give an address over the Internet for a special offer. For example, the coupons I get mailed to us through smartsource.com and upon.com are sent to our P.O. box. Then if you do enter any contests that don't require the disclosure of extensive personal information, you can give the P.O. box as your address.

SPECIAL ACCESS PERMISSION

Many sites that offer coupons or other promotional freebies require that you fill out an application to get into that site. However, some sites take that application process one step further. Beware of any site that asks you to give them permission to download software onto your computer beyond the initial setup. Make sure you understand the purpose of that software.

For example, when you sign up for free e-mail with Juno, they will send you a disk to set up the program. Additional updates are accepted at your discretion. They will notify you that there is an update available, and you can update your files at will. However, by giving any Internet business permission to periodically update your software, you are not the one controlling the updates—they are. While most Internet businesses will only use this privilege for legitimate updates, you have still given them permission to alter your software while you are online.

ONLINE RETAILERS—CHOOSE WISELY

Here are ten tips on how to choose a reputable online retailer and protect yourself when purchasing online:

1. You should be able to contact the retailer through a variety of methods, including e-mail, telephone, and live interactive chat.
2. The retailer should prominently display customer service options throughout their Web site so you have no difficulty finding them.
3. You should expect responsive and prompt replies from your retailer regardless of how you contact them.
4. The customer service agent should be knowledgeable and equipped to answer your questions.
5. Steer clear of new companies. If a company is new, chances are they are still working out the kinks at your expense.
6. Look carefully at legal disclaimers. Some say they have the right to take up to three weeks to notify you if they're out of stock, which could make you three weeks late on your project.
7. Beware of early billing. Some stores invoice you before you receive the merchandise. Make sure your credit card is charged at the same time the produce is shipped and not before. And if you get a second invoice before you get the item, cancel the order.
8. Pay by credit card instead of debit card or check. Using a credit card provides more legal protection if a dispute arises.
9. Read the warranty before buying an item, and check for limits on the company's liability if something goes wrong with the item.
10. Make a printout of the Web page, the item being pur-

chased, the warranty, and any messages between you
and the seller.

AUCTION SITES

We talked a little about these sites in chapter 11. The top auction sites
are *www.ebay.com, www.auctions.yahoo.com*, and *www.auction-
watch.com.* Here's some advice for buyers (adapted from *USA Weekend
Magazine*, January 2, 2000).

✓ Know what you're looking for before you go. The number
of items can be overwhelming.

✓ Don't shop at auctions if you have a problem with compulsive buying or debt.

✓ If an item needs a picture to verify its authenticity or condition and there's none, or if a generic photo is shown,
skip it. Be wary of auctions with poor grammar, mis-
spellings, and overhyped pitches. If it sounds too good
to be true, it usually is.

✓ Look for the sunglasses icon, which indicates that a seller
is assuming a different identity than they previously
used online.

✓ At every auction site, buyers can give feedback about sellers and vice versa. Before bidding, check the seller's
feedback rating and avoid sellers with low scores.

✓ Read the sales policy carefully. If it is vague or extremely
strict, be wary. Look for specifics on shipping, insurance, and payment.

✓ Don't pay in cash. For items that cost more than $150,
consider using an online escrow service like i-Escrow.
It works like this: The buyer pays i-Escrow. The seller
then ships the item to the buyer. If the buyer approves
the item, i-Escrow pays the seller. The buyer and seller
must agree upfront to use an escrow service and may
decide to share the escrow fees. Ultimately, however,
the buyer is responsible for payment. The fees are non-

refundable and range from 2 to 4 percent of the value
of the transaction.

✓ Make a printout of the page, as outlined in number 10 on
page 149.

As you surf the Net, just remember that to avoid the tidal waves, you
must be on guard and not be cradled into a false sense of security. Let
wisdom and prudence guide you, and you'll avoid meeting cybersharks
in cyberspace.

**"Fervently I think that many times one
feels oneself to be secure and suddenly
one's world falls down like a pack of
cards in a matter of seconds."**

—GUILLERMO VILAS,
ARGENTINEAN TENNIS PRO,
SPORTS ILLUSTRATED INTERVIEW

CHAPTER FOURTEEN

Take Me to the Funny Farm

Tips When You're MOO-vin' On

We were lost on a country road in northern New York. However, we weren't *so* lost that Bob felt the need to ask for directions. After all, we'd only been lost, driving aimlessly with five active, hungry children for about two hours. My Beloved has to be lost for about three hours and down to a gallon and a half of gas in the tank before he feels it's finally time to ask for directions. Of course, that leaves me praying with all the fervency I can muster that we won't run out of gas before we find a station.

I don't understand my husband's sense of direction sometimes. I mean, when he's in his jet, he can find a target the size of a postage stamp, but he misses the turnoff for the rural road we're supposed to take and we end up lost. I just don't understand him. I'm not like that. I can follow and give *great* directions.

For example, if you were coming to my house, I would first find out where you're coming from. Are you coming from the mountain side of Alamogordo or the flat side? (Don't you hate it the way men always ask for that north and south stuff?)

If you're coming from the mountain side, then you just take the highway that leads into town. (I can't remember the name of it, but it comes into town from the mountain side.) That highway will turn into a street that will go right by the White Sands Mall. Every woman knows that malls are the best landmarks in the whole town. If you get lost, you can always shop.

The mall should be on your right, I mean your left, you know, the *other* right. Go past the mall until you see a small zoo on your right. If you see the zoo, you know you're going the right direction. Then, you go to the Kentucky Fried Chicken. Restaurants are the second best landmarks because you can snack along the way if you get turned around. Take a left at the KFC and you'll go by the Hampton Inn (hotels are the third best landmark because if you're lost and tired you can always rest a while), which will be on your right. You know, the *other* right.

The road will go by a pretty white house with red-and-white checkered curtains and yellow flowers in the flower bed (unless it's in the fall—then the flowers won't be there). Just keep going. If you get to the golf course, you've gone too far and you're on the wrong side of town. Keep going until you come to one (or it *might* be two) stop signs. When you see a house with a bunch of plastic ducks out front, turn right at that road. We are the second house on the right, unless you count the first house, which is really on the other street because we are kind of on the intersection. If you count it that way, then we're the first house on the right. No, the *other* right.

You can't miss our house. It's a two-story. Actually, there are lots of two-story houses on our road. But ours is the one with the Americana-style wreath on the front door and a garden in the backyard. Of course, you can't see the garden from the road—but it's there nonetheless. Our house is real easy to find—you can't miss it. Maybe you ought to bring your cell phone in case you get lost.

I just can't understand why Bob gets lost, especially when I'm giving him directions…

The day we were lost in rural New York we never did find our destination, but we did find the place of our destiny. As I was calling out directions and praying for a gas station, we turned a bend in the road and there it was—in living color. The Funny Farm.

I'm not kidding. There was a farm with bright white letters on the big red barn that said, "Welcome to the Funny Farm."

"Look!" I shouted as soon as the words came into view. "We've got to stop! We have to take our picture by that barn!"

Bob groaned, but he knew from my tone of voice that stopping was inevitable. He walked to the farmhouse to ask permission to take our photo by the barn. The gracious farmer and his wife allowed us the favor as I herded the tired and cranky children out of the car.

As it turned out, the Funny Farm was really a dairy farm filled with lots of reminders that cows lived there. Joshua and Jonathan found this evidence right away as Bethany was grossed out and Daniel wondered why he had such a weird mom. Ever helpful Philip led the way to the barn, pointing to the land mines that we needed to avoid.

Bob trudged out after us, and as the kids and I posed ourselves amongst the mud around the barn, he snapped the picture.

I don't always hear real well, but I *thought* I heard him mutter, "I always knew we'd end up here."

Well, as I've said before, you either learn to look at life in a funny way or you'll end up on the funny farm. When it comes to visiting new places, we've been there, done that—many, many times. As of this writing we've just made our eleventh move in thirteen years. By the time this manuscript goes to press, we might live somewhere else.

As a veteran of many travels, I've learned a few tips on moving as well as traveling with children. I've also learned that when family members are content, it will save you money. You'll be less likely to compensate for the tiring move with pricey placebos. Here are some savvy strategies to save your sanity on your scenic safari.

BE CONTENT

In the New Testament, Paul learned to be content in every situation. When moving, it is very easy to become discontent. After all, you have to make new friends, find a new church, handle the sheer physical exertion of a move, and basically start over. I have found that when I focus on the pain of moving, then I'm more likely to overspend at the department store to make up for what I'm missing.

That is why Paul told Timothy: "But godliness actually is a means of great gain, when accompanied by contentment" (2 Timothy 6:6 NASB). The combination of godliness with contentment will be demonstrated vividly in a person who doesn't require material goodies in order to cope with life.

> If we can focus on what we *have*, rather than on what we *think* we need, we will save money before, during, and after every move.

If we can focus on what we *have*, rather than on what we *think* we need, we will save money before, during, and after every move.

Reasons for Contentment

When we move to a new area, sometimes it is hard to even think of the positive aspects of a move. But there are some advantages to being new. Some of these tips have been adapted from Susan Miller's wonderful book on moving *After the Boxes are Unpacked* (Focus on the Family Publishing).

- ✓ You have a completely clean house before you move in.
- ✓ You have the opportunity to share some of the stuff you don't need with others who need it (why not give that high chair to Goodwill?).
- ✓ You'll unpack items you can use, but forgot you had— thus saving you the expense of buying them again.
- ✓ Maybe some of the old clothes you've held onto for twenty years have come back into style! (They probably won't fit you, but they may fit your teen.)

✓ You have more control over time because you don't have old commitments.

✓ Nobody has seen your wardrobe, so it's like getting a brand new one every time you move!

✓ You have the opportunity to reprioritize your life.

✓ Moving will give you a better education by broadening your perspective along with your horizons.

✓ As Anne of Avonlea said, "Tomorrow is always new, with no mistakes in it." You have a chance to be known for who you are today and not what you were yesterday.

✓ All those things that are old to you about yourself and your family will be new and exciting to others.

SAVING MONEY ON YOUR MOVE

Whether you move yourself or use a moving company, you could save as much as 50 percent by doing your homework before you move.

Moving Companies

Even if your company or Uncle Sam pays for your move, you do have some latitude on the quality of the move. Even though the military moves us, we always ask the moving companies to bid on what is oftentimes called a "Code Two" move. This special kind of move costs more because extra care is given in the packing materials and preparation of the household goods. They will shrink-wrap our fabric-covered furniture and put bubble wrap around the wood furniture. Oftentimes a competing company will offer to do a Code Two move for a Code One price.

Collecting Boxes

If you know you are going to move yourself, then start collecting boxes in advance to save on the purchase of boxes. If you see a house that just sold up the street, ask the new occupants if you can collect their boxes when they unpack. People often just put them outside for the movers to come back and collect for discard. The dish barrels from professional movers are a must! These are extra-sturdy boxes with tons of packing paper to handle fragile dishes and glasses. You might even want to call a moving company for "seconds" in boxes. Some companies have a policy of never reusing those boxes they collect from people whom they just moved. For some breakables, professional packing materials will make the difference in whether that item arrives intact or broken.

Banana boxes from the grocery store make the very best box for moving many kinds of household goods. The smaller size and built-in handles on the side make for easy carrying by children and teens—so everyone can help. Boxes for printer and copy paper also work well. They're easy to come by at printers, always clean, very sturdy, the lids lift off, and a nice size.

> **Banana boxes from the grocery store make the very best box for moving many kinds of household goods. The smaller size and built-in handles on the side make for easy carrying by children and teens—so everyone can help.**

Original Boxes

Save the original packaging that products came in. The TV, VCR, computer, stereo, and even collectibles such as Lladros (lovely statues from Spain) or artwork will ship more safely in their original boxes.

Wardrobe Boxes

If you have a choice between a lay-down wardrobe box and a hang-up box (where they actually have a rod and your clothing and coats hang in the box), go for the hang-up box. A lay-down box will wrinkle everything, and you'll have to put it all back on hangers, costing you hours and hours of time in ironing and hanging.

Custom-Made Boxes

If you lost that Lladro box or bought it at a garage sale and want it to make it safely to its destination, you can ask the moving company to custom-build a box for your collectible. My lovely Lladro ballerina that I got as a teen in Spain has made it through fourteen moves now.

Ditty, or for Nonmilitary Types, a "Self-Move"

In the military, we often have the option of moving ourselves for a lower price than the moving company would charge (and keeping the difference for our labors). You may also have this option with your company. However, there are several items to consider. First, you'll need to crank *all* the figures, including the total compensation you can expect from this move versus the total expenses of gas, truck rental, self-insurance, tolls, and other unexpected expenses. When we were first married, Bob and I made $800 for a very small move with minimal labor (most of the stuff was in boxes anyway). That was worth it to us. The last time we checked on a ditty, a fifteen-hundred-mile move with twelve thousand pounds of household goods would only yield five hundred dollars—obviously not worth it!

> There are wonderful values to be had for first-time customers; take advantage of all of these that you can.

Don't forget about insurance either. When you move yourself or pack anything for the movers yourself, you usually take on the risk. Most tenant insurance policies will cover a self-move, but you need to make sure. If the moving van caught on fire, who would pay? (That happened to one of our friends.)

SAVING MONEY IN YOUR NEW TOWN

There are wonderful values to be had for first-time customers; take advantage of all of these that you can.

- ✓ **Welcome Wagon:** The local Chamber of Commerce can help you find this service if they don't find you first. They will have coupons, special offers, maps, and other helpful items to assist you in the new area.
- ✓ **Local map:** These are usually free from the Welcome Wagon or the Chamber of Commerce. Keep a map in each car or you'll waste time, gas, and brain cells.

✓ **Car insurance:** Depending on your automobile insurance company, this might be a good time to shop around for the best policy. But if you have tickets or an accident on your driving record, it may be better to stay where you are. Before you cancel your existing policy, call several agents for quotes on a new policy—and be truthful about your driving record. As a former agent, I saw too many people who didn't mention an accident on their record because the other person was at fault.

✓ **Homeowner's/Renter's insurance:** Even if you are living somewhere temporarily, you'll likely need a renter's policy, so call around for the best value. Make sure that your collectibles (jewelry, guns, antiques, vintage cars, stamp/coin collections, etc.) are covered if they exceed the maximum coverage on your policy.

✓ **Health insurance:** Don't let this one fall through the cracks or the costs could be astronomical. Accidents seem to abound during moves. When we went from Mississippi to New Mexico (the second time), one-year-old Joshua fell from a bunk bed when the movers were there and had to have his lip sewn back on. Then, when we were en route in Abilene, Texas, he toddled face-first into the trailer hitch and got stitches in his forehead.

✓ **The postman doesn't ring twice:** Make sure your forwarding order is in place before you move, and after you move, introduce yourself to your new mail carrier. Let him or her know all the aliases in your family. This could save money on late fees and other penalties due to rerouted mail. Our carrier knows Jonathan (aka Sweetpea), Joshua (aka Conan, the Baby Barbarian, or a Mighty Man of God), Bethany (aka Bunny), Philip (aka Cello Man), Daniel (aka Damien), Ellie (aka Eleanor, Her Majesty), and Bob (aka Robert, K-Bob).

✓ **First-time customer:** It pays to invest in your new local newspaper, even if it is an 18-page publication. In our tiny paper this week, there are ads for the following savings for first-time customers: pest service (a must in New Mexico); a free week of workouts at the local health club (a must for every woman who has had enough children to make up a basketball team); a discount for massage therapy (a must for moms who move with children); a discount for new Internet customers (a must for anyone researching a book on saving money); a discount for new cell phone customers (a must for the long drive to the airport in El Paso that goes through a desolate wasteland); free dry cleaning (a must for a Sweetpea who wears his good black suit to go on a nature walk with his Sunday school class); and a free haircut for new customers (a must for those bad hair days).

"Like a shepherd's tent my dwelling is pulled up and removed from me."

ISAIAH 38:12 NASB

CHAPTER FIFTEEN

Pay It on Down

Paying Down Debt

The tiny woman took the platform with a large microphone in her small hand. As the music began to play, I noted that the big stage seemed to envelop the petite dark-haired young woman. The backup choir seemed excited, anticipating what was coming. When her cue arrived, she held the microphone to her lips and wonder immediately swept through the auditorium. Her voice was ten times the size of her stature as she belted out the upbeat song. The five-foot-tall woman had a fifty-decibel voice. It reminded me of the television commercial where there's a man seated in a chair and the stereo television is blasting him with tornado-like winds.

I sat in the pew, my hair flying behind my head, due to the force coming from the voice of my friend Madeline. I'd never heard the old-time gospel spiritual she sang, but the choir had. They clapped and laughed and danced in their places as she belted it out.

Send it on down,
Send it on down,

Lord, let the Holy Ghost,
Come on down!

I thought the rafters were going to come on down that day. Even though that event happened almost five years ago, I still can feel the power in that room when my girlfriend sang. Every chance I get, I bring this kindred spirit with me to sing her songs of exhortation to our audiences.

The way Madeline sings is the way she lives her life. She's a powerful prayer partner, a power-packed mom-on-the-run, and a powerfully precious friend. Over the years, she has stirred up many dreams in me that had lain dormant. She helped create a desire in me to seize each day and live it for the One who would rather die than live without me.

> "The increase in the American divorce rate can be tracked on a curve matching the growth of debt in this country."—Larry Burkett

I introduced my girlfriend to you in order to make a power point. Just as Madeline sang, "Send it on down," the same kind of power exists for us to be able to pay down debt in order to abide by solid financial principles. While debt is bondage, there's freedom in owing no man. In his best-selling book *Debt-Free Living*, Larry Burkett said, "It is interesting that the increase in the American divorce rate can be tracked on a curve matching the growth of debt in this country." Debt doesn't benefit a marriage or a family, and it certainly doesn't benefit your finances. You may want to consider the following.

REASONS TO AVOID DEBT

✓ Debt makes you a servant to the lender (Proverbs 22:7).
✓ Debt borrows from your future.
✓ Debt hinders sharing with others.
✓ Debt limits ministry.
✓ Debt erodes resources, through high-interest payments.
✓ Debt promotes impulse buying.

On the other hand, those who are debt-free have the ability to give generously in order to meet the financial needs of others. There are fewer arguments over money in a household with a low debt liability. You can answer your phone and not worry about having an answering machine to screen calls from creditors. The anxiety over floating the bills to make the minimum payments will not exist in a home that follows sound Biblical financial principles.

EXPANDING DEBT

Some people find themselves sinking into deeper debt in anticipation that pay raises will cover the payments. Many families are simply not aware of how overwhelming a debt is until it's almost too late and they find themselves in bankruptcy court for debts they cannot repay.

My friend Jaye Ann told me about the time she was in Wal-Mart waiting in line to make a purchase. The woman in front of her was in her early twenties and was holding up the line due to a credit card problem.

"Oh," the young woman said indifferently, "that card is probably maxed out—try this one," she thrust another card into the cashier's hands as she continued, "and if that one doesn't work, we can put part of it on the first and the other part on the second."

The youthful woman was not disturbed as she remarked nonchalantly to Jaye Ann, "Oh, I have almost all my credit cards at their limit. I just pay the minimum balance each month and use it up to the limit again."

She raised her chin, as if to defend herself, "I may be at my credit card limit—but I'm able to get whatever I want."

This young woman knows nothing about delayed gratification. She could be the poster child for a debt-laden society. This destructive mindset has as its motto: "All that matters is getting what you want when you want it." They don't realize that one day this increasing debt will make them pay a price much higher than they should be willing to pay.

Here is a chart that vividly indicates the accumulating debt load for a family who spends only a hundred dollars more per month than they earn. We are assuming an average credit card interest of 18 percent compounded monthly for fifteen years.

Year	Amount Overspent	Accumulated Interest	End-of-Year Balance
1	$1,200	$104	$1,304
2	1,200	463	2,863
3	1,200	1,128	4,728
4	1,200	2,157	6,957
5	1,200	3,621	9,621
6	1,200	5,608	12,808
7	1,200	8,217	16,617
8	1,200	11,572	21,172
9	1,200	15,818	26,618
10	1,200	21,129	33,129
11	1,200	27,714	40,914
12	1,200	35,821	50,221
13	1,200	45,749	61,349
14	1,200	57,855	74,655
15	1,200	72,562	90,562
Totals	**$18,000**	**$72,562**	**$90,562**

This chart vividly illustrates how a modest amount of accumulating debt can cause a family's finances to self-destruct. The family indicated would more than likely have destroyed itself financially well before the fifteen-year point.

Warning Signs

You may not know if you really have a debt problem yet, so here are some indicators that you are heading for a financial fall.

✓ Using credit card cash advances to pay for living expenses.
✓ Using and depending on overtime to meet the month's expenses.
✓ Using credit to buy things that you used to pay for in cash (groceries, gas, clothing, etc.).

✓ Using the overdraft protection plan on your checking
account to pay monthly bills.

✓ Using savings to pay bills.

✓ Using one credit card to pay another.

✓ "Floating" the bills: delaying one bill in order to pay another
overdue bill.

✓ Using another loan or an extension on a loan to service your
debt.

✓ Using a cosignature on a note.

✓ Paying only the minimum amount due on charge accounts.

OVERCOMING DEBT

Is there hope for those who already have a sizeable amount of debt? Is there any use even *trying* to manage debt? The answer is a resounding YES! Getting out of debt may be easier than you think, even for major debt, such as a house. Here are some tips to get debt, as Madeline sang, "on down":

The Power of Prayer

Bob and I have experienced the incredible miracle of answered prayer in the area of seemingly insurmountable debt. When we got married, we had forty thousand dollars in consumer debt. We were like many other young people who didn't realize the price we were paying for instant gratification.

We purposed to get out of debt and made immediate changes in our life-style to accomplish this. We also purposed to tithe 10 percent of all we made. We ended up living on less than 25 percent of one income in order to accomplish these goals.

Within two years we were debt-free! Incredible? Yes. Impossible? No.

With God, all things are possible. He has laid out the plan for financial freedom in His guidebook. By following His principles, you, too, can become debt-free. I can't promise that you will reduce your debt as quickly as we did. But the message and the ministry of God's plans are so much higher than man's plans. He will lead you to your unique place of financial freedom. Even though the process may be challenging, you will not regret the result.

Family Meeting

It usually takes more than one family member to get a family in serious debt. Even if one person does most of the spending, the other members usually tolerate the destructive behavior in some way.

A family meeting is a time to write down goals on paper so you will have a tangible and objective standard to work toward. The goal you set should include (1) how to stop spending more than you make, (2) how to pay the interest on the debt you have accumulated, and (3) how to repay the debt.

> **With God, all things are possible. He has laid out the plan for financial freedom in His guidebook. By following His principles, you, too, can become debt free.**

Budget and Pay the Tithe

If your family does not have a budget, then refer to page 190 of *Shop, Save, and Share* or a standard budget from Larry Burkett of Christian Financial Concepts. Their Web site is at *www.cfcministry.org*. Make sure your tithe is included in this budget.

No More Debt!

If your family members cannot commit to the standard of no more debt, then perhaps it would be wise to seek professional counseling. Financial mismanagement may simply be a symptom of other unresolved issues. The next chapter can help you locate a counselor near you.

I would recommend that you cut up all but one or two credit cards and cancel all other open credit accounts. This will help minimize the temptation to buy on impulse as well as serve to keep you within your goal of acquiring no new debt.

The credit card you keep should offer a grace period of at least twenty-five days. It should only be used for convenience and it should be paid off within twenty-five days, or you might need to eliminate that card too.

If you or family members lack the discipline to use this credit card properly, it should be kept in a drawer at home and not carried in your wallet.

Face the Facts

A critical part of assessing your situation is to list all the following information on columnar paper. You may even want to use one piece of paper for each creditor.

Creditor
Balance on the account
Minimum payment
Number of payments left
Interest rate
Item purchased
Payment due date

Once this information has been documented in one place, it will be easier to ascertain your true debt load and develop a systematic plan to get out of debt.

If you or family members lack the discipline to use this credit card properly, it should be kept in a drawer at home and not carried in your wallet.

Simplify

If you have a serious debt problem (as indicated by the warning signals and the exercise above), you need the help of a professional and should refer to the next chapter. Modest debt can usually be handled by a lifestyle simplification plan.

The easiest step is to reduce variable expenses, those monthly expenses that are not fixed like mortgage and car payments are. The fact that you are reading this book indicates you are already on your way to simplifying.

The bottom line is that you may have to do without in some areas, which can be somewhat painful if you've developed the attitude of the young Wal-Mart shopper from earlier in the chapter.

A more dramatic approach would be to reduce your fixed expenses by trading down in a home and/or car in order to get out of debt. This is an issue that your family will need to decide based on your desire to become debt-free and the severity of your financial situation.

If you will reduce your standard of living to allow for a monthly debt reduction program, it will be that much easier to become debt-free. You will also need to commit to applying *all* extra income from the simplification process toward the debt.

Here are some unexpected sources of income that should be applied toward debt reduction.

- ✓ Inheritance
- ✓ Income tax refund
- ✓ Overtime
- ✓ Bonus
- ✓ Insurance dividend refund
- ✓ Pay raise
- ✓ Any other unexpected additional income

Don't forget that if you have purposed to become debt-free in accordance with the biblical admonition to do so and you've dedicated this area to God, you should look for those unexpected incomes as a means of God's provision to reduce your debt.

Debt Consolidation

If you are going to consolidate your accounts, then purpose to do this only to lower the rates and *not* in order to extend debt. It's important to be sure that you don't add to your debt by extending it, even if it is offered.

You should only go to this option under the watchful eye of a financial counselor.

CREDIT CARDS

How do you know if you are getting a good value for the credit cards you currently have? You want a card that charges a low rate (not just as a temporary introductory rate either) that is fixed (not subject to increase), with no annual fee.

Don't be deceived by some of the so-called reward cards either—do the math on those cards. For example, most cards that offer frequent-flier miles require that you earn twenty-five thousand miles (at one mile per dollar = $25,000 spent) in order to buy *one* ticket (which averages $250 to $300). This means you are earning only one cent for every dollar you spend. These reward cards also subliminally encourage you to overspend on your credit card.

For a list of credit cards by category (low rate, no annual fee, etc.), go to *www.bankrate.com* or *www.cardtrak.com*. Other tools that are available to help you get the card that is right for you are *www.getsmart.com* and *www.creditcardgoodies.com*.

Paying the Principal

I am the first to admit that I'm not a financial planner. I'm just a mom who wanted to stay home with her children and developed a plan to do so. My plan was based on Biblical principles and some of my great-grandma's commonsense strategies.

> **Don't be deceived by some of the so-called "reward" cards—do the math on those cards, and you are earning only one cent for every dollar you spend.**

While I do believe that there is "wisdom in many counselors" and I devote an entire chapter to how to find those counselors, I also believe that if we desire wisdom, God will give it to us (James 1:5).

You can buy an expensive "pay-down kit" from a financial planner or you can just follow some simple steps and watch your debts diminish. Here are a couple of strategies to pay down the principal, rather than just managing the interest.

Pay the original minimum on each credit entry from the *Face the Facts* section on page 169. As you continue to make payments, you will find that the required minimum payment amount is reduced. Don't pay this new lower required amount, but continue paying the original minimum payment; you'll be paying off the principal and saving on interest by paying the debt off early.

Pay the least first. Organize your debts with the shortest pay-off time as the first priority on the list. Once this debt is paid, then apply the total amount of that payment (that you no longer have) to the next bill on your list.

Pay your mortgage principal. If you habitually pay your required monthly mortgage payment *plus* the principal on the next month's payment, you can pay off your mortgage in about half the time. Look at your original mortgage loan and see how little of your initial payments go toward the principal. You are mainly paying the interest.

On the other hand, if you habitually make the monthly payment plus pay the principal for the next month, it will only increase your payments by a margin (depending on your mortgage payment). All of those additional dollars go directly to the principal. This allows you to pay down the principal rapidly, and with proper planning, you could end up paying a thirty-year mortgage off in only fifteen years!

> **If you habitually pay your required monthly mortgage payment *plus* the principal on the next month's payment, you can pay off your mortgage in about half the time.**

If you want precise amounts and the exact timing on how to pay your mortgage in half the time, you can invest in a financial calculator (available at electronics stores), contact a volunteer financial counselor, or visit a Web site that makes these calculations for you, such as *www.interest.com/hugh/calc/mort.html*.

BUY DOWN YOUR MORTGAGE RATE

If you get an unexpected bonus or source of other income, it makes sense to buy down the rate of your mortgage loan. You can do this by paying points (one point is equivalent to 1 percent of the loan amount). This means that on a $100,000 30-year fixed-rate mortgage at 8.5 percent, you could lower the rate to 8 percent by paying $2,000 up front. Go to *www.homepath.com* to help you explore this "what if" situation. See how various changes to loan terms, income statements, and interest rates affect your mortgage. As long as you stay in the house for five years, you'll recoup the money.

Paying down your mortgage is a good idea when rates are not projected to come down over the next few years. If there's a prediction of falling rates, then it would be wiser to use your buy-down money during a refinance to get a lower-than-low rate.

REBUILDING GOOD CREDIT

A bankruptcy will stay on your credit report for at least eight years. Even once you've rebuilt credit after this severe kind of damage, you won't be able to qualify for rock-bottom mortgage rates. According to Jean Sherman Chatzky, financial editor at *USA Weekend Magazine* (Jan. 21, 2000), these are the things you'll have to do to rebuild your credit rating.

✓ **Close accounts you don't use.** To lenders, charge accounts or home-equity lines of credit mean you could go on a spending spree at any time.

✓ **Don't hit all your credit limits.** If you're using 80 percent or more of your available credit, it's a sign to lenders that you're overextended.

✓ **Limit inquiries into your credit record.** Minimize the number of times you apply for credit, because each inquiry will appear on your credit report, whether you get the credit or not. Keep in mind that all inquiries for one purpose, such as a mortgage, will count as one.

✓ **Don't miss payments.** Automate as many payments as possible if you can keep up with these automated payments in your accounts at home. If you make sure the funds are there, you will never be late on payments. Companies from health clubs to utilities have these services available.

✓ **Check your credit report.** Order a copy from any of the major credit bureaus: Equifax (1-800-685-1111), Experian (1-888-297-3742), or Trans Union (1-800-888-4213). These reports cost about $8. If you live in Colorado, Georgia, Maryland, Massachusetts, New Jersey, or Vermont, or if you've been denied credit before, you qualify for a free copy annually. It makes sense to take advantage of this service.

**"Diminish your wants
or augment your means."**

—BENJAMIN FRANKLIN

CHAPTER SIXTEEN

True Confessions of a Debt-Monger

Finding Affordable Financial Counseling

Janice was born to a domineering mother and a skirt-chasing father. Her abusive dad left her and her mom when she was an adolescent. Janice compensated for her lack of a father figure in several ways: through promiscuity, being competitive, controlling and manipulating others, and through things. Yes, things.

Her mom couldn't afford to keep her in the clothing she felt she deserved. So she decided that when she was old enough, she'd get everything she wanted—and figure out how to pay for it later. She even developed the strange idea that God wanted her to have all those things she never had.

She said, "I decide what I want, then I ask God to help me get it."

In her first marriage, Janice got herself and her husband into a massive amount of debt. She was trying to fill the void within her that she thought things could fill. When he couldn't keep up with her spending patterns, she got a wealthier husband.

Hubby number two had deeper pockets than number one. He paid all the debt she couldn't pin on hubby number one. Sadly, within four years, Janice and hubby number two were into debt to the tune of two hundred thousand dollars. She even let their car insurance go unpaid for six months, and their phone got disconnected, while their family made a very good income. When she had children, she started saying she was doing it for them. She called it "giving them what I never had."

Not surprisingly, her second marriage ended in divorce over finances. In between husbands, she filed for bankruptcy—and each time she blamed men, victimizing herself as a means of coping with her problems. She also brought her children into her financial problems.

No amount of child support or spousal support could solve her problems. Years of therapy did nothing for her either. Nor did hubby number three. Her compulsive spending became so great, she resorted to forging signatures on loans and a series of lies to cover her self-destructive steps. Someone else was always responsible for Janice's problems.

"Janice" could just as easily be known as Bill or Cindy or Nancy or Thomas. The name may change and some of the facts may vary, but the story is sadly the same: people using money and things to fill the void that only God can fill.

God knows the financial problems you have, and He knows why you have them. He knows what you've done in secret that not even your dearest friend knows. He knows how you've tried to justify yourself and how you've tried to cope. He knows it all and He *still* desires to have a relationship with you. He's made a provision for this relationship through His Son, Jesus Christ, and you can have it today.

If you're not sure about how you relate to God, why not stop where you are, find a Bible, and read the book of John. In that book, you will find out how to fill the void that money, sex, and things haven't been able to fill.

Even today, I pray for Janice and the others I've met with similar variations of her story. It would bring my heart great joy to hear that Janice has finally found God. Not a man-made God of her own imagination, but the God of the universe—the person who loved her so much He'd rather die than live without her.

I know that this true story is a radical departure from my "kids smear chocolate all over the kitchen floor" type of story. It's not the "Ellie gets to a formal tea and discovers she's wearing two different shoes" kind of event. This is a departure because there are times when I meet hurting people and there's little humor to be found in their lives.

As a matter of fact, there are times in my life when coping is difficult, like when I have to move (yet again) and leave friends, a community we've grown to love, and our church family to start over (again). It's also no picnic to compartmentalize Bob flying in a war situation in harm's way. But I have found a way to cope, one that gives me hope. This hope is available for people like Janice and other hurting people. God can take the challenging (and even ugly) things of our past and create something good.

> There are trained, caring, and competent financial counselors all over the country who are eager to help you find your way back home.

One of God's provisions for your finances is a book like this one. There are also other authors and books that can be a great resource (see the appendix). One other tremendous provision for you can be found in financial counseling. There are trained, caring, and competent financial counselors all over the country who are eager to help you find your way back home. All you have to do is ask.

The following organizations can help you consolidate your bills into one lower monthly payment to get out of debt. They can help you reduce your interest charges by as much as 20 to 50 percent. These two things will help save thousands in finance charges alone.

They can also help remove the pressure from creditors to eventually help free you from financial bondage. All of these tools are used to the end goal of helping you to become a more responsible steward of your finances.

REALISTIC EXPECTATIONS

You didn't get in the terrible financial shape that you're in overnight, and you won't get out of it instantly either. Sometimes people get discouraged after they've gone for financial counseling for a few months because the results are not happening quickly enough.

Getting a grip on your finances is a gradual process. So don't expect your bills to magically disappear under a sprinkling of fairy dust.

This having been said, I do think that it is wise to pray that God will provide opportunities to become debt-free even sooner than the experts say is possible. However, you will need to commit to this so if that Christmas check for five hundred dollars comes in from Aunt Ruth, you have already committed to putting it toward your debt load. God honors those who honor Him.

> **Getting a grip on your finances is a gradual process. So don't expect your bills to magically disappear under a sprinkling of fairy dust.**

FINDING SOME HELP

It is critical that you find counselors you can trust. I've heard too many horror stories about people who were taken in by those who just wanted to take advantage of them. Don't confuse credit counselors with "credit-repair" groups that offer to wipe out negative information from your credit report. Not only is that impossible, but credit-repair organizations often charge high fees, and these groups are all over the Internet. My junk e-mail accounts get at least twenty daily offers to "erase your bad credit history."

There are some specific steps that a good, solid financial counselor will take with her clients. One of the first questions you should ask is "How much will this cost?" to make sure that the service is free. Before you meet with a financial counselor, ask her what the step-by-step process involves. These steps were taken from Larry Burkett's best-selling book *Debt-Free Living*. They include:

✓ Determine the actual spending level at present.
✓ The counselees will keep a record of every expenditure they have for the next month.
✓ The counselees will maintain their budget each and every month.

Along the way, a trained counselor will help with interest reduction, debt consolidation, and debt collectors.

Counselors from Your Church

More and more churches are taking advantage of programs such as the one highlighted by Christian Financial Ministries to train church members to help others in this area. Ask your pastor if there is someone who could mentor and assist you with your financial difficulties. Many businesspeople or other qualified individuals in the church would be more than willing to help and would be flattered by the idea that you would approach them.

Another advantage to finding a person from your local church is the accountability factor and regular contact. There can also be a oneness in prayer as you work through the situation together. The person who ministers in this area will actually "own" (in the figurative sense) a part of your family's financial recovery. The counselor invests his or her time, energy, prayer, and wisdom, and the debt-free result will be extremely gratifying for the counselor who has helped the distressed family.

I do believe that those who have been given much in terms of financial opportunity and experience have also been given much in terms of ministry opportunity. If you fit into this category, why not consider offering your expertise as a ministry through your church? You could make the difference in many lives.

Christian Financial Concepts/Crown Financial Ministries

This is Larry Burkett's ministry site, which merged with Howard Dayton's Crown Ministries and is now called Crown Financial Ministries. It is chock-full of great biblically-based resources. They also offer training to people who have a burden to teach financial concepts. Not all of these resources and services are free, so be sure to go through the checklist I've outlined later in the chapter. They can put you in touch with one of these classes or counselors in your area. For more information you can contact them at their Web site at *www.cfcministry.org*, or write to:

Crown Financial Ministries
P.O. Box 2377
Gainesville, GA 30503-2377

Trinity Credit Counseling

Trinity is a nonprofit, fully licensed agency specializing in credit consulting and debt management for consumers nationwide. You will need to review the rest of this chapter and ask the appropriate questions listed, such as fees, etc. You can contact them at 1-800-758-3844 for confidential information or look them up at their Web site at *www.trinitycredit.org*.

> **Keep in mind that these counselors may not understand the concept of tithing. But hold fast to that principle.**

Counselors from Your Work

You may be able to get help from your employer. Some businesses have a financial counselor on their staff and others provide outside counselors as part of employee benefits packages.

In the military, there are financial counselors who will help military personnel and their families on an appointment basis. The Air Force has the Family Support Center, and the Army has the Army Community Services center. The Navy, Marines, and Coast Guard all have a similar office as well. This counseling is not private, however, and severe problems will be reported to the commander. So some families choose other confidential resources.

Keep in mind that these counselors may not understand the concept of tithing. But hold fast to that principle.

FORMAL CREDIT COUNSELORS

Open your Yellow Pages to the Credit and Debt Counseling section. In the phone book I'm looking at there are fifteen counselors listed. Ask the Better Business Bureau about the local office of any service you are researching. Once again, these counselors may not see the value of tithing, so keep that in mind. Also, some of these organizations have a charge for their services, so be sure to find out how much they charge. Costs can vary from no charge to fifteen hundred dollars when you enter a formal program.

Another thing to consider is that if you use a formal counseling service and they have to take drastic measures to reduce your debt load, this can leave a blemish on your credit report that is almost as damaging as bankruptcy. Your accounts may be frozen, so you can't use your cards. But counseling is still the best option for some people.

The following secular organizations may charge a fee, but they also have a good reputation. The first organization doesn't charge for the counseling portion, but there are handling fees of anywhere from eight to eighteen dollars depending upon the number of accounts you have. The last two charge fees based on your situation.

- ✓ National Foundation for Consumer Credit (nonprofit organization). More than 1,450 Neighborhood Financial Care Centers nationally. 1-800-388-2277 or *www.nfcc.org*.
- ✓ Debt Counselors of America (a flat rate includes about fifteen counseling hours). No local offices; they work with clients online and on the phone. 1-800-680-3328 or *www.dca.org*.
- ✓ Debt Relief Clearinghouse (a consortium of five services). Rebates half the money it's paid by creditors to those who pay well. 1-800-433-2843 or *www.debtreliefonline.com*.

Questions to Ask Formal Credit Counselors

Some organizations will allow you to take a financial planning course even if you're not in formal counseling, and that would be beneficial. When you're selecting a formal credit counselor, such as the three listed above as examples, you need to ask the following questions:

- ✓ What will this cost?
- ✓ Can I track my progress? (Debt Counselors of America has an online service that allows clients to see when a check was received and when it was sent to creditors.)

✓ Do I get rebates? (Debt Relief Clearinghouse offers such rebates.)
✓ Do I have to have a certain amount of debt to work with you? (Some groups won't touch you unless you have a minimum amount of debt.)
✓ What are your qualifications? (If you're entering a drastic program, you want to make sure that your counselor has more than just a few hours in a classroom.)

"The rich rule over the poor, and the borrower is servant to the lender."

—PROVERBS 22:7 NIV

CHAPTER SEVENTEEN

I Got Me a Right Good Ed-gee-ca-tion

Finding Education Money from Preschool to Post-Grad

Even though I've lost a lot of my Texas accent, people say I still have some of it, and that's OK with me—I'm proud of my home country of Texas. I will admit that my accent comes back again pretty strongly when I'm visiting Texas or when I talk to someone from back home. Bob can always tell when I've been talking long distance in the middle of the day (it's a guy thing—they think the only time a woman has to talk long distance is after five o'clock or on weekends). But, somehow, Bob always knows. The encounter usually goes something like this:

He comes home and I greet him with, "Why hiiiii, hunny, how ya'll doin' tuday?"

He frowns slightly, "Ellie, have you been talking long distance to Texas again *in the middle of the day*?"

I try to tap-dance around the question a bit, "Whyyyyy, whut makes ye' think thaat, darlin'?"

People in New Mexico don't talk as funny as people in New York. I think it has something to do with the fact that New Mexico is right next door to the Lone Star State.

Believe it or not, despite the fact that New Mexico is so close to Texas, there are still an amazing number of people who don't speak fluent Texan. For example, one day we were at a party thrown by our friends, Jan and Mike McMinn. They live out in the country, surrounded by wide open spaces in Tularosa, New Mexico. I was standing by the sliding glass door next to a woman named Ailene, whom I didn't know very well. As we looked out the window at the McMinn property, I was trying to identify the trees on their land. One tree looked like a pecan tree, but I wasn't sure.

Pointing to the tree in the distance, I asked, "Is that there a pe-caan tree?"

Ailene smiled and nodded but didn't say anything, so I repeated the question in my Texas drawl, but slowed it down a bit so she'd understand.

"I said, is that a pe-caaan tree?"

As other people laughed and talked in the noisy room, Ailene got a strange look on her face and spoke, "Yes, yes, Ellie, we're in the *country*."

She didn't speak fluent Texan and the way we sometimes run our words together can be confusing, so Ailene thought I was saying: "We're in the country! We're in the country!"

Yep, I don't get out much.

The main thing that I dislike about my accent is that people tend to assume I'm not very intelligent or I'm uneducated because I talk differently. Which is not true. Why, I've got two college degrees. I've got me a right good ed-gee-ca-tion! So ya'll listen up!

College is one of the largest expenditures for families in their middle-age years, and it is one that could saddle the parents or students with years of bondage due to extensive debt. College is even more expensive if you pay double by paying for it on credit. It is much cheaper if you pay as you go.

Owing forty thousand dollars worth of student loans is not a good way to start life in the workplace. Young marriages start out with two strikes against them when both of the parties enter the marriage with excessive education loan debts. Remember that the number one cause of divorce is arguments over finances.

Any time you can minimize your expenses for education, you're a step ahead of the game. The following tips cover education costs for school-aged children all the way to advanced college degrees.

HOMESCHOOLING

For seven years I homeschooled my children. I did so for many reasons, but primarily because I thought it was the best for them at the time. One of our boys wasn't reading right away, and I knew he'd get labeled in a conventional classroom. He eventually started reading in third grade and has caught up in that subject.

> Ask your homeschool group to have a used curriculum swap/sale. The best time to do this is in March or April, so you'll have adequate time to order the other materials you couldn't pick up used.

Another reason I chose this option was because we moved a lot and this provided continuity for the children. A final reason for homeschooling was the cost of private schooling. At the time, we couldn't afford this expense for multiple children. The following tips for homeschooling parents should help to cut costs.

Used Curriculum

Once you've decided on a curriculum, ask your homeschool group to have a used curriculum swap/sale. The best time to do this is in March or April, so you'll have adequate time to order the other materials you couldn't pick up used.

The main thing to keep in mind with a used curriculum is if it will work for you. What good is a textbook if the student workbook is out of print and you can't order a new one? This means you would have to develop your own workbook, and we're talking many, many hours to develop this. Homeschooling is enough of a challenge without adding these additional chores. You have to carefully consider the financial and time trade-offs when purchasing used curriculum.

New Curriculum Fairs

It is very important not to duplicate a curriculum or purchase materials that will not work for your homeschool. This is a waste of money and the one area where homeschoolers are likely to blow their budgets.

If you can go to a curriculum fair with several distributors, it would be worth the trip. *Before* the fair, try to get catalogs from the major distributors (call 1-800-555-1212 and ask the operator for the distributor's phone number).

Do your homework by looking over the catalogs and writing down the materials you would like to order for the coming year. Pay attention to which textbooks, lesson plans, teacher's guides, and quiz keys you need to look at in person and indicate these on your list with an asterisk.

The reason you want to look at some of these resources is that you may not need to order the lesson plan if the materials seem to be self-explanatory. If you have a good grasp of mathematics, for example, then you may already know how to teach addition and won't need the teacher guide. I didn't really need these additional resources until my children were in the second and third grade, depending upon the subject.

I learned very quickly, when my oldest was in the third grade, that a mathematics workbook teacher's key was worth nine dollars a year so I wouldn't have to do every fraction and long division problem.

If you are not yet confident in teaching your children at home, then you might feel better ordering the full curriculum. If you are more experienced or have a good grasp of teaching, there are a lot of materials that you can avoid purchasing while not compromising the integrity of the material your child is learning.

Postage and Handling. When you order from a curriculum fair or a special demonstration set up in a local hotel conference room or church, you will usually avoid sales tax and postage and handling fees.

Multiple Children

If you have more than one child and know you will be homeschooling them for many years, you may want to pay special attention to "last edition" indicators in your favorite catalog. The curriculum publishers will usually indicate in their catalogs when they are revising the curriculum. If you already have a teacher's guide, key, and lesson plan text, you might want to consider ordering additional student workbooks for your younger children as well. You might have to pay a little more this year, but it saves you from having to buy another expensive teacher's curriculum for that subject.

When you are schooling many children, you can think in terms of investment. I ordered Abeka Bible teaching aids for a variety of series and topics and taught those subjects to all of the children at once. They were good investments and can be used outside of homeschooling for Sunday school classes or neighborhood summer Bible clubs. Learn to think in terms of investment, whether you're ordering teaching equipment, desks, curriculum, or supplies.

Share Your Used Curriculum

Jessica, a homeschooling friend of mine, schooled two children all the way through high school, and they are now young adults she is quite proud of. She said that when she was done with her youngest child's curriculum, she always looked for a family that could use it and gave it to them. Jessica found that when she gave these things away, she always either had enough money to buy next year's curriculum or someone gave her the new set of textbooks.

Library Resources

Some friends I know used the library for the majority of their curriculum, but there are limitations to this approach. For one thing, there's far more planning, organizing, and research involved in this approach. You would have to spend approximately an extra ten hours a week (depending upon your organizational skills) in order to take advantage of this approach for the majority of your curriculum needs.

On the other hand, the library does offer free access to computers, readers, and resources for book reports and research papers. Your child can also request information from other libraries via an interlibrary loan. There are computer programs that access thousands of periodicals for research information.

PRIVATE SCHOOLS

We believe in meeting the needs of each of our children on an individual basis. Last year, the time was right and the finances were available, so we put our children in a private Christian school. Each family has to prioritize its financial resources and decide what is worth scrimping for. We now drive much older vehicles, wear clothes from garage sales, and take modest vacations because our children's education is worth the sacrifices in other areas.

> **Be aware of the fact that the majority of private schools must have a series of fund raisers and other requests for money on a regular basis. Add a buffer of 15 to 20 percent of the tuition you will pay to allow for these additional requests.**

If you've never had your child in a private school, you need to be aware of the fact that the majority of private schools have a series of fund raisers and other requests for money on a regular basis to meet operating expenses and to fund special projects. You can participate to the degree your family feels comfortable, but I would advise you to add a buffer of 15 to 20 percent of the tuition you will pay to allow for these additional financial requests.

Saving in Private School

Surprisingly enough, there are ways to save—even in private schools.

Multiple child discount. We have used two private schools so far, and they both had a multiple child discount. The first child paid full price, the second was 15 percent off, the third was 20 percent off, and all other children were free. So we could send our children on a "five for three" special! Of course, price isn't going to be the driving factor in selecting a private school, but it is certainly worth looking at before you choose, especially if you have a large family.

Teacher's benefits. Many Christian schools offer free or reduced tuition for the children of teachers, teacher's aides, librarians, office workers, and facilities management workers. If you are working outside the home and want to send your children to a private school, you may want to consider a job change. Even if you are not licensed to teach in your state, you could work in a different area in the school, even part time.

Scholarships/grants. Some Christian schools have scholarship programs based on financial need that could be yours for the asking. Some states even have financial assistance from private corporations (we're not talking government money here). Talk to the financial counselor at your local private school and see what options are available.

Individual needs. This year my children are in a private Christian school, but next year they may be homeschooled again or some may be at home and some may be in a public school. On an annual basis, we try to determine and act upon what we feel is best for each of our children individually.

COLLEGE

Have you ever sat in on a financial planner's workshop? At the risk of stepping on some toes, the one part I strongly disagree with is the part about financing our children's college education. The discussion usually goes something like this:

"How many children do you have?" they ask, dry erase marker in hand.

Bob and I know what's coming next as we answer, "Five."

"Oh my, now that's a lot of children. Tell me, do you want your children to go to college?"

The way they ask the college question is phrased more like, "Well, if you're a good parent, you will want to provide for your children's college education. This is what decent parents do for their kids."

Bob and I pull up our shields as we get ready for the response to our answer of "Yes, we want them to go to college, but we think they should earn it. We don't feel that being good parents means we give them four years in college at our expense."

Following are some tips to help put college in perspective and some ways to get that education without hocking your future to do so.

Earn It!

Bob and I have discovered that those things that mean the most to us in life are the things we earned. When I earned the money for my first car (an old Datsun B210), I took good care of that car. When my parents broke from the norm for my younger brother and gave him a classic '58 Chevy pickup truck, he wrecked it within a year. Bethany had a friend whose grandparents lavished her with ten American Girl dolls. Bethany worked six months for hers and we matched her funds. She takes great care of the doll. Her friend leaves the dolls scattered around their house.

> **Those things that mean the most to us in life are the things we earned. Kids paying for their own education are upset when classes are canceled and work or study on weekends.**

Growing up, I had one family member who got college scholarships and minimum student loans to get his sheepskin. The parents paid for the first semester of a sibling's college, and he partied it away—never completing the course work for a single class. You can see this pattern in today's colleges. Sometimes, the kids who are there at their parents' expense are the ones who cut classes and party on weekends. The kids paying for their own education are upset when classes are canceled and work or study on weekends.

My husband, Bob, got the very best education by going to the U.S. Air Force Academy. He worked throughout high school to get good grades and cultivated a well-rounded life experience to get into that institution. While there, he worked eighteen-hour days doing military studies, athletics, or academics. Those who begrudge his success as an officer don't fully appreciate that he very much paid for his education with blood, sweat, and tears. He likes to say he graduated as a D.G. (which is not "Distinguished Graduate" but "Did Graduate!").

SAVING FOR COLLEGE

Start Early

Please don't get me wrong. I don't think there's anything wrong with parents helping their child go to college; I'm just opposed to parents providing a full free ride without the child earning a portion of his education.

It's wise to start putting away money for college early—while they're still babies. You may want to start a custodial account at your local bank. These are irrevocable gifts to the child and up to $700 per year of the investment income is tax-free. Once the fund has grown beyond $10,000, you're probably better off putting additional capital in either an education IRA or one of two state tuition programs (see below).

Education IRA

This is a relatively new program that is available through banks and brokerages. This option allows annual contributions of up to $500 per child under 18, provided the donor meets certain income criteria. No taxes are owed on withdrawals used for college expenses as long as the student is under age 30. The only drawback to this plan is that you may not be eligible for education tax credits later on. It would be best to consult IRS Publication 970 or visit *www.irs.ustreas.gov* on the Internet before investing in this plan.

Prepaid Plans/State Tuition

With a prepaid plan you can avoid future increases by buying credits in advance at today's rates. Most states will allow you to redeem the cash value of the credits at other institutions, including private colleges and out-of-state public schools. You may want to look at other options, depending on the current tuition inflation rates. This plan is tax-deferred. To further investigate this plan or the next one (Savings Account), you can call 1-877-277-6496 or visit *www.collegesavings.org* on the Web.

State-Sponsored Tuition Savings Accounts

These accounts can be used to pay for any accredited college or university. In this savings account the funds are managed professionally by state employees or contracted investment firms. The main drawback is that once you invest, you forfeit control and can't close the account without a large penalty.

The main advantage of this plan, as well as the prepaid state tuition plan, is that they have a tax-deferred status. The earnings are taxed at the student's lower rate as they are withdrawn.

OTHER OPTIONS TO CONSIDER

Just because a high school graduate is accepted to the college of her dreams doesn't mean she is entitled to go to that school. College should be a matter of what the family can afford, not what kind of school your child can get into. Students and parents need a reality check in this area. Acceptance into college needs to be balanced with an acceptance of what you can afford without becoming indebted for the next twenty-five years.

> **College should be a matter of what the family can afford, not what kind of school your child can get into. Students and parents need a reality check in this area.**

Some people think, "I'll just figure out what I want and then try to figure out how to pay for it." The people spouting this kind of dogma are usually the same people who are in debt up to their eyeballs.

Community Colleges

The first two years of basics can be completed at a junior college or community college and then transferred to a four-year university, which will issue the diploma. The diploma doesn't indicate that the graduate paid a fourth of the cost of school those first two years. All you have to do is check with a counselor at the four-year university to make sure those courses will transfer.

Advanced Placement

While a student is still in high school, in the summer before school starts or even after they have started classes, they can take advanced placement tests. The fees on these tests are nominal, but a student can receive credit for a variety of subjects and have those credits apply toward a degree. All it will require are some hours of study and preparation. I received an entire semester of credit for advanced placement in Spanish. *¿Cómo que no?*

College Classes in High School

Another option that saves big money is to take college courses—at little or no additional expense—while still in high school. (In some parts of the country this is called Post Secondary Option, or PSO.) Talk with your school's counselor or principal to determine if this option is available for your student. Here are just a few Web sites you can visit for more information:

✓ *www.hsc.org/chaos-highschool.html#college*
✓ *www.powerstudents.com/highschool/hs_askexperts/*
  1198h.shtml
✓ *www.houghton.k12.mi.us/highschool/hsstudent-hand-*
  book.htm #Dual Enrollment

Military Options for College

Military Academies: In these institutions, the education is free, but cadets pay for their education with very hard work. In addition, they are paid around seven thousand dollars a year. A military academy is not for everyone—it is extremely challenging academically, physically, and emotionally. Only the top 10 percent of eligible applicants will get into major service academics (U.S. Air Force, West Point, Annapolis). They are the créme de la créme, and grooming for these institutions begins early in high school. A résumé that includes a degree from any of these schools is extremely impressive in corporate America.

If your child aspires to go to one of these academies, he will need to do well academically, show leadership ability (they look for outside activities that indicate leadership), and have an athletic aptitude. The student will need to contact your representative or either of your two senators for a letter of nomination. There is usually a competitive interview and application process for these nominations. After the highly competitive nomination is secured (children of retired military personnel may receive a presidential nomination and forego the nomination process), then they must again compete before a board at each military institution.

In addition to the nomination process, each ROTC from colleges and high schools will send twenty students each year, eighty-five enlisted soldiers on active duty may be admitted, and eighty-five in the reserves can be admitted annually. So going through the actives or reserves may be another way to get to an academy.

ROTC (Reserve Officer Training Corps): These programs offer scholarships to future military officers at local colleges. Some ROTC scholarships go unused because of a lack of applicants.

Active Duty/Reserve Military: By joining the military, a young person can learn a trade and earn money for college as well. When I interviewed an Army recruiter, the college benefits package was so attractive it made me want to enlist! (But Bob wouldn't let me!)

Basically, a person would take the ASVAB test to determine their aptitude for college and for other enlistment purposes. If an individual scores less than 50, they qualify for the Montgomery GI Bill, which is a contributory fund. The soldier contributes $100 per month for the first twelve months ($1,200 total) and a minimal commitment to the Army of two years would yield $15,696 in college funding. Increased commitment would yield up to $19,200 total. However, if they score higher than 50, the Army considers them college material, and they qualify for the Army College Fund. This fund has the same contributory funds as above ($1,200 total), but they get anywhere from $26,500 to $50,000 for college, depending on whether they sign up for a two-, three-, or four-year term.

The Air Force, Navy, and Marines offer similar packages, but this gives you an idea of what you can get for your enlistment into the military. The current benefits packages vary, so check with your recruiter. Keep in mind that military living is not for those who are timid and laid back. These people lay their lives on the line to protect our nation's freedom, and the service they provide our nation is more than worth the benefits they receive for college tuition.

Frugal Alternatives

State Schools: There are plenty of fine state schools that offer reduced tuition for residents. The price difference between a state and private school is astounding. You will find that all expenses can be covered (including room and board) at a state school for the same price as tuition alone at a private school.

Living with Family: Room and board are oftentimes the most expensive part of college. By living with parents, grandparents, or other relatives, a student can pay as he goes in school because he doesn't have this major expense. We have no problem with one of our children living at home while earning his way through college.

Work-Study Programs, Employee Benefits, Corporate Benefits: Check with the college of your choice and see if they have work-study programs available for students. These are federal programs that provide jobs for students on campus and the college administers the jobs.

> The price difference between a state and private school is astounding. You will find that all expenses can be covered (including room and board) at a state school for the same price as tuition alone at a private school.

Most colleges have plenty of jobs that don't involve teaching. These schools oftentimes allow children of employees to receive free tuition. One of my best friends went to Texas Christian University (TCU) that way, and another retired Air Force friend paid for his son's college by choosing to work at a small college.

Last but not least, if you haven't finished your education and always wanted to, ask your employer if they have benefits that will pay for courses. Usually this is done as a reimbursement for the courses you take, and there are qualifying factors that they may impose.

Delay for a Year or Two: Bob and I counseled a young lady who graduated from high school at age sixteen and immediately went to Columbia University. The financial pressures were unbearable when combined with her age, the distance from her home, and living in a big city. In addition, the demanding course work added more pressure to this student. After her sophomore year, she took a two-year sabbatical to work full time and earn money to pay for school. She's back at Columbia, and the pressure is greatly reduced from that of a couple years ago. She doesn't have the tension of working all those extra hours while in school, and she now has much more time to study. She will graduate soon and have minimal debts for her excellent education due to keen financial decisions on how to pay for college.

Knit Your Way Through School—Assorted Scholarships: In the Family Support Center at our base, the education staff will research scholarship information for people seeking to go to school. A friend of mine got two, one-thousand dollar scholarships from the American Wool Association because she listed her hobby as knitting. This scholarship had gone unawarded for two years because no one applied!

Go to the library and look at *Paying for College Without Going Broke*, by Kalman A. Chany. This is a handbook for minimizing out-of-control college costs. The book includes advice for special circumstances from single parents to independent students. It also gives information about how to find scholarships, how to find the best lender for occasional educational loans, and information on the recent tax law's impact on financing college.

The National Scholarship Research Service is an organization that has been around for twenty years. You can do your own search on their Web site at *www.800headstart.com*, or they can do a search for you for $185 (this service is done free on most military bases). You can also contact them at 1-707-546-6777 or at their mailing address: 5577 Skylande Boulevard, Suite 6A, Santa Rosa, CA 95403.

Internships: Check out *The Internship Bible*, by Mark Oldman and Samer Hamadeh, at your local library. A new edition is published every year. This resource gives thumbnail sketches of essential information on nearly every internship in the country—more than ten thousand opportunities every year. The book tells prospective interns about application deadlines, compensation and perks, selectivity, and more.

There are also quite a few Christian programs and schools that can give you information about their internship programs. Focus on the Family has one of the most selective and comprehensive programs in the Christian arena; call 1-800-A-FAMILY for more information. The Home School Legal Defense Association also has a great program for students; contact them at 1-540-338-5600.

———————————

"A student once asked the president of his school if there was a course he could take that was shorter than the one prescribed. 'Oh yes,' replied the president, 'but it depends on what you want to be. When God wants to make an oak, He takes a hundred years, but when He wants to make a squash, it only takes six months.'"

—MILES J. STANFORD,
PRINCIPLES OF SPIRITUAL GROWTH

CHAPTER EIGHTEEN

'Tis a Gift to Be Simple

The "Attagirls" and Simple Living

One of the major challenges of having so many school-aged children is visits to the dentist. Regular checkups, occasional fillings, pulling teeth to make room for more, sealants, spacers, broken sealants, broken spacers…you get the idea. This past fall I had twelve dentist appointments in five weeks (that's 2.4 visits a week).

On my first appointment, Linda, a dental hygienist, was cleaning my teeth. She looked at the name on my chart and asked, "Are you the same Ellie Kay that wrote a book on saving money? I ordered it from Crossings Book Club."

I was surprised and delighted, but I've always wondered why they love to ask you questions when you still have that suction tube in your mouth, "Warrl, yaa, yaa, daa me."

It's awfully hard to be poised and graceful when you sound like you have a mouthful of marbles.

She smiled as she got another glob of tutti-frutti-flavored toothpaste on the polisher. "Are those stories true about your youngest boy, Joshua?"

She was rudely interrupted by a child's loud voice coming from the next cubicle, "Hey! Whut ya doin'? I think ya' oughta' brush my teefh some more! You missed dat spot right dere!"

I heard a faint reply from the other hygienist that indicated she knew her job and they really were done. Joshua continued, "Do I get a toy? Can I have two toys since I been so good? I have been awful good, ya' know!"

I smiled sheepishly at Linda, who had her fingers in my mouth, and rolled my eyes toward the sound of Joshua ranting on the other side of the wall.

Linda was just finishing when Joshua, his fist full of toys, walked into the room, his hygienist following behind him.

He announced, "I done now, Mama!" He licked his lips, "I tink she missed a spot, but she done pretty good. I got my toys and I is ready to go now, Mama."

As I wiped my mouth and ran my tongue over my freshly polished teeth, I thought of the song Joshua had just learned in his four-year-old class at school and asked him, "Do you want to sing your good-bye song for the ladies?"

He loved to sing his "good-bye song" from preschool and usually gave command performances.

His brow furrowed in concentration as he loudly sang:

Goodbye now, goodbye now,
The clock says we're done.
We'll see you tomorrow,
God bless everyone.

The women smiled at his cute performance, and Linda asked, "So, Joshua, what time does the clock say when you're done?"

He frowned and stammered, "Uh…uh." He looked as if she'd asked him a trick question.

Suddenly, he looked at her with a mischievous smile, shrugged his shoulders and shouted, "I don't know—our class don't have a clock!"

If you didn't like these kid stories, you wouldn't still be reading them in chapter 18, would you? One of the universal appeals of kid stories is that almost everyone can think of at least one funny story of when they were a kid, what their kids have done, what you've heard a kid say in Sunday school, or what your grandkids have done.

There is great value in recounting these stories. For one thing, they make you laugh when you could scream. They also make you relive some pleasant memories. They may even serve as blackmail material for your grown kids—that's of some value, isn't it?

These stories are especially important because they bring about laughter at the simple things in life. Humor is a simple pleasure that is readily available if you will slow down and look around. While stress is a part of life, living simply is one way to minimize stress and conflict while bringing out the best in others. Simplicity is a value that can save us money every day.

> If we simplify, we can live beneath our means, thereby having extra to save and invest.

When we can learn to be content with simple things, we are less likely to buy more stuff and spend beyond our means. If we simplify, we can live beneath our means, thereby having extra to save and invest. None of this will happen if we cannot catch the vision of how gratifying it can be to adopt the "less is more" view of life. The added benefit of simplifying is that we will de-stress our lives in the process.

Here are some simple-living stress busters guaranteed to create a happier, more healthful lifestyle. These tips are from a group of my friends who are also authors and speakers. We call ourselves the "Attagirls" because we're always trying to offer simple encouragement. My mom offers the final tip in this chapter.

THERE IS A BRIGHT SPOT

Whether you're running errands, going to work, or chasing after toddlers in a grocery store, you'll run into people who can spoil your day. However, there really *are* people out there who genuinely want to be of service. Look for and be grateful for these kinds of people—they are out there.

TAKE A NAP

My good friend and mentor, Becky Freeman, said in *Peanut Butter Kisses and Mudpie Hugs*: "One way you know you're growing up is when you think of bedtime as a luxurious reward at the end of a long day, rather than an ominous cloud hovering over your parade."

DARE TO BE CONTENT

"It's silly to think that a relaxed, happy person lacks motivation. You *can* be content and still be energized. Why, just look at my role model—the *Energizer* Bunny," says Ellie Kay, a simple mother of five.

TAKE A MINI VACATION

Whether it's a quiet cup of tea when the babies are sleeping or a rare afternoon of window shopping, it's important to schedule a break in our week of endless responsibilities in order to retrench and refresh ourselves. Rachel St. John-Gilbert, my free-lance editor-friend said in *Seasons of a Woman's Heart*: "How often the responsibilities and tasks of everyday life have my compass pointing due east, while my heart cries out, 'Go west, young woman!'"

MAKE THE MOST OF THE MUNDANE

I met Lynn Morrissey when I submitted stories for her beautiful day-book, *Seasons of a Woman's Heart*. She put it so well when she challenged women in her first book with: "Are you making the most of each moment God gives you? Mundane routines become sparkling experiences. Chance meetings become divine appointments. As you *live on purpose*, every season becomes sacred with meaning. Make moments matter!"

SEEK GOD WITH ALL YOUR HEART

A relationship with God can seem like a complex issue, but it becomes simple if you listen with your heart. Brenda Waggoner, licensed professional counselor and author of *The Velveteen Woman*, said it best: "It is our *hearts* that respond to God's wooing voice rather than our intellects."

GO FOR THE CHOCOLATE TRUFFLE

OK, I'll admit it, I'm a chocoholic. I'd quit this habit, but I'm no quitter. Much to my delight, I found a wonderful application for my hip-expanding habit in my friend Kali Schnieders's book, *Truffles from Heaven*. She said, "Every truffle has its own nougat center message from God. The work of life is to get that message." To get every delightful taste of God's purpose for life, we must search out His personalized message. I think of that every time I eat a chocolate truffle, speaking of which, I think I'll just go and find one....

SHARE YOUR HEART

Sharing has always been a big part of my life. There's nothing like sharing something simple to bless others and reduce stress in our lives at the same time. I found a friend who can relate to this in Jane Jarrell, the author of many books, among them a delightfully practical one

> There's nothing like sharing something simple to bless others and reduce stress in our lives at the same time.

called *Love You Can Touch*. She said it so well: "When I was growing up I knew what the tantalizing aroma of a coconut pound cake filling our home meant. Either a family member was celebrating a birthday or a friend was having surgery or a new baby was about to make his entrance into our world. In a home where gift-giving was a treasured thing, cake-baking to mark an 'occasion' was a ritual. The same is true in my house today. Whatever the event, happy or sad, it is always a perfect time to offer love you can touch."

BE TRUE TO YOUR DREAMS

My mom was in her sixties before her childhood dream came true of having one of her stories published. She put her writing on hold while she valiantly raised children full time, served in her local church, and worked part time in order to financially support mission work. It was my privilege to edit and submit some of her stories for publication. It was difficult to know who was happier when they were accepted, the writer or the editor!

In the midst of a hectic lifestyle, it's so easy to forget those dreams. But we need to be like a child who never forgets a promised ice cream cone or trip to the zoo. If pursuing our hopes will not be at another's expense, then we need to remember those dreams of long ago.

It's as my mom, Paquita Rawleigh, said in *Treasures of a Woman's Heart*: "A trusting child will love you forever. Do not disappoint him."

Look back at the child you were, the dreams she had, and do not disappoint her.

"One teacher I sat under put it in these words: 'The one who says it most simply knows it best. Anybody can make the simple difficult, but it takes a gifted teacher to make the difficult understandable.'"

—CHUCK SWINDOLL,
THE TALE OF THE TARDY OXCART

CHAPTER NINETEEN

Random Acts of Kindness

Changing Your World

After seven years of marriage, Cynthia and her husband finally had a baby, and oh, what a baby! After six hours of labor, Sammy made his grand entrance—all *eleven pounds* of him! Cynthia was ecstatic, but her joy was short-lived when her husband abandoned them when little Sammy was only three months old. She didn't plan on being a single mom—she didn't want to be a single mom—but suddenly, that's what she was.

Added to the overwhelming adjustment of motherhood and instant singlehood, Cynthia also had the financial burden of providing for her son. Yet she still wanted to spend as much time with him as possible. One evening, as she sat crunching the numbers at her desk, she realized that despite her three part-time jobs, there would still be a five hundred dollar shortfall each month. There was no money in savings. Armed with a deepening faith, this brave single mom decided to trust God to be "a father to the fatherless and a husband to the widows." She also purposed to continue to tithe out of her meager income.

Every morning, she applied the Psalms as a healing balm to her wounded heart. Every night, as she nursed Sammy, she claimed Psalm 37:25 (RSV), speaking it out loud: "I have been young, and now I am old; yet I have not seen the righteous forsaken or his children begging bread."

God provided in miraculous ways for that young mom. Weekly, someone provided groceries for her and her child. One month, an unexpected insurance refund arrived to make up the shortfall. Opportunities to house-sit helped her make the house payment. An anonymous cash gift arrived in the mail. By the end of that first critical year, Cynthia found that she had never missed giving her tithe and she had never skipped a bill payment. Not only were all her needs met, but, by some miracle, the single mom managed to put a thousand dollars into a savings account!

Incredible?

Yes.

Impossible?

No.

This true story is not as rare as you might think. In the offices of *Shop, Save, and Share*, we receive hundreds of similar accounts of God's provision for those in need. In fact, the *share* aspect of *Shop, Save, and Share* is the heart of our work. When people learn to save 50 to 85 percent off their food bill, they have an abundance to share with others in need. They do this by being wise with their money and by holding their material things with open hands.

God has said that when we're faithful in little things, He will give us stewardship over much. What about you? Have you had opportunities to share with others? It could mean sharing your time with a young mom by watching her children. It could mean taking groceries and leaving them anonymously on another family's porch. It could even

> When people learn to save 50 to 85 percent off their food bill, they have an abundance to share with others in need. They do this by being wise with their money and by holding their material things with open hands.

mean donating your older car to the Salvation Army or other nonprofit organization.

One thing is certain: When you give to the Lord, you will never be able to outgive God.

Here are some other testimonials that could inspire you in this area of sharing.

Kelli Ruiz from New Mexico: "I was skeptical as to whether Ellie's plan would work for me before I attended a live seminar. I wasn't sure the coupons would be for things we needed. I prayed about it and felt like it could be a very effective way for me to save my family money, so I decided to give it a try. The month before I started couponing, I paid $542.83 for groceries, the month after I only paid $281.76! I've even given away seven bags of groceries and toiletries, and still have an abundance of items—more than I've ever been able to keep in my pantry before!

"In eight weeks I've saved $588.72 which enabled us to afford health insurance for the first time. I have a health problem that could eventually be critical and now I have the means to afford the testing and treatments." *Author note: Two months after Kelli got insurance, she fell and had a major break in her leg. The insurance saved the family from financial devastation.*

Ursula Mixson from Tulsa, Oklahoma is one of the many single parents we hear from who have caught the vision of saving to share. She wrote: "Hi Ellie! This is the first time I've accessed your Web site. I'm a single mother of two with a determination to eliminate debt. I used to say that I didn't have the time it took to cut, sort, and organize coupons. Even when I did take a few coupons to the store, by the time I got ready to pay for my groceries, I would forget I had coupons. But now I realize that the hours I spend working overtime on my job, I could be using to save money and spend more time with my children. Thanks for the insight!"

Robert from Columbus, Mississippi: "There was a man named Peter in our Sunday School class who had been out of work for quite some time. He'd shared this as a prayer request week after week. We watched him diligently pursue job interviews to no avail as his sense of worth plummeted. One day, we felt led to anonymously donate about eight bags of groceries.

"The next week, Peter came and shared an amazing story. He said his daughter had signed them up to bring a cake to the school carnival. He knew they couldn't afford the cake mix, frosting, and oil. That afternoon, he found the bags of groceries that someone had quietly left. Inside the bag was cake mix that required only water and frosting. Peter told us, 'My hope had failed as I cried out to God and asked "Why can't I find a job? Don't you care about me, God?" Then God provided for these little needs, and when He did, I realized He cared about all my needs, too.'" Robert wrote back later to say that Peter found work the next month, but Peter would never forget how precisely God provided for his family's needs. It's an amazing thought that God would use you and me to be His arm of compassion and love to those around us.

> **It's an amazing thought that God would use you and me to be His arm of compassion and love to those around us.**

Heather from California posted this online review at *www.barnesandnoble.com*. "This book changed my life. My husband and I were having the same fights over and over again. It was all about the dreaded topic of money. He thought I didn't try hard enough and I thought he spent money foolishly. Then we got *Shop, Save, and Share*. It really challenged us to make some drastic changes. We realized we truly could cut corners in ways that weren't too painful. It truly wasn't that difficult to shave hundreds of dollars off our monthly food budget and simplify other areas of our lives. We have found we have lots of (free) groceries to pass along to other people who need them.

"By reaching out to others, we've taken the focus off of ourselves and our (former) problems. My husband really appreciates the teamwork philosophy. Our marriage is better than it has been in a long time and we don't argue about money all the time. Thank you, Ellie, for making a difference in our lives by writing this book. I hope that those children you support in India can one day meet you—you are one incredible lady!"

Charlene Hollaway from Aberdeen, South Dakota wrote: "Today I was returning telephone calls. One of them was from a member family in our homeschool group. She told me about the hardship another family was experiencing: DH [devoted husband] working two jobs, wife working in the evenings and homeschools during the day. And still they are without regular meals, etc. She asked if we might be able to contribute a meal? Immediately I thanked God for *Shop, Save, and Share*. Of course I would take a meal…. But had I not been reading your book, I would not have been prepared in my heart to take groceries, clothes for her children, toiletries, laundry supplies, etc. It just so happened that we had cleaned out closets this week and had the clothes ready, and their children just so happened to be similar in ages to many of our children. It also just so happened (hmm…there must be some coincidence here???) that I haven't done my shopping yet this week—so even though I don't have a large surplus to choose from, I can shop with her family in mind, as well as my own.

"Thank you, Ellie Kay, for shopping as unto our Lord, saving for your family's needs, and sharing your ideas with the rest of us."

Jessica Nichols from New Mexico said the sharing part of *Shop, Save, and Share* sometimes requires creativity. She and her husband lived in Korea when he was in the Air Force. Every morning she'd watch a little four-year-old boy, wearing only a shirt, eat from her trash can. "I had heard that the Koreans were a proud people and wouldn't eat food if you made sandwiches and set them by the trash cans—they would know you are giving them food.

"So, every payday, we'd buy extra loaves of bread, and my three-year-old and five-year-old would help me make peanut butter and jelly sandwiches. We'd take them and smush them and tear them apart, so they would look like rejects. Then we put them back in the bread bag and tied the top. We'd dump coffee grounds nearby to make it look like it was trash and put it in the back alleyway.

"As we secretly watched from the bedroom window, we saw the little boy scream in delight to his mama (they lived in a tent up the alleyway) that he had found food."

These are such powerful examples of how God prompts people to share with those in need and to be better stewards of His resources. I don't have room to share all of the stories—how people are setting up food pantries in inner cities, others are taking goods into Mexico, and others are sponsoring children in Third World countries.

I'd love to hear your story too. We all have a story to share about God's provision—some of those stories have already been played out in our lives. But millions of those stories are yet to be written.

What will God write through you?

"Bring the whole tithe into the storehouse, so that there may be food in My house, and test Me now in this," says the Lord of hosts. **"If I will not open for you the windows of heaven and pour out for you a blessing until it overflows. Then I will rebuke the devourer for you."**

—MALACHI 3:10–11 NASB

CHAPTER TWENTY

"Give Me All Your Money!"

Tips to Stewardship

As the Coupon Queen, I have a royal court that will oftentimes travel with me. Our seminars are unique, challenging, informational, and *way too much fun*! On stage, you'll meet Mongo, a grocery nomad; Kim, a refined southern gentlewoman who goes cuckoo over coupons; and Kyong, a military bride who provides groceries for her poor Korean minister.

Wendy Wendler (who helped research chapter 5 in this book) is our product manager at Shop, Save, and Share. She's also a home decorator, a wondercook, and the head of security—yes, security, because she used to be a deputy sheriff in life before babies. Consequently we call her "Princess of Quite a Lot."

Wendy has taught me to be conscious of security issues at home and when we travel. Before we talked about security, there were two times when someone followed me home. Wendy said I did the wrong thing each time. (You should never go home if you're being followed. Instead, you should drive to a mall, the police station, or a busy parking lot and immediately exit your car and go in.)

Thanks to Wendy, I now know how to drive defensively, walk safely, and talk to strangers. But nothing prepared me for my recent trip to Hollywood.

It was one of the rare trips I took alone—none of my princesses could come and Bob was swamped at work. I was a little concerned about staying alone in a strange hotel, even though it was a decent place to stay. I spent the afternoon in my hotel room, working on my computer before the evening's television taping. At one point, the maid tried to come in—even when I had the "Do Not Disturb" sign posted at the door! This scared the wee-wee out of me.

A little while later, I heard a tapping at my window. I wasn't on the first floor, so I couldn't figure it out. I walked over to the window and peeked around the blinds. There, on an incredibly tall ladder, was a man at the window! He had on workman's dungarees and was washing windows—but why would he pick *my* window to wash when I was already scared? I called the front desk, and they hadn't heard of anyone washing windows. But it must have been all right because they didn't send security personnel to my rescue.

I tried to remind myself that God would send His angels to protect me, but I couldn't figure out why a maid and window washer came instead! I was so exhausted from worry that I decided to lie down on the bed and watch a little television. I found an old movie, *The Maltese Falcon*, and started watching it. I was so tired, I soon drifted off to sleep.

The next thing I remembered I was sitting up on my bed because someone had broken into the room! My heart was beating wildly as I couldn't believe that there were footsteps in my hotel room's short hallway. Soon, the person would be around the corner! I glanced desperately around the room for a weapon of some sort and my eyes fell on the metal lamp.

I stayed perfectly still, so my intruder wouldn't know I was alerted to his presence as I heard him take slow, deliberate steps in the hallway. My eyes were riveted on the corner of the hallway from where he would soon emerge. I prayed desperately as my mind raced to remember Wendy's self-defense training.

The first thing I saw were his brown shoes, then he emerged around the corner with a gun in his hand. He had an ugly, sinister face with a large scar along his cheekbone.

I screamed, "JESUS!"

As soon as I screamed, the man was suddenly gone because I'd woken up. You can imagine my feeling of terror as I lay on the bed, the television set still playing, and realized it was all a terrible dream. I called Bob on the phone, and he prayed with me as I calmed down. I went on to the studio later that night and the rest of the trip went just fine—no robberies, no mishaps, no more misplaced fears.

My experience on that trip serves as a dramatic example of what can happen to us when we focus on the negative and allow our minds to run away with us. And yet, do you know that many people do the same thing when it comes to the application of proper principles of biblical money management?

Some people I've talked to seem to think that if they yield their finances over to the principles found in the Bible, they will lose control of all they own. They fear some celestial robber will invade their lives and force them to turn over all their assets to a commune or something. Others just don't want to yield their desires and self-control to another's authority. This results in an inner conflict over money management, with the most common outcome being that these people will find themselves losing control of their finances anyway—often to their own harm.

Back in the mid-eighties, when I was a very young woman, I read Larry Burkett's book *Your Finances in Changing Times* and Ron Blue's *Master Your Money*. I learned some principles that I've found to be true and timeless in their approaches to finances. I'd like to share what I learned so many years ago from these great authors that has made all the difference in our family's finances.

Here are the four basics of Biblical money management.

1. GOD OWNS IT ALL

A lot of Christians believe this, but few really live it. If you really believe that God owns it all, then that gives Him the *rights* of ownership while we have the *responsibility* for His things in our possession.

When we lived on base housing for so many years, it was very clear that Uncle Sam owned that house. We were required to water the grass, trim the lawn, and generally maintain the home in good working order. If we didn't, there would be penalties imposed—Bob could get a reprimand from his commander or we could even be evicted from the base. There was no doubt that Uncle Sam owned the house because of the natural consequences of our violation of housing regulations.

For goodness' sake, there was even a regulation that we couldn't hang Christmas lights on our home because Bob could fall off the roof and break his neck. Now that really frustrated me—in government housing, Bob didn't even have the right to break his neck.

> If we really believe that God owns the "home" and we are just stewards, then we won't make permanent changes to any of our finances without seeking His counsel and advice. Financial decisions are some of the most spiritual decisions you'll ever make.

If we really believe that God owns the "home" and we are just stewards, then we won't make permanent changes to any of our finances without seeking His counsel and advice. Financial decisions are some of the most spiritual decisions you'll ever make.

Look at your credit card receipts, checkbook, or budget, and you'll find out who you *really* believe owns your stuff. People can fake Christianity in a lot of ways, but they can't fake the bottom line in their finances. That's why they get so angry when someone tries to challenge them in the area of personal finance.

Here are a few questions that you can ask yourself to help determine if you believe that God owns it all.

✓ When you have a beautiful dress your daughter has outgrown, what is your first thought? Do you want to sell it or give it to someone else who could be blessed by it?

✓ Have you ever considered giving away an automobile (to your church or school, Salvation Army, Vietnam Veterans of America, Disabled American Veterans, Goodwill, Easter Seals, etc.), or is it struggle enough to let your kids' friends ride in your vehicle?

✓ What about something as basic as the tithe—do you obey in that area?

✓ Have you ever taken a meal to someone who needs one?

✓ When you hear of a family who doesn't own a washer and dryer, would you consider letting them use yours, or do you dismiss it as too much of a bother?

> Do you regularly tithe off of all you own? If you are watchful, you will find that you have opportunities to give of your clothes, groceries, material goods, and even your time.

✓ When you have a garage sale, do you try to make money, or do you try to find people whose needs can be met by giving them your stuff?

✓ Are you bound by the 10 percent tithe, or can you give beyond that marker?

✓ If your family finances were to dramatically decrease due to loss of employment, illness, or downsizing, would your marriage survive, and would your kids be able to come alongside and help?

✓ When you have an unexpected check arrive in the mail, do you pray about how God wants you to use it, or is your first thought "What can I buy?"

✓ Do you regularly tithe off of all you own? If you are watchful, you will find that you have opportunities to give of your clothes, groceries, material goods, and even your time.

This list is by no means all-inclusive. Every single one of these areas are real-life issues that we—or people we've counseled—have faced. The true indicator of whether you believe God owns it all is when you learn to hold "things" with open hands.

2. WE ARE CONSTANTLY GROWING

In Philippians 4:11–12 NKJV, Paul said: "Not that I speak in regard to need, for I have learned in whatever state I am, to be content: I know how to be abased, and I know how to abound. Everywhere and in all things I have learned both to be full and to be hungry, both to abound and to suffer need."

> Our attitudes toward money are a witness to the world of our faith in God.

Because of the nature of man and his relationship with money, this is an area in our lives that is constantly changing and in which we grow. Paul had to *learn* to be content—it didn't come naturally. So we, too, have to learn that God will use money and material wealth in our earthly lives as a tool to mature us.

Ron Blue said in *Master Your Money,* "Money is not only a tool, but also a test." Our attitudes toward money are a witness to the world of our faith in God. I like to call sharing with others "Christianity in practicum." Just as Christ sought to meet people's physical as well as their spiritual needs, we can use our financial and material resources to meet the needs of others and to share the love of God with them.

3. THE AMOUNT IS NOT THE ISSUE

Carolyn, from Denver, wrote to me and said: "I am a single parent with a warmhearted three-year-old daughter. We'll be giving 'Old Mother Hubbard' style—as you call it. We sponsored the creation of five holiday food baskets for families who need help. I have found that I can share at least a bag of groceries each month with my local food bank. This sense of empowerment is your doing!"

Carolyn didn't have much, but she used what she had. The empowerment she's talking about comes from God, and He uses people like you and me to communicate these ideas to others. God doesn't care how much you have—financially, intellectually, timewise, educationally, or emotionally. If you will yield these resources to Him faithfully, He will give you stewardship over more, just as Matthew 25:23 NKJV says, "Well done, good and faithful servant; you have been faithful over a few things, I will make you ruler over many things. Enter into the joy of your lord."

Ron Blue wrote: "The amount you have is unimportant, but how you handle what you have been entrusted with is very important." So don't fret if you don't have much, just be faithful and you will see what God will do.

4. FAITH IN ACTION

Just as I've said before, our faith in action is Christianity in practicum. When we practice our spirituality with our finances, then we are abiding by this principle of money management. In one of the most practical books of the Bible, James tells us: "If a brother or sister is naked and destitute of daily food, and one of you says to them, 'Depart in peace, be warmed and filled,' but you do not give them the things which are needed for the body, what does it profit? Thus also faith by itself, if it does not have works, is dead" (James 2:15–17 NKJV).

Get the picture here?

Let's say you talk to someone who says, "My husband just got laid off work and we're running out of groceries."

You express sincere compassion as you reply, "Oh, I'm so sorry, I remember what it was like when my husband was out of work five years ago. I'll pray for you. Have a nice day!"

How does that response express your Christianity? It sounds good and prayer is the most important part of solving anyone's problems, but you've got plenty of food in your pantry. Your husband isn't laid off work. Don't you think that your faith in action could be a little more practically expressed by saying, "I've got some groceries I'll drop by later and we'll continue to pray for your situation. Furthermore, let me show you some ways I've learned to stretch a dollar at the grocery store"?

Meeting people's needs is faith in action.

I can't believe it! We're at the end of the book already! I've been doing an incredible juggling act to get this manuscript in by the deadline, and I have to confess, I'm glad we're almost there. But, on the other hand, I'm a little sad to see this book come to a close.

I just took a break from the writing to go and debone some chicken. I don't know about you, but I loathe deboning chicken. I boil it and let it cool, then I've got to get rid of the bones. As I was working over the sink, trying to hurry through the task so my family could have some chicken Dijon tonight, I started grumbling, "I don't have time for this, I need to get back to the computer. I wasn't *called* to debone chicken; this is *not* my purpose in life."

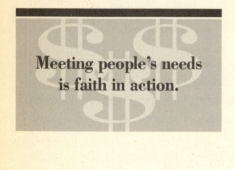

Meeting people's needs is faith in action.

Now you know how arrogant I can be sometimes, though I realized that my family needed to eat—whether the book was done or not. Our lives are filled with mundane tasks that add up to important issues—like eating!

You may not be called to excel in financial issues; managing money may not be your perceived purpose in life—it may seem like a necessary evil to you. But it is significant and critical, and the way you manage money will add up to important issues—like financial freedom!

Thanks for picking up this book and thanks for reading it all the way to the end! Please let me hear from you—I'd love to hear your stories. I'd like to close with my motto verse, which truly captures the heart of what we do. May God richly bless you as you shop to share.

A P P E N D I X

Books and Resources

Barnes, Emilie, et al. *Beautiful Home on a Budget.* Eugene, OR: Harvest House Publishers, 1998.

Blue, Ron. *Master Your Money: A Step-By-Step Plan for Financial Freedom.* Nashville, TN: Thomas Nelson Publishers, 1997 (revised).

Burkett, Larry. *Your Finances in Changing Times.* Chicago, IL: Moody Press, 1993 (revised).

———. *Debt-Free Living: How to Get Out of Debt (and Stay Out).* Chicago, IL: Moody Press, 2000 (revised).

Cole, Rebecca. *Paradise Found: Gardening in Unlikely Places.* New York: Clarkson Potter, 2000.

Country Accents Farmer's Almanac. *501 Household Tips.* GCR Publishing Group, 1993.

Dacyczyn, Amy. *The Tightwad Gazette.* New York: Random House, Inc., 1993.

———. *The Tightwad Gazette II.* New York: Villard Books, a division of Random House, Inc., 1995.

———. *The Tightwad Gazette III.* New York: Villard Books, a division of Random House, Inc., 1997.

Freeman, Becky. *Peanut Butter Kisses and Mudpie Hugs.* Eugene, OR: Harvest House Publishers, 2000.

800 Household Hints and Tips. Boca Raton, FL: Globe Communications, 1995.

Hillier, Malcolm. *The Book of Container Gardening.* New York: Simon & Schuster, 1991.

Hunt, Mary. *Debt-Proof Living.* Nashville, TN: Broadman and Holman Publishers, 2000.

Kay, Ellie. *Shop, Save, and Share.* Minneapolis, MN: Bethany House Publishers, 1998.

Miller, Susan. *After the Boxes are Unpacked.* Colorado Springs, CO: Focus on the Family, 1998.

Morrissey, Lynn, ed. *Seasons of a Woman's Heart.* Lancaster, PA: Starburst Publishers, 1999.

Schneiders, Kali. *Truffles from Heaven.* Colorado Springs, CO: Chariot Victor Publishing, 1999.

Swindoll, Chuck, ed. *Tales of the Tardy Oxcart.* Nashville, TN: Word Publishing, 1998.

Go On and Laugh!

Two Warm Reads From a Pair of Wise and Witty Women

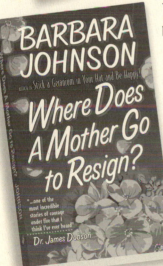

Didn't My Skin Used to Fit?
by Martha Bolton

Living, Laughing, and Loving After Forty!
A full-time comedy writer for Bob Hope, Ann Jillian, and others, Martha Bolton's attitude is that when you can't stop the crow's-feet from walking all over your face, it's time to laugh about it. And that's her goal in this humorous yet insightful book on life after forty. Don't let those birthdays get you down. After all, the longer you live, the more there is to laugh about!

"Didn't My Skin Used to Fit is a laugh-out-loud look at life past the forty mark. If you're already there, you'll identify with it. If you're almost there, it'll let you know what you're in for."
—Mark Lowry, comedian, singer, and songwriter

Where Does a Mother Go to Resign?
by Barbara Johnson

The True Story of God's Work in the Life of Humorist Barbara Johnson
From the beloved author of *Stick a Geranium in Your Hat and Be Happy!* comes the original story of the tragedy Barbara Johnson and her family experienced—including the crippling of her husband, the death of two sons, and the disappearance into the gay lifestyle of a third. Through their pain, they set out on a personal journey of survival and restoration that included a steady diet of laughter, joy, and hope. And through the sharing of their story, thousands of other families have found their own way back to hope and joy and laughter.

"…one of the most incredible stories of courage under fire that I think I've ever heard."
—Dr. James Dobson

◈ BETHANYHOUSE

11400 Hampshire Ave S. Minneapolis, MN 55438
(800) 328-6109 www.bethanyhouse.com

Pigs Might Fly

**Other APPLE® PAPERBACKS
you will want to read:**

Pigs Might Fly

by

Dick King-Smith

Drawings by
Mary Rayner

AN
APPLE®
PAPERBACK

SCHOLASTIC INC.
New York Toronto London Auckland Sydney Tokyo

ISBN 0-590-32876-X

12 11 10 9 8 7 6 5 4 3 2 1   4   4 5 6 7 8/8
Printed in the U.S.A.   11

CONTENTS

Contents

Pigs Might Fly

1

Taken Away

"Oh, no!" cried Mrs. Barleylove miserably. "Oh, no!"

"What is it, dear?" came the voice of Mrs. Gobble-spud next door. "One dead?"

"No," said Mrs. Barleylove. "Not yet anyway."

Mrs. Barleylove was a pedigree Gloucester Old Spots, a flop-eared white pig spotted with black blobs of color, as though a giant had flicked his paintbrush at her. During the night she had given birth to eight babies, seven of them all of a size, round and strong-looking and already plumped out with their first milk. But the eighth, she now saw, was a poor spindly little creature, half as big as the rest, with a head too large for its scrawny body and a look of hopelessness on its face.

It was a runt, a piglet born for some reason far smaller and weaker than its brothers and sisters. In different parts of England they are called by different names—cads, wasters, or nesslegraffs. In Glousstershire they call them dags.

There was a rustling and a scrabbling in the next sty, and Mrs. Gobblespud's head appeared over the wall.

"Oh, dear me," she said. "Oh, dear me, Mrs. B. Oh, I am sorry. It isn't just a smallish one, is it?"

"No," said Mrs. Barleylove. "It's a real dag."

Most of the Old Spots sows in the range of nine sties had probably had a dag at some time in their careers as mothers. It wasn't thought of as a disgrace, something to be whispered about, because it didn't seem to be anyone's fault. But it was thought to be a pity, a great pity, for every sow's ambition was to rear a fine litter of healthy, evenly matched youngsters, and as the news spread that morning, there was much worried grunting and rolling of eyes and shaking of long, droopy ears.

The servant wouldn't like it either, they said to each other. They thought of the Pigman as a servant since he did nothing but minister to their wants; he fed them, he watered them, he cleaned them out and brought them fresh bedding. They spoke of him

—and to him, though he could not understand this—simply as "Pigman," as a Roman nobleman might have said "Slave." Pigman wouldn't be pleased about Mrs. Barleylove's dag, for dags, if they survived, grew very, very slowly and were more trouble than they were worth.

Mrs. Barleylove's neighbor on the other side was called Mrs. Swiller, and she was leaning over her wall, gossiping with the next lady down the line, Mrs. Swedechopper.

"It's not just that it's a dag, Mrs. Swedechopper," she said sadly. "From what I can see of the poor little soul, it's deformed."

"Deformed, Mrs. Swiller?" said Mrs. Swedechopper in a tone of horror. "Why, what do you mean?"

"Well, its front feet aren't right."

"Not right?"

"No. They turn inward. And they don't look like pig's trotters. More like dog's feet."

Mrs. Gobblespud, too, had noticed this further piece of misfortune for poor Mrs. Barleylove and had told her neighbor, Mrs. Maizemunch, and everywhere heads were sticking up as the sows rested their forefeet comfortably on their boundary walls and discussed the situation. Only at Number Five, in the center of the row of sties, was no head raised, for Mrs. Barleylove still stood sadly contemplating her misshapen child, while its seven brothers and sisters squeaked greedily around her legs, begging her to lie down and give them more milk. When she did so, the dag was knocked down in the general rush and lay for a moment upside down in the straw, his curious clubfeet waving helplessly.

Even when he righted himself and tried to feed, he was continually pushed aside by the others and got very little. From Mrs. Troughlicker at Number One to Mrs. Grubguzzle at Number Nine, everybody was convinced of one thing. Pigman would never let this one stay.

"Pigman'll take him," they said.

"No doubt about it."

"Stands to reason—with feet like that."

"Poor little thing."

"Pigman'll take him away for sure." And gloom hung over the pigsties like a black cloud.

The sows never quite knew what happened to a dag or, for that matter, a piglet badly hurt by being stepped or lain on by its mother. They knew that the servant came and removed such an unfortunate, so they simply spoke of it as being "taken away"; they were unaware of the hardwood club the pigman kept in his shed to deal out merciful death to the weak and the wounded.

Before long, the distant clank of buckets and good smells blowing on the wind told them that the servant was bringing breakfast. The low grunts of

concern changed to loud, impatient yells as the dag was forgotten in the excitement of feeding time.

"Hurry up, Pigman!" shouted the sows.

"Stir your stumps, you lazy thing!"

"He's too slow to catch a cold!"

And Mrs. Troughlicker at Number One, who would be the first fed, champed her jaws with a noise like clapping hands, and great dribbles of spit ran out of her mouth.

When the Pigman had completed his duties and Mrs. Grubguzzle's head was deep in the trough at Number Nine, he returned to Mrs. Barleylove. Earlier that morning he had seen that the birth was finished and all seemed well, but he had not yet examined the litter. Of course, he immediately saw the dag and gently and without hesitation picked it up and popped it into the deep pocket of his old apron, unnoticed by the sow busy at her breakfast. If he had wanted to examine or remove a healthy piglet, he would have clamped its mouth shut to prevent its squeals bringing the mother rushing to its defense, but this one, he thought, didn't have the strength for even a squeak.

In the shed he looked at it more closely. In all his long experience he had never seen a piglet with such funny forefeet. The little points of the tiny hooves were turned inward toward one another, so that the shape of the foot was not sharp but rounded, as Mrs. Swiller had said, like a puppy's.

Now Gloucester Old Spots are a rare breed of pig, and the Pigman occasionally gave in to the temptation to spare the life of a dag if it was a female. A little sow piglet, or "hilt" as he called it, just might grow, even if very slowly, to make a breeding sow one day. But little boar piglets, called hogs, he wanted nothing to do with if they were born weak.

Not only was this one a hog, it also had those awful feet. Hanging on a rusty nail was his hardwood club, and the Pigman reached for it.

Not IT, but HE

Strangely enough, people who keep pigs very often seem to look like them. The Pigman was a huge fat person, with short legs and a big stomach. His face had several chins, a squashed nose, and little dark glinty eyes. He also had enormous hands, and in one of these he held the dag as one might hold a bunch of flowers, its bony sad-looking head and curious fore-feet sticking out above his curled fingers. He shifted his grasp to hold the creature by its hind legs, its head now hanging down, and took a good grip on his club with the other hand. At that very moment he heard a scuttling noise at the other end of the shed, and, turning, he saw a rat running across the top of one of his meal bins.

Now if there was one thing the Pigman hated, it was a rat. Rats, as far as he was concerned, were worthless, greedy, cunning thieves, plotting from dawn to dusk to steal the food of his beloved pigs, and the sight of a rat was enough to make him forget everything else. He dropped the dag headfirst on the floor and lumbered toward the meal bin, grunting with fury.

The first thing the dag saw, when he had picked himself up, was bright sunlight outside the door, and he tottered toward it and fell down the concrete steps into the yard. Once outside, he heard in the distance the contented noises of full-fed sows and the squeals of piglets fighting for a place at the milk bar, and he turned that way. He was weak and confused and hungry and unhappy. But he was also

determined and wanted his mother and was going to find her even if, as seemed likely, it killed him.

He plodded on on his dog feet and eventually reached the door of Number One, where he had just enough strength left for some feeble squeaking. Mrs. Troughlicker's head appeared over the door.

"Upon my soul!" she cried. "It's that little dag that Pigman took away! Mrs. Barleylove! Mrs. Barleylove! It's your dag! It's little Daggie Dogfoot!"

There was an uproar along the row as every sow lurched to her feet, those with piglets shaking them off and scattering them in screaming confusion. Soon on every front door there rested a pair of trotters, and above each a large drop-eared face gazed down at the object outside Mrs. Troughlicker's sty.

Above the hubbub came the deep urgent grunting of little Daggie Dogfoot's mother at Number Five. When Mrs. Barleylove had finished breakfast, she had nosed her newborn litter and, though she could not count, had found them all fat and level and had known that Pigman had taken one away. Now, by some miracle, here he was again, not a dozen yards from home.

"Daggie!" she called. "Daggie! Come on, son! Don't give up now."

Slowly the exhausted baby began to cover the last lap, wobbling along past Mrs. Boltapple at Number

Two, then Mrs. Swedechopper, then Mrs. Swiller, till at last he stood swaying with weariness at the door of Number Five.

"Mommy," said Daggie Dogfoot, "I'm tired. And I'm hungry. Let me in."

Mrs. Barleylove would have broken down the door without a second thought if she had been able to, but it was strong and opened inward. Rooting frantically at the bottom of it in a vain attempt to lift it off its hinges, she discovered that there was a narrow gap between its lower edge and the concrete, a gap not wide enough to get her snout through or to allow a fat piglet out, but just sufficient perhaps to let a very thin piglet in. She scraped away all the straw from it and snorted madly under it as though she were trying to sniff Daggie in like a vacuum cleaner.

"Come on, baby," she said. "Just get your head through, and the rest'll come easy."

"Go on, little one!" shouted Mrs. Grubguzzle at Number Nine, and she was echoed by Mrs. Grazegrass, Mrs. Maizemunch, and Mrs. Gobblespud, as well as by the ladies whose doors Daggie had already passed.

"Go on, baby!" they shouted. "We're all behind you!"

And through the combination of their support and his mother's urging and his own determination, with a last desperate effort Daggie Dogfoot somehow

squeezed his head beneath the door and scrabbled with his funny forefeet and pushed with his skinny hind legs and found himself at last back home. He lay exhausted while with tender grunts his mother carefully licked him all over. All down the line there rose a chorus of snorts of relief, and Mrs. Swiller and Mrs. Gobblespud got off their doors and up on their boundary walls for final words of congratulation.

"I love it!" cried Mrs. Gobblespud. "What a brave little pig it is!"

Mrs. Barleylove looked up from her licking.

"Begging your pardon, Mrs. Gobblespud," she said slowly and severely, "it isn't an 'it.' He's a 'he.'"

"She's right," said Mrs. Swiller. "And not just a 'he.' I reckon he's a hero." And with a few last good wishes both ladies returned to their duties.

Fortunately, by the time Daggie had made his way back to the pigsties, his mother had not only finished her own breakfast but had also given his brothers and sisters theirs. So now she was able to push and prod and nose their well-fed little bodies into the inner covered part of Number Five, to barricade the opening with her great spotted back, and to offer the whole range of the milk bar to one thin, tired little body.

And how he drank! Moving along the line, scrabbling at his mother's side with his puppy's feet, he drank and drank and drank. And as he drank, color seemed to come into his skin, and his tummy blew out like a drum, and some sparkle crept into his dull eyes. Ten minutes later, when the Pigman looked over the door, he found it hard to recognize his late intended victim.

The Pigman's pursuit of the rat had led to much moving of bins and sacks, which in turn had exposed other rats. And from this followed much swearing and heavy breathing and wild swiping with the hardwood club, and cries of "Dratyer!" and "Dangyer!" and "Blastyer!" At the end of it all he was hot and sweaty, and the rats were laughing in their runways, and quite a lot of time had passed.

He looked around the doorway end of the shed, expecting to find the dag hiding somewhere, then searched the yard, and finally, seeing no sign of him, walked down to the sties in case the piglet could by any chance have found his way home. He leaned on the door of Number Five and shook his head till his three chins wobbled.

"I'd never have believed it," he said to himself, mopping his face with a red spotted handkerchief. "That kid's got some guts. But all the same he'll never be no use to no one, nohow. He'll have to go." And he slid back the bolt.

Now Mrs. Barleylove, busy at breakfast and unaware of the fact—though resigned to the possibility —that one of her children was to be taken away, was one thing. Mrs. Barleylove interrupted while feeding that hero of a child was another.

Heaving herself to her feet with a violence that threw a surprised Daggie far to one side, she ran at the servant, swinging her head and champing her jaws together so that a froth of bubbles ran out over her tusks. The chomping and her furious grunting combined to make a noise that sounded to the Pigman like "Out! Out! Out!" which, in fact, was exactly what she was saying. At the same time, Mrs.

Swiller and Mrs. Gobblespud reared onto their walls and also shouted angrily at the servant.

"You leave him alone, Pigman!" they roared.

"Poor little fellow!"

"Tackle somebody your own size!"

"Dirty fat man!"

For just as we say "dirty as a pig" or "fat as a pig," so pigs repay the insult the other way around. And all along the row, from Mrs. Troughlicker to Mrs. Grubguzzle, the cry went up, "Dirty fat man! Leave him alone!" while nine pairs of jaws champed and nine pairs of eyes glittered.

The Pigman got out of Number Five remarkably quickly for a man of his size. He knew all about the damage an angry sow can cause, and it was a different kind of sweat that he now wiped from his brow.

"Dratyer!" the Pigman cried, and "Dangyer!" and "Blastyer!"

He waited until the fuming Mrs. Barleylove had gotten off the top of her door, and then he bolted it and lumbered off, grumbling to himself. Let her keep the horrible little dag, he thought, it'll die soon enough and save me the trouble. Blasted old sows!

And as men often do when they feel that women-folk are too much for them, he walked across the yard to seek the company of another male, for the Gloucester Old Spots boar lived opposite. The boar

: 17 :

came to his door and gave his usual order.

"Hey, you, Pigman. Scratch my back." And the servant, of course, obeyed. He's not a bad guy really,

thought the boar. Does what he's told.

He's a good old guy, thought the Pigman. "Aren't you, old man?" he said. "Not like those nasty old sows."

And indeed, except that one was spotted and one was not, they looked very much alike as they stood and chatted, each in his own tongue.

3

Pigs Might Fly

Time passed, and Daggie Dogfoot not only survived but grew. He did not expand visibly like his litter mates, but by cunning and agility he secured a fair share of his mother's milk. For example, he would persuade her to lie across a corner in which he was already waiting, or stand alongside the concrete feeding trough so that he could scramble onto its rim for a high-level drink which the others couldn't reach; their slippery sharp-hooved forefeet did not allow them to balance there.

The Pigman became resigned to Daggie's survival, and persuaded himself he had kept the creature out of kindness, as a mascot. Well aware of the look in

Mrs. Barleylove's eye and the sound of her threatening grunts, he left the dag severely alone.

Mrs. Barleylove's neighbors spent a lot of their spare time leaning over their respective walls to watch. Unlike the Pigman, who was merely pretending, they really did regard Daggie as a mascot, as did all the other mothers; no piglet had ever before been "taken away" and then come back, and there seemed something magical, almost mystical, about this, and also about his feet, which appeared at the moment to be an advantage to him rather than the reverse.

"I love him!" said Mrs. Gobblespud one morning after watching Daggie do his King-of-the-Castle trick on the trough. "He's smart, isn't he, Mrs. B.?"

Mrs. Barleylove only grunted, but inwardly she swelled with pride. She had never believed in having favorites among her many children, but she had to admit to herself that this one was special.

"No offense," said Mrs. Swiller, "but his little feet have changed, haven't they?" And indeed, though the hooves on Daggie's hind feet remained normal, the grotesquely inward-curving horny parts on his front feet had fallen off, leaving even more puppy-like round pads. This seemed to make him more surefooted, so that when the litter played a game of tag, racing around the smooth, clean-washed concrete of the outer enclosure after Pigman had mucked out, it was always Daggie who stayed on his feet, while his stronger brothers and sisters often slipped and skidded onto their sides.

Mrs. Barleylove had half a mind to take offense at such a personal remark, but she quickly realized that it was well-meant, and anyway she wanted her neighbors' opinions.

"Yes, they have changed," she said. "To tell you the truth, ladies, I'd be glad to know what you think. You may think I'm crazy, but I've caught myself wondering if he isn't somehow"—she paused and looked around to make sure that Daggie was not listening. He had run off with the rest to roughhouse in the straw inside, so she went on—"somehow . . . special?"

"Special?" said Mrs. Swiller.

"Well, born for some purpose."

"Purpose?" said Mrs. Gobblespud.

"What I mean is," said Mrs. Barleylove, "he was taken away, wasn't he?"

"Musta been," they said.

"And yet he came back?"

"For sure," they said.

"So that's kind of . . . special?"

Long droopy ears slap-slapped against fat faces as the two ladies nodded vigorous agreement.

"And his front feet?" said Mrs. Barleylove.

"Different," said Mrs. Swiller.

"Curious," said Mrs. Gobblespud.

"Special?" asked Mrs. Barleylove.

There was a pause.

"Do you mean," said her neighbors, "special feet . . . for some purpose?"

It was Mrs. Barleylove's turn to nod. There was another pause, during which the neighbors glanced a little anxiously at each other over her head. It occurred to them simultaneously that this was going a bit too far. Mrs. Barleylove's concern for her dag was leading her to flights of fancy. Special feet for some purpose? No, no, that was too much of a good thing.

"Well . . . no, dear, not really," said Mrs. Gobblespud in a kindly voice, "I mean, I know they're not like other piglets' front feet, but . . ."

"What Mrs. G. means, dear," said Mrs. Swiller soothingly, "is that you shouldn't worry about the little fellow's feet. I mean I don't personally think they're going to be a hindrance to him, but as for having been made like that for some purpose—well, that's about as likely as that . . ."

". . . pigs might fly," finished Mrs. Gobblespud.

As Mrs. Swiller had hesitated, Daggie Dogfoot had been on the point of coming out from the inner part of the sty, impelled as children often are by the certain feeling that adults are talking about them. All he heard in fact were the three last words. What's more, his mother and her friends fell silent the moment they saw him, so he was sure he had been right.

"Good morning, Auntie Swiller, good morning, Auntie Gobblespud," he said politely. And then, "Can I have a milk shake, please, Mommy—quick, before the others come back?"

The sows' conversation thus abruptly terminated, the neighbors dropped back off their walls, and Mrs. Barleylove lay down hastily, anxious to please her darling.

Even as he gulped down milk, Daggie was thinking hard. Pigs might fly, he thought, and they were definitely talking about me; that must mean *I* might fly. The other piglets came dashing out at that moment and scrambled and shoved and stamped all over him, but he hung on determinedly until he was finished, and then climbed up and lay down on the huge rubbery cushion of his mother's side.

He looked at his curious feet, about which the others had already begun to tease him, though he did not mind, for he was glad to be alive. He looked up at the blue sky. A sparrow flew over the sty with a whir of wings; a little higher, a flock of starlings made their way across the yard; higher still, the swallows cut lovely circles in the air, and above them all, so high that his baby eyes could hardly see them, the swifts raced, black and crescent-shaped,

screaming their joy at the wonder of flight.

I . . . might fly, thought Daggie Dogfoot. He sat up on his mother and beat his forelegs together experimentally, but nothing happened. Perhaps it's taking off that's difficult, he thought. Perhaps once you get up there, it's easier. He looked up into the sky again and tried to imagine himself up there, legs beating away somehow or other, ears flapping, curly tail stretched out straight behind him as he soared and glided and swooped.

Perhaps if I got up somewhere high, he thought, so that I could jump off and then start flying. I'm sure they were talking about me. I'm sure I could do it. I will do it—you see if I don't. Just give me half a chance.

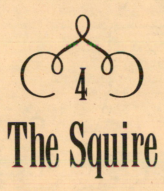

The Squire

The boar was, of course, the most important person around, partly because he was an incredibly well-bred and aristocratic Gloucester Old Spots, and partly because he was the father of all the children born. His real name was Champion Imperial Challenger III of Ploughbarrow, but the sows all knew him as the Squire. His sty, which was opposite the row of nine, had a sloping veranda-type roof to keep the rain off his noble back, and the Pigman, being large, had to duck under this whenever he went in; the sows appreciated the fact that the servant always bowed low before the master.

The Squire kept in touch with his wives by means

of occasional conversations across the yard when he felt like it and the wind was not too strong. He would stand against his door and poke his head out under his veranda roof and shout at them in his

bluff, jolly way. Sometimes he would address them generally, and then everyone who was not actually engaged at that moment in feeding babies would come respectfully to their front doors and bob their heads up and down deferentially. Sometimes he would single out an individual.

One morning some weeks after Daggie Dogfoot's birth, the Squire's deep coughing grunt was heard, and the rattle of his door as he heaved his bulk up onto it.

"It's the Squire!" they all said to their neighbors, and waited in awestruck silence. The boar cleared his throat.

"Ah, hhhrm, Mrs. Barleylove, dear lady. A word with you."

"Here I am, Squire," said Mrs. Barleylove.

"The latest children, my dear. I hear from sparrow talk that you have a litter?" The sparrows carried all the gossip around the farm.

"Y-yes, Squire."

"All well, I trust? Chips off the old block?" There was a moment's pause, and a shudder of anticipation ran down the row of sties. But Mrs. Barleylove was equal to the occasion.

"All well, I thank you, Squire," she replied, with hardly a tremor in her voice.

"Good," said the Squire. "Keep up the good work." He got down off his door, while all the ladies ducked their heads again and disappeared with a whistling sound, which was made up of eight small sighs of relief and one large one.

It was not that the Squire didn't know about dags. He knew only too well, because a litter sister of his had been one. He had never forgotten waking up one morning when he was a baby, to find the poor spindly little thing stretched out cold and lifeless beside him, and because of this he was always terrified that one of his own children might be born a dag.

So he always asked the same question, "Chips off the old block?" and the sows never let him down. He never knew that occasionally the chips were very small and either died or were taken away, and as for the occasional hilt whose life the Pigman saw fit to spare, the Squire would not set eyes on it until it was weaned and on its way to other quarters. If it survived that long, it would have caught up a bit in size and be nothing worse than the smallest of the litter. But what on earth would he say about Daggie Dogfoot?

Mrs. Barleylove's neighbors tried to find a tactful way to approach the subject. They began with praise.

"Isn't he active?" said Mrs. Gobblespud admiringly as she watched Daggie, his mind on flight, leap from his mother's back and land upside down in the remains of breakfast at the bottom of the trough. "You must be proud of him, Mrs. B."

"Any mother would be proud of him," said Mrs. Swiller. And then, greatly daring, she added defiantly, "And any father, too."

There was a long, awkward pause, and it seemed to the neighbors that Mrs. Barleylove's white parts grew a little pink and her spots turned slightly blacker.

"I don't know what to do, ladies," she said at last. "Squire's bound to set eyes on him sooner or later. He'll go raving mad."

"It'll be sooner than later though, won't it?" said Mrs. Gobblespud. "They'll be crossing the yard in a week or so, won't they?"

"Crossing the yard" meant weaning time, when the eight-week-old piglets left their mothers and went to the store pens on either side of the boar's sty. Later the hogs would go to the fattening pens, and the hilts to other quarters till they were big enough to be sold for breeding.

Daggie, though he had not been listening closely to the conversation, had, like children everywhere, picked up the awkward bits.

"Who's Squire, Mommy?" he asked.

"The Squire is your father, dear, a very fine gentleman."

"Why will he go raving mad?"

"Oh, your father's a hot-tempered person," said

Mrs. Swiller quickly. "He gets very angry with the servant if his meals are late."

"Well, what does crossing the yard mean, Auntie Swiller?"

"Oh, you'll like that, Daggie," put in Mrs. Gobble-spud soothingly. "That's when all you young ones go off on a lovely vacation and your mother gets a nice rest."

Mrs. Barleylove's other seven piglets jumped up excitedly at this and ran around the sty, squealing, "A lovely vacation! A lovely vacation!" But Daggie Dogfoot sat on his thin backside, and a tear ran down one side of his big head.

"I don't want to leave my mommy," he said, and another tear ran down the other side.

At that moment Mrs. Barleylove made up her mind, quite firmly, that she would not allow this humble, undersized deformed child of hers to cross the yard. Always before, like all the other mothers, she had allowed the servant to drive the weaners away without protest, indeed with a sigh of relief after two months' hard work. This time it would be different, for this child was different, and her heart ached at the sight of those two great tears. The servant could take the other seven, but not her Daggie. Just let him try!

Two weeks later he tried. He opened the door of

Number Five and, holding a sheet of corrugated iron in front of him like a shield, he shooed Mrs. Barleylove into the inner part of the sty while the litter ran out into the yard. A grunt and a rattle on the other side told everyone that the Squire was at his door to inspect his offspring as they crossed. But when the Pigman had shut up Number Five again, he could count only seven fat weaners frisking about outside. He looked back in and saw the dag peeping out from between his mother's legs. He started to open the door again, but immediately Mrs. Barleylove rushed forward, champing and snorting, as fierce as one of her wild woodland ancestors.

"Dirty fat man!" she shouted. "Leave him alone!"

"Dratyer!" cried the Pigman, and "Dangyer!" and "Blastyer!"

But he backed away quickly, and then turned and lumbered off after the rest.

"Keep the miserable thing then!" he shouted back over his shoulder. "It'll never be no use to no one, nohow!"

He rounded up the others, drove them into a V-shaped funnel of hurdles he had put up, then into one of the store pens, and shut them in. He mopped his face with his red spotted handkerchief and went to talk to Champion Imperial Challenger III of Ploughbarrow.

"Hey, you, Pigman. Scratch my back," said the Squire. And, as usual, the servant obeyed. They held a conversation, and it was fortunate that they spoke different languages.

"Fine bunch of youngsters, Pigman," said the Squire. "Fat as you are by the time they're grown, I bet."

"You've got a horrible little dag left over there, old man," said the Pigman. "That bad-tempered old sow's welcome to him."

And what a welcome Daggie Dogfoot was having, for his mother still had plenty of milk left for one, and now the whole milk bar was his and his alone.

At last, full to the brim, he fell asleep by his mother's side, and dreamed that he and she and his father the Squire were all flying, trotter in trotter, through a warm and milky sky.

Resthaven

The sows usually had two litters each year, in the spring and in the fall, and so twice a year, after weaning her piglets, every mother enjoyed what Mrs. Gobblespud had called a good rest. As soon as a newly weaned litter had "crossed the yard," the sow would expect the servant to open her door and then a gate at the upper end of the cluster of farm buildings. This gate was the entrance to a small field which the Pigman unimaginatively called the Pig Ground, but which the ladies always referred to as Resthaven.

"Not long now," a harassed mother would say to her neighbor at about the seventh week of nursing.

"Soon we'll be going to Resthaven. Not that I won't miss the kiddies."

"No, but you have to get away. Besides, it gives that lazy Pigman time to give the house a good cleaning."

Resthaven was a small triangular patch of rough hillside, sloping down from a point at the top to a long base bounded by a brook. The other two sides were fenced with pig wire, and right in the center stood a great old oak. Most of the upper part of the little field was dotted with ant heaps.

The morning after Daggie's brothers and sisters had left, the Pigman came to Number Five and opened the door. Normally on these occasions one or two heads might pop up along the row, and one or two shouts be heard of "Have a nice time!" But this time it was different, for no one remembered a piglet ever going to Resthaven, much less a dag. By the time Daggie had politely said good-bye to Auntie Swiller and Auntie Gobblespud, every other head was up to get a look at this strange baby. As Mrs. Barleylove made her stately way off after the lumbering servant, with Daggie trotting behind her, many and heartfelt were the good wishes that followed them, though softly spoken so as not to wake the Squire.

For Daggie, everything was new and wonderful. No sooner had the servant closed the gate than the little piglet cried, "Oh, Mommy! Isn't it exciting? Can I go off and explore?"

"Go where you like, darling," said his mother. "But be careful of the water at the bottom of the field. Pigs can't swim, you know."

Pigs might fly, though, thought Daggie Dogfoot gleefully to himself as he ran off over the summer grass. Especially if they could find somewhere high enough to jump off.

Mrs. Barleylove, watching her darling with pride, was quite amazed to see how fast he made his way around Resthaven. When Daggie arrived at the very top of the wedge-shaped field, he climbed up on the highest of all the ant heaps. He turned to face downhill and saw his mother looking up toward him. "Watch me, Mommy!" he yelled, and leaped off. He nose-dived into the grass, turned a somersault,

rolled over a few times on the steep slope, and landed on the next ant heap six feet away.

"Yes, dear. Very clever," called Mrs. Barleylove tenderly, and went to the oak to look for acorns.

By the end of that first thrilling day, Daggie was pretty sore. He had climbed onto and jumped off everything he could find, every bank and ridge in the rough field, every ant heap, and several stumps of felled elms. But every effort had resulted in a crash landing, and now, in the warmth of the August evening, he was not only bruised but a little despondent.

He and his mother had just left a shallow place at the edge of the brook, where they had drunk their fill, and now they stood together at a point farther along the bank, a high point where the stream had cut away the side over the years as it made a swirling turn. Here they were about fifteen feet above the water, and behind them the slope of Resthaven was steep and short-grassed for some distance.

Suppose I started back up there and ran really fast, thought Daggie. "Mommy," he said, "did you say pigs couldn't swim?"

Mrs. Barleylove, like all her kind, had been brought up to believe the old sows' tale that a pig attempting to swim will cut its own throat by the awkward action of its sharp-hooved forefeet, and she explained this to her son. She was comfortably full of acorns and roots and grasses and berries, as well as the ration of pignuts the servant had brought, and she gazed dreamily down at the winking water without really thinking what she was saying.

"But I haven't got . . ." began Daggie, and then some instinct checked him.

"What, dear?" said Mrs. Barleylove absently.

"Er—I haven't heard that before," said Daggie quickly. "I mean, I didn't know that."

"There are lots of things you don't know, my son," said his mother in the way mothers always do.

And there's something that you don't know, too, thought the dag to himself. Which is that if I started back up there and ran really fast . . . Pigs *might* fly, he said to himself, Auntie Gobblespud said so. I just wish I had the chance to consult an expert before trying. Daggie had thought a good deal about getting expert advice and had often asked the birds who hopped around Number Five. But the sparrows, when he questioned them, only answered, "Cheep! Cheep!" in an impudent way, and the starlings simply piped rudely at him. Once a big crow had perched on the sty wall, but in reply to the piglet's questions only said, "Garn!"

Suddenly, as he stood by his mother high above the brook, there was a whistle of wings, and over their heads flew a black-and-white bird with a bright red bill and cheek patches and wide webbed feet with sharp claws at the ends of the toes. Beating its wings rapidly, it braked and dropped on the surface in a shower of water drops that gleamed golden in the sunlight. Wagging its tail feathers from side to side, it swam rapidly about. It drank and then showered itself with water by splashing with its wings.

Flying *and* swimming, thought Daggie. Too much!

"What's that bird, Mommy?" he asked. "I've never seen one like that before."

"There are lots of things you've never seen before, dear," said his mother in the way mothers always do. "That's a duck."

"Where does it come from?" asked Daggie.

"Oh, Pigman keeps some," said Mrs. Barleylove. "For their eggs, I think. After all," she went on

reflectively, "even servants have to eat, I suppose. Let them eat eggs."

"May I talk to it, Mommy?" said Daggie Dogfoot eagerly. "It won't hurt me, will it?"

"It won't hurt you," said his mother. "But I don't suppose you'll get much out of it. They're stupid things. Probably won't understand a word you say."

But when Daggie ran down to the shallow place and called to the duck, it immediately turned and swam toward him with a pleasant expression on its neat face.

6

Felicity

"Good-mor-ning-duck," said Daggie Dogfoot very slowly and loudly—the proper way to address foreigners. "May-I-ask-you-some-thing-please?" The duck, which had been walking toward him up the sandy shallows with a quick rolling gait, hopped onto a low willow branch, gripped it comfortably with her clawed feet, settled her feathers, and considered the piglet with bright eyes.

"Absolutely anything you like," she answered in a quiet musical voice.

"Oh," said Daggie, surprised, "Mommy said you wouldn't . . ." He stopped, confused.

". . . wouldn't understand a word you said?"

chuckled the duck. "Well, your mother obviously doesn't know much about Muscovy ducks."

Daggie gulped. "Please," he said, "what is a . . . Muscovy duck?"

"Well," said the duck, "we're a tree-perching variety—that's what these are for." She raised one foot to show the curved claws. "Originally from South America."

Daggie's world had expanded enormously since leaving Number Five, but it was still very small. He imagined South America to be the next field beyond Resthaven.

"Anyway," said the duck, "what did you want to ask me?"

Daggie took a deep breath. He looked up at the steep bank to see if his mother was there, but she had moved away.

"Do you think," he said slowly and carefully, "that pigs might fly?" The duck opened her bill wide, and then hastily closed it again. Then she opened and closed it rapidly perhaps a dozen times, making a soft quot-quot-quotting noise.

"Well, do you?" asked Daggie.

"I think," said the duck, "that almost anything *might* happen. Though I have never actually heard of a flying pig. Who put the idea in your head?"

"My auntie," said Daggie. "Well, she was our next-door neighbor, really, but I called her Auntie.

She said it, you see, and I'm pretty sure they were all talking about me."

"So it's you that's going to . . . fly?" said the Muscovy.

"Hope so."

"Have you tried yet?"

"Oh, yes, quite a few times. But I can't seem to get airborne. That's why I'm so excited about this place." And Daggie proceeded to explain to his new friend his idea of the steep downhill take-off and the leap from the top of the high bank into glorious soaring flight. "D'you think I could do it?" asked Daggie Dogfoot.

The bright-eyed duck looked thoughtfully at this strange creature before her. She looked at his big head and his hard thin little body and his skinny backside. She looked down at the sand and saw the three sets of prints in it—her own webs, the deep slots of the heavy sow, and the third strange set of tracks of two tiny slots and two pawmarks. The idea of a modest lecture on the qualities necessary for flight occurred to her, but she dismissed it immediately in the face of the determination that shone on the piglet's features.

"I think you're going to try," she said. And looking at the deep pool the current had gouged out below the steep bank, she added, "It's not a bad place to try, either. I assume you can swim?"

Daggie looked puzzled.

"Pigs can't swim," he said. "I'd have thought you'd know that. I'm not talking about swimming. I'm talking about flying."

The duck hopped off the willow branch and walked over to Daggie. Pretending to dig in the damp sand with her bill, she shot a close look at the piglet's forefeet. I wonder, she thought. His high-flown ambitions are going to flop, that's for sure. But something else quite novel might come out of it.

"Tell you what," she said. "I'd love to see the—er —maiden flight. Would you mind?"

"Not a bit," Daggie replied excitedly. "That's exactly what I wanted—an expert to be around to give me tips. I mean it isn't just the take-off. I may need some help with landing."

Once again the duck made that soft quot-quot-quotting noise with her bill.

"Yes," she said. "Though coming down is really the easiest part. By the way, what does your mother think about all this?"

"Oh, she doesn't know," said Daggie. "I thought I'd try it very early in the morning while she's still asleep. How about tomorrow?"

"All right," said the duck. "I'll be in the pool here at sunrise tomorrow. By the way, I don't know your name."

"Daggie Dogfoot," said the piglet.

"Right," said the duck. She slipped into the water and began to paddle off upstream.

"Wait a minute," Daggie called after her. "How will you get here that early? Won't you have to wait till Pigman lets you out?"

The duck stopped paddling and floated back toward him on the current.

"Pigman?" she said.

"Yes, the servant," said Daggie. "You know, that dirty fat man."

"Oh, you mean Duckman," said the Muscovy. "Oh, no, I don't go in the shed at night with the rest of them. I roost in a tree."

You might suppose Duckman just keeps us for the eggs we lay, she thought, but I've seen him before now go into the shed with an empty sack and come out with it full and kicking. I'm not taking any risks. And off she swam again. She was almost around the next bend in the stream before Daggie realized he did not know her name. He ran through the shallow water onto the bank and galloped along till he caught up with her.

"What's your name?" he shouted down.

"Felicity," said the duck.

"That's a funny name," shouted Daggie. "What's it mean?"

"Happiness," said the duck, and paddled away past the boundary of Resthaven and out of the piglet's sight.

Happiness, thought Daggie as he made his way toward his mother, who was lying under the oak tree. Life seems to be full of it. Living in this lovely place, and making such a nice friend, and tomorrow . . . wheeeee!

Mrs. Barleylove woke up from her nap at his squealing arrival. "Where have you been, baby?" she asked. "Talking to that duck?" She grunted with amusement.

"Yes, Mommy," said Daggie excitedly, "and she's awfully nice, and she's called Felicity, and"—he took a deep breath—"she's a Muscovy from South Amcrica."

"That's nice," said Mrs. Barleylove. "You come and take a rest now. You don't want to overtire yourself. Tomorrow's another day."

But as Daggie Dogfoot lay by his mother's side

and dozed in the sheltered warmth of Resthaven
while the afternoon shadows lengthened, he knew
that tomorrow wasn't just another day. Tomorrow
was the day he had been planning for ages and ages,
a whole two weeks, a quarter of his life. Tomorrow
was the day he would fly. And Felicity would be
there to help him. His mouth spread in a grin of pure
joy, he fell soundly asleep.

Gosh!

Felicity woke early the next morning on her usual perch. This was the thin branch of an alder tree sticking out over the stream. She had chosen it not only because it was completely fox-proof, but because she liked the never-ending music of the running water, singing her to sleep with its bubbling lullaby and waking her each day with its gurgling song.

She stretched her wings, one after the other, pushing out each in its turn to its fullest extent so that the big flight feathers stood apart from one another, as a human might stretch his fingers wide. Then she flapped her wings vigorously as she stood on the branch and shook herself all over. She felt very happy.

She began to think about her new friend, Daggie Dogfoot. He's going to get a ducking, she thought with amusement, and then it suddenly struck her that a ducking might easily turn into a drowning. She jumped off her alder branch and flew rapidly downstream toward Resthaven. She was suddenly worried that the piglet might have been too impatient to wait for her.

However, as soon as she reached the little sloping field, she could see that everything was in order. Under the oak lay a mountain of spotted flesh, which was Mrs. Barleylove still asleep. And at the top of the steep slope above the high bank, a small spotty figure danced with impatience, pawing at the ground with his round front feet as though he were a puppy on an invisible leash.

"Hello, Felicity!" cried Daggie as the duck glided over his head. "Take-off in two minutes. O.K.?"

A minute and three-quarters later the first rays of the rising sun came over the eastern bank of Resthaven and shone on the rough bark of the oak tree and on the smooth, closed, white-lashed eyelids of Mrs. Barleylove. She opened her eyes, stretched, heaved herself to her feet, and looked around for her beloved boy. She had hardly focused on him, high above her on the slope, when, to her absolute horror, she saw him begin to run downhill at great speed, faster, faster, faster, till at last he leaped out over the high bank of the stream and disappeared from her sight.

Felicity had positioned herself close under the Resthaven bank of the brook, directly underneath the take-off point. She knew that the impetus of his downhill run would take Daggie well out into the middle of the pool, and, head cocked upward, she waited, ready to go instantly to his aid.

Suddenly the quiet of the morning was shattered by an anguished scream from the horrified watcher under the oak tree, and in the same instant, high above the waiting duck, a small spotted shape shot out from the top of the bank and seemed for a frozen fraction of time to hang suspended against the clear blue sky. Legs working frantically, ears streaming behind his head, ridiculous tail whipping around and around like an eggbeater, Daggie Dogfoot enjoyed a split second of level flight. Then his heavy head came down to point him at the pool, a squeal of fright burst from him as the dark water rushed up to greet him, and, "Eeeeeeeek—kersplosh—glug!"—he was gone from view.

When he rose to the surface, he was facing the opposite bank and could not see the reassuring figure of the Muscovy duck, who by now had swum close to him. He could see nothing but what seemed an ocean of water, of which he had already swallowed a lot, and on top of the newfound knowledge that pigs couldn't fly came the awful realization that they couldn't swim either. He knew this. Mommy had said so. Mommy, whom he would never see again.

"Heeeelp!" he squealed. "Heee-gurgle-glug!" and down he went again.

As soon as he surfaced for the second time he

heard two voices. One was his mother's, shouting desperately from the shallows where she stood belly-deep after a thundering gallop from the oak tree.

"Save him! Save my boy!" yelled Mrs. Barleylove in agony.

The other was a quiet voice which spoke in his ear.

"Keep still," said the quiet voice. "Don't struggle. Don't talk. Keep your mouth tight shut. Breathe through your snout. Run after me. Just run as though you were on dry land," and Felicity set off for the far bank, which was by now the nearer of the two. She wagged her tail encouragingly and glanced back over her shoulder at the piglet.

Because of the confidence in the duck's voice, because even in the midst of his panic he still had spirit and courage, and because there was nothing else to do, Daggie obeyed. He clenched his teeth, tipped up his head so that his nostrils pointed skyward like the twin guns of a surfaced submarine, kicked with his hind legs and paddled like mad with his doggy feet, trying hard to imagine that he was galloping through the grass.

To his amazement, he began to move forward through the water after the duck, at first slowly, then faster as he gained momentum and confidence, and finally so fast that, before they reached the far

bank, he was even with her and they touched bottom together in a little reedy inlet.

They looked at each other and their eyes shone, Felicity's with amusement and pleasure, Daggie's with relief and triumph as realization swept over him.

"Pigs can't fly," said Daggie. Felicity shook her head.

"But there's one pig," said Daggie quietly, "that can," said Daggie more loudly, "SWIM!" shouted Daggie Dogfoot at the top of his squeaky voice, and off he went, all by himself, toward his mother on the Resthaven bank.

Mrs. Barleylove had continued throughout to yell, "Save my boy!" pausing only when it seemed he had reached safety. Now here he was back in deep water again, and she began to squeal as before, until two voices reached her ears.

"Calm yourself, madam," said one voice, as the duck, who had flown quickly across over the head of the swimmer, landed beside her. "He's all right. Just listen to him." And as the sow quieted, she heard the other voice, the voice of her fast-approaching son.

"Mommy! Mommy!" came the cry over the gentle lapping of the pool. "Look at me! I can swim! It's easy! Watch!" and as she stared, open-mouthed, the small figure came paddling nearer and nearer, pushing up a little bow wave in front of it with the speed of its progress.

Still Mrs. Barleylove did not really understand what had happened since the sun had awakened her. As soon as Daggie was out of the brook and shaking himself like a water spaniel, she turned and made off up the bank toward the summit, scolding as she went in the way that mothers do when their children have given them a bad fright.

"Silly boy!" she said. "Naughty boy! Come quickly and run around in the sunshine or you'll catch your death of cold. I told you not to go down by the water. You're never to go there again, understand? Never. I don't know what your father would say if he knew," and so on, until, receiving no reply, she turned and found that she had been talking to herself.

Slowly the incredible truth dawned on Mrs. Barleylove. Her poor undersized deformed child was

swimming, really swimming, swimming beautifully. "Special feet for some purpose," eh? If only the
neighbors could see him now!

"Oh, Daggie darling!" she called down. "How
clever you are!"

How happy I am, thought Daggie, to have such a
lovely mother, to swim in this beautiful sparkling
stuff, to be with my friend whose very name means
happiness. And he paddled around wildly, while
every little fish in the pool formed its mouth into a
perfect round "O" of wonder. The rails in the reeds
tut-tutted their amazement. The heron at the top of
a downstream willow squawked his disbelief. A
brilliant kingfisher gave an admiring whistle, and a
passing green woodpecker laughed hysterically. And
up the line of the brook flew a solitary swan, the
sound of his great wings expressing exactly the
surprise of all. "Gosh!" was the noise they made.
"Gosh! Gosh! Gosh! Gosh!"

8

The Truth Comes Out

The news traveled fast, by air mail of course, for the woodpecker shouted it to his mate in her nesting hole, and starlings resting in upper branches heard it. Later they discussed it in wheezy whistles as they bathed in the yard trough. Sparrows, searching the floor for small seeds, listened to the starlings, and then, of course, told everybody. By midday there was only one creature who did not know the story of the swimming piglet, and that, of course, was the Pigman, too stupid to understand animal language. The Squire knew, as the sows soon found out.

Mrs. Swiller and Mrs. Gobblespud were conversing across the empty outer run of Number Five, now brushed and scraped and washed clean by the servant, and smelling strongly of disinfectant. They were recalling a conversation of a few weeks ago.

"Do you recall what she said, Mrs. G.?" grunted Mrs. Swiller.

"That I do, Mrs. S.," replied Mrs. Gobblespud, "that I do. Special, she said. Special feet, that's what she said. And do you remember what we said?"

"That I do, Mrs. G.," answered Mrs. Swiller. "Sure as my name's Rosie Swiller, I do. 'Special feet for some purpose,' that's what we asked if she meant. Nonsense, we thought."

"Just imagine!" said Mrs. Gobblespud. She paused. "Always said he was a clever little chap," she went on.

"Brave, too," said Mrs. Swiller.

"Never heard of any Ploughbarrow pig swimming, never."

"Never heard of any pig swimming."

"What'll Pigman say when he finds out?"

There was a short silence, and then with one horrified voice they said, "What'll Squire say when he finds out?"

The words were hardly out of their mouths when they heard the deep grunt and the rattle of the door on the other side of the yard. Mrs. Swiller and Mrs. Gobblespud slid back off their walls and stood very still in their sties, heads lowered, breath held. If they had had fingers, they would have crossed them. Neither wanted in the least to hear her name called if the boar started asking questions. As it turned out, no one was to escape.

"Ladies!" barked the Squire in his loudest voice. "A word with you all, if you please. My apologies if any of you are in the midst of your duties, but I want you all on parade in one minute."

At these stern words there was a tremendous noise of hustling and bustling and shuffling mixed with the squeals of rudely disturbed piglets, and within thirty seconds eight pairs of trotters reared up onto eight front doors, and above them eight large, anxious faces peered across at the lord and master.

Only at Number Five, of course, was there no face, and it seemed to the nervous sows that the Squire's angry gaze was directed at this space rather than at any one of them. After a moment, however, he shifted his look to Number One, and then slowly, deliberately, swung his heavy head to scrutinize in turn each face, all the way to Number Nine.

At last he spoke. "It has come to my attention," he said, "that something very strange has been going on, doncherknow. What?"

No one answered, so he went on. "Now I'm going to get to the bottom of this, so I shall ask each of you in turn. And I don't want any shilly-shallying. Understand?"

"Yes, Squire," chorused eight worried voices.

The Squire looked directly at Number One again. "Mrs. Troughlicker," he said, "the sparrows are talking about a swimming pig. What do you know about it?"

"Not a great deal, Squire," said Mrs. Troughlicker uncomfortably. "There are rumors."

"Mrs. Swiller?"

Mrs. Swiller hesitated, and glanced nervously across at Mrs. Gobblespud.

"Well, Mrs. Swiller?"

"It isn't one of mine, Squire. They're all here, dry as a bone, every one," and Mrs. Swiller forced a kind of snorting laugh.

"No laughing matter," said the Squire severely. "Mrs. Gobblespud?"

"Pigs can't swim, Squire, we all know that," said Mrs. Gobblespud in a strained voice. "Not if they're normal," she added thoughtlessly.

"Normal? Normal?" said the Squire loudly. "What child of mine has ever been other than normal? What are you talking about? What's she talking about, Mrs. Maizemunch?"

"Don't know, Squire."

"Mrs. Grubguzzle?"

"Don't ask me, Squire."

"But I do ask you," shouted the Squire angrily. "I do ask you! I'm asking all of you. Except, of course,

Mrs. Barleylove," and he shifted his gaze back to the door of Number Five.

Nobody said anything.

"Well, she's at Resthaven, isn't she?" asked the Squire. Eight heads nodded. The Squire began to lose patience again.

"You're not telling me," he shouted, "that Mrs. Barleylove's been swimming in the brook, are you?"

Eight heads shook and eight faces struggled to keep straight at this question.

"Well then!" roared the Squire. "I saw her last litter cross the yard with my own eyes, and a fine bunch they were. Any father would be proud of them. And," he added as an afterthought, "any mother, too. So if she's not swimming, and she has no youngsters with her, will you kindly tell me who in the name of Saint Anthony is this swimming pig?"

Now Saint Anthony is the patron saint of pigmen, and when the sows heard the Squire swear so dreadfully, they knew that the issue could no longer be avoided. It would have to come out sometime. It had better come out now.

"Well?" said the Squire.

"Well, Squire," said Mrs. Swiller and Mrs. Gobblespud together. "This last litter, Mrs. Barleylove . . . had a . . . dag," they finished in a kind of whisper.

There was an awful silence, broken only by the sound of the Squire grinding his tusks. The sows could not see his eyes, hidden by his drooping ears, and of this they were glad.

At last he spoke, very softly. "Go on," he said.

Mrs. Swiller swallowed. "Usually, you see, Squire," she said, "when a . . . dag's born . . ."

"Usually?" interrupted the Squire in the same soft voice.

"Doesn't happen very often, of course," put in Mrs. Gobblespud hastily, "but most of us, one time or another . . ."

"I see," said the Squire heavily.

"And then," said Mrs. Swiller, "the servant takes it away."

"Takes it away?"

"Well, the mother never does see it any more."

"But this one came back!" said Mrs. Gobblespud excitedly, and at this the rest could not contain themselves but joined in in a babble of voices.

"Wouldn't be beat!"

"Squeezed under the door!"

"Then Pigman came again!"

"Dirty fat man!"

"We told him!"

"And later on he came again!"

"When the others crossed the yard!"

"And she told him!"

At last the hubbub died down, and there was silence again, this time unbroken.

After a while the Squire spoke. It seemed to the sows that he sounded old and tired.

"This . . . dag, then," he said slowly, "is down at Resthaven with Mrs. Barleylove?"

"Yes, Squire," they all replied.

"It must be the swimmer, then?"

"Yes, Squire."

"Extraordinary. Extraordinary. Boy or girl?"

"Boy, Squire."

"Boy, eh? What's he called?"

"Daggie Dogfoot."

"Daggie what?"

"Dogfoot."

"Because . . . ?"

"Yes, Squire."

"Which is presumably how he . . . ?"

Eight heads nodded, and nine minds imagined the scene in the brook. "Extraordinary," said the Squire.

His natural courtesy reasserted itself, and he said in his normal bluff, hearty voice, "I'm obliged to you, ladies. Please return to your duties, doncherknow."

But after the sows had disappeared from sight, the boar still leaned on his gate. He felt shocked. But he also felt in some way relieved, for it is better to admit some facts, even hard, bitter facts, than to go on pretending that they don't exist. Most of all perhaps, as he stood there in the late afternoon sunshine, he began to feel proud.

Daggie Dogfoot, eh? he thought to himself. Taken

away but fought his way back. And swimming! Swimming like a fish, apparently! Extraordinary! By Saint Anthony, said the Squire to himself, I'd like to meet the little guy.

The Race

Daggie spent nearly all that day in the water, coming out only for a drink of milk or to eat some of the pignuts the servant threw down. The Pigman noticed nothing. We see only what we expect to see, and he did not dream that he was a slave of a swimming pig.

Mrs. Barleylove had already come to look on Felicity as a combination nurse, aunt, instructress, and lifeguard. Mrs. Barleylove stood on the bank watching teacher and pupil with a silly grin on her big fat face.

Felicity concentrated on Daggie's streamlining, to begin with. She wanted him lower in the water, but he was having trouble with his nose. Like all pigs, his nostrils faced directly forward out of the flat end of his snout and the water simply rushed up into them.

"Why doesn't the water go up *your* nose?" spluttered Daggie, after much trial and error.

"Oh, we've got a sort of valve thing we can shut to stop it," said the duck. "Just as you can shut your eyes if you don't want to see something." She paused, considering. "Perhaps you've got one too?" she said.

"Try and see," called Mrs. Barleylove. "After all, my dear," she addressed Felicity, "I can put my snout deep in a trough full of slops and gobble away without having to take it out."

So Daggie tried, first on dry land, thinking very hard about pinching the insides of his nostrils together, while Felicity peered up his nose. After a while she thought it was working, so they went in the water, and it was!

Then Felicity redesigned Daggie's swimming action. His otter-like forefeet were just fine for the job. But his hind feet, used as though running on dry land, lacked the necessary drive.

The duck taught him to stick his hind legs straight out behind him and beat them up and down in the water alternately, as fast as he could, keeping them stiff, barely breaking the surface.

They reached this stage by the end of the first day, and a long day it seemed to a very tired piglet curling up by his mother's warm side under the oak tree at dusk.

Oddly enough, as the Muscovy was settling to sleep on her alder branch, she heard, farther up the valley, a thin, hard cry in the coming darkness. "I-zaak!" it sounded like. "I-zaak!" Must warn Daggie about otters, she thought drowsily. Don't want him mistaken for a big fish.

For the next few days they worked hard at improving Daggie's style, and on the morning of the fourth day Felicity swam down early from her alder tree and found Daggie already practicing in the pool.

"Hello, Felicity!" shouted Daggie. "I've just been warming up. You said something about a final trial today."

"Well," said Felicity, "I thought we might have a race. I mean you've taken to the water like a duck, as the saying goes. Let's see if you can beat one."

"Hey!" Daggie said. "You're a real swimmer. You've been doing it all your life. I'm only a beginner. You'll wallop me."

I'm not so sure of that, thought the Muscovy.

"It's just for fun," she said. "Just to see how you perform over a longer distance. I thought we could start from the end of the pool and swim upstream as

far as the Resthaven boundary fence. The current's
not running all that strongly because we haven't
had rain for a long time. And it's a pretty straight
course. About two hundred yards overall, I think.
O.K.?"

"I'm game," said Daggie. "Wait while I get
Mommy to watch."

"Well, don't bring her here," said Felicity. "Ask
her if she'd be kind enough to go to the finish line.
Ask her to stand on the bank by the fence and act as
judge."

Five minutes later duck and pig floated side by
side at the lower end of the pool. They saw the big
spotted shape of Mrs. Barleylove come down to the
bank and stand waiting. A little way up the kingfisher sat on his root.

"We'll use him as a starting signal," said Felicity.
"When he moves, swim."

They fixed their eyes on the blazing little bird, and
Daggie braced his hind feet against the bank behind
him, ready to push off to a good start. He quivered
all over with excitement.

Suddenly, in a burning streak of color, the kingfisher flashed away upstream, and they were off!

For a time they were even, and Felicity, thrusting
as hard as she could with her broad webbed feet,
began to think that she had overestimated this
prodigy, for though she could see out of the corner of

her eye that he was swimming beautifully, doing in
perfect style everything that he'd been taught, she
felt she had the better of him. For a moment she even
considered slacking off a bit, to let him win and give
him confidence. Then she caught his eye, and it
seemed to have a twinkle in it.

Suddenly, at about the halfway stage, Daggie

Dogfoot changed gears, and Felicity realized that he'd only been playing with her. Twice as low as before his body went in the water, twice as hard as before those otter's feet pulled, twice as fast as before those outstretched hind legs beat, and he shot away in front of her with the speed of a salmon. She could hear Mrs. Barleylove behaving as an impartial judge certainly should not, urging Daggie on to further efforts with loud proud squeals, and she saw her jump for joy, all four feet off the ground, as he crossed the finish line, fifty yards ahead.

By the time the duck finished, the piglet had been able to climb out of the brook, shake himself all over, be licked by the judge, and call encouragement to his puffing, panting teacher. *He isn't even out of breath*, thought Felicity as she clambered out and waddled up to mother and son.

"How about that, madam?" she puffed. "Aren't you proud of him?"

"Any mother would be," said Mrs. Barleylove. And any father, too, she thought. At least I hope he will.

10

Izaak

A mile upstream was a mill, the very mill that ground the barley meal for the pigs, and beside it was a great pond that gave the waterpower to drive the mill wheel. It was from this pond, some nights before, that the thin, hard cry had reached Felicity's ears as she dropped off to sleep. The animal that had made the cry was a big otter, in the best of health and the worst of tempers. And the reason for his anger had been his lack of success in realizing a long-held ambition.

The millpond was deep and dark, with a bed made of thick mud and the rotting of a million leaves dropped into it over many autumns. Big fish lived in it, tench and carp and pike; and of these last there was one absolute monster, so otter lore had it, a pike half as long as a man, as fierce as a wolf and twice as cunning. Often in his travels between the sea and the hills, this particular otter had spent some time by the millpond with one idea in mind—to find this monster and kill him and eat him. And on that particular night he had come close to doing it.

Searching the deepest, darkest corner of the thickest tangle of weeds, the otter had suddenly seen, motionless beneath him, a long barred shape with narrow wolf jaws and cold, hard eyes, a shape even longer than himself—and he was thirty inches from the end of his nose to the tip of his rudder.

Quick as he was, the long barred shape was quicker, leaving behind it a swirling fog of rotten leaves and a cloud of soupy water and strings of gas bubbles and an angry otter.

"I-zaak!" the otter had cried in his fury as he hauled himself out by the black oak sluice gates all slimy with mosses. "I-zaak!"

The otter spent several days by the millpond, enjoying some easy fishing but without further sight of the monster pike. And then, on the day after Daggie and Felicity had had their race, he decided to move on downstream.

He slipped down with the last of the night, past the farm buildings, under Felicity asleep on her alder branch, past the finishing line of the race, and into the reach that led to the pool beneath the high bank. Sometimes he swam on the surface; sometimes only a string of bubbles showed his progress.

But suddenly he saw something that not only made him lift his round tomcat's head right up out of the water, but actually land and stand up in the grass on his hind legs, peering and sniffing and moving his head from side to side as though he simply could not believe his eyes. In the pool ahead, swimming rapidly from side to side with a racing turn at either bank, was a pig! It wasn't a very big pig by the look of it, no longer than the otter's body without its rudder, but it was, undoubtedly, a white pig with black spots. And it was, undoubtedly, swimming.

Now otters have a tremendous, if rather twisted, sense of humor, and they love jokes, especially bad jokes. One of the jokes that this otter enjoyed very much was giving people sudden awful frights. As everyone knows, a good way to give someone a sudden awful fright is to appear, from nowhere, when you're least expected, and, better still, to make a fearful noise at the same time. A big grin came over the otter's face, and he dropped down and slid into and under the water.

Daggie was in the exact middle of the pool, swimming along without a care in the world in the

peaceful silence of the early morning, when suddenly, right beside him, a grinning whiskery face
popped up, opened a wide mouth to show a battery
of sharp white teeth, and shouted, right in his ear,
"I-ZAAK!"

Daggie felt three sorts of feelings, all at the same
time. Startled because of the sudden noise, afraid
because of the rows of teeth, and angry because he
was startled and afraid. Of the three he quickly
decided that he was mostly angry, and he trod water
and said in a shrill, breathless voice, "I don't know
who you are, but this is my pool and you have no
manners frightening people like that, and I'll tell my
Mommy and Felicity, and anyway your breath stinks
of fish."

Now otters make all sorts of noises, from loud
ones when they are angry or want to frighten someone, through chitterings and chatterings, to lovely
fluty whistles when they are playing or calling to one
another from afar. But when they think something is
really very funny, they laugh quite silently.

To Daggie's astonishment, that is what the creature in front of him proceeded to do, splitting his
hairy face wide open, and rocking to and fro in the
water with his webbed forepaws clasped against his
chest. He laughed so much and rocked about so
wildly that eventually he sank below the water and
swallowed some mouthfuls. Spitting and puffing, he

came back to the surface and at last calmed himself enough to speak to the piglet.

"Sorry, old pig," he spluttered, still grinning broadly. "Sorry if I scared you."

By now Daggie had gotten his breath back, and he said with a sort of quiet dignity, "I'm not an old pig, I'm a young pig. And I'm not just a pig, I'm a pedigree Gloucester Old Spots. And my name is Daggie Dogfoot, son of Champion Imperial Challenger III of Ploughbarrow."

The otter's mouth fell wider and wider open during this recital, but whether in astonishment or in preparation for another round of silent laughter Daggie never knew, for at that instant there was a whistle of wings and Felicity splashed down between them.

She had been so busy with Daggie's training that she had quite forgotten to mention the subject of otters to him, as she had realized with horror when this one's shout had awakened her. Now she faced the danger bravely, determined to protect her little friend. There was a moment's pause, and then all three animals spoke at the same time.

"Are you all right, Daggie?" said Felicity. "Who in the water is he?" said Daggie. And "Hello, old duck," said the otter, and dived beneath the surface.

As the friends swam rather rapidly to the Resthaven bank, they answered each other's questions.

"Yes, I'm all right," said Daggie. "Why shouldn't I be?"

"Because that's an otter," said Felicity. "Great hunter. Kills anything and everything that swims —fish, frogs, eels, ducklings. Never heard of it bothering piglets, but then piglets don't usually swim. You'd better keep away from him."

"Well, he didn't hurt me," said Daggie. "He just seemed to find me rather funny. I can't think why."

As they talked, they could see strings of bubbles bobbing up as the otter searched the pool, and after a moment more he surfaced, smooth as oil, and walked out onto the sandy hollow below them.

"No fish in there, old pig," said the otter cheerfully, "and don't say there are, 'cause there aren't. Must have driven them away with all that swimming practice of yours. What's a pig doing swimming anyway, old duck?"

"I taught him," said Felicity shortly. "What's your name, if I might ask?"

"Izaak," said the otter. "And don't think it isn't, 'cause it is. My friends call me Ike, and don't say they don't, 'cause they do."

There was something very nice about the otter, despite his fearful fishy breath. Perhaps it was his cheeriness. Perhaps it was his odd way of speaking. Or maybe it was the growing certainty that he was not in fact an enemy to them that made the two friends suddenly warm to him.

"Sorry I spoke so rudely to you, Mr. Izaak," said Daggie, "but you did give me an awful shock."

"That's all right, old pig," said the otter. "I'm fond of a good laugh and don't say I'm not, 'cause I am." He turned to Felicity. "Going back to this business of him"—he nodded at Daggie—"swimming. From what I could see, he's pretty good on the surface. I never expected to see a pig swim, old duck, let alone swim as well as that, and don't say I did, 'cause I didn't."

"Yes, he is good," said Felicity. "But then he's lucky enough to have been born specially equipped," and she pointed with her bill to Daggie's forefeet.

"Let's have a look, old pig," said the otter, and

after a close examination he sat back with a long, low whistle, and looked thoughtfully at the piglet.

"Tell you what," he said. "I was going to the seashore for a break, but I'm not in a hurry. Now am I right in thinking you haven't done much underwater work?"

"Not much," said Daggie. "Just the surface dive."

"It's nearly all been surface work," said Felicity. "I'm afraid I'm not much good down below."

"No, but I am," said the otter.

"And don't say you aren't . . ." said Daggie quickly.

". . . because you are," finished Felicity, and they all laughed in their different ways, the otter silently, the duck quot-quotting, the piglet giving little squeals.

"Seriously," said the otter, "I could teach you a lot, old pig, if you'd like. You have no webs, and no rudder to speak of, so you'll be a bit slow on the turn. But I could teach you a lot about breath control and use of currents and general aquabatics. We'd have you catching big fish in no time."

"Well," said Daggie doubtfully, "I'd love to have lessons from you, Mr. Izaak, but I don't actually eat fish."

"Nonsense!" said Felicity sharply. "You mean you haven't eaten fish—yet. Just think, if this gentleman is kind enough to teach you . . . after all, pigs are omnivorous."

"What's that mean, old duck?" said the otter.

"Means they can eat anything and everything."

"She's clever, isn't she, old pig?" said the otter. "They say eating fish is good for your brains, though it doesn't seem to have done me much good," and he swished around in another fit of silent laughter.

So it came about that Daggie Dogfoot acquired a second teacher and right away began more lessons, so that by the time Mrs. Barleylove, who had slept through everything, rolled down to the brook for her morning drink, she found Daggie was more under the water than on it. And often when his head popped up, there was a round brown whiskery one beside it, and sometimes his squeaks of delight mingled with the stranger's lovely fluty whistles. Felicity explained everything to her, and because it was all right with Felicity, it was all right with her.

All that day Daggie played with and learned from his new tutor, occasionally coming to the bank to see if his old tutor approved and was not upset, and she did and she wasn't, and his mother beamed her usual fatuous smile of pride.

In the afternoon swimmers and spectators moved upstream a little, and the otter caught a big trout, taking it in a lightning upward swirl too fast for the eye to follow. He pulled it onto the bank and offered Daggie first bite ("From the shoulder—the flesh is sweetest there, old pig"). Daggie was too polite to

refuse and afterward glad that he hadn't, for it was
delicious. Between them they ate most of the best of
it, as they were hungry from their exertions. When
they had returned to the brook, Mrs. Barleylove ate
the rest—head, tail, bones, and all—till not a scale
was left.

When the light began to fade, the otter said he
must be going.

"See you tomorrow, old pig," he said. "You're
learning fast."

"Oh, I really enjoyed that," said Daggie. "The underwater training, and the trout, and, of course, meeting you. Thank you so much, Mr. Izaak."

"Good night, old pig," said the otter. "But I told you before, and don't say that I didn't, 'cause I did—my friends call me Ike."

"Thanks, Ike," said Daggie happily.

The Flood

Daggie did not see his new friend Ike the next day, because overnight the weather, which controls everything in the country, changed completely. As Felicity had said before the race, they hadn't had rain for a long time. But not an hour after the otter had slipped away upstream, the heavens opened and proceeded to make up for their stinginess by such a display of generosity as none of the animals had ever known before. It rained heavily all that night, and went on without stopping for two more days and nights.

The sows in their sties kept to their inner compartments, venturing into their soaking outer runs only for food. The Squire, of course, was dry under his veranda roof, but the constant stream of water flowing across the yard from higher ground worried him. He was not concerned for himself, but he couldn't help thinking about the strange son of whose existence he had just heard. He hoped that that existence would not be ended in an untimely way, for he knew that boys will be boys, and this one sounded particularly adventurous. The brook will be swollen, thought the Squire. I hope the kid stays on dry land.

He spoke to the servant about it, but the Pigman, more hideous than ever in yellow oilskins and rain hat, was too stupid to understand his master.

At Number One and Number Two Mrs. Troughlicker and Mrs. Boltapple stood upright at their front doors and looked anxiously over the yard. It was covered with a stream of fast-running water, as indeed were the outer runs of all the sties. Only inside, where each sow had a raised wooden platform six inches high, was there still a dry space for them and their piglets. Mrs. Troughlicker spoke first.

"I don't like it, Mrs. B.," she said in a worried voice. "I've never seen rain like this."

"What can we do?" asked Mrs. Troughlicker.

"I'll be butchered if I know," said Mrs. Boltapple. "If only the rain would stop!"

But the rain did not stop. On the contrary, even as

they spoke, it began to come down heavily again, and the ladies hastily retreated indoors.

The Pigman stood at the door of his shed and looked down at the water, now almost over the lower of the two concrete steps. Behind him he heard rats squeaking among the bins, and his red face grew redder at the sound of his enemies' voices. But even as he turned to reach up for his hardwood club and do battle, a big buck rat came running out of the gloom of the shed and scampered right over his boots and out the door. It fell into the water and swam rapidly away. And as the Pigman watched, open-mouthed, half a dozen more rats of all sizes dashed past him and into the water and away. Something he had heard long ago, at school perhaps, came into his mind. A sinking ship, he thought. Rats leaving a sinking ship.

At that instant the westerly wind, which had been blowing hard from the sea far down at the foot of the valley, dropped for a moment, and in the ensuing lull the Pigman heard a sound from the other direction, from the upper eastern end. It was a muttering that grew to a grumbling that grew to a mighty rumbling. Straining his eyes through the driving rain, he stared back at the brook to where it curved into view around some trees two fields away.

Suddenly, to his horror, he saw a great wall of

brown water coming around this bend, and he knew in a flash what must have happened. The sluice gates have gone, thought the Pigman, the millpond's burst. And for once in his slow, lumbering life he acted quickly.

He grabbed a sack of pignuts, jumped off the steps of the shed into the six-inch-deep water, and splashed his way to the sties. He flung open door after door: Mrs. Troughlicker's, Mrs. Boltapple's, Mrs. Swedechopper's, Mrs. Swiller's, missing the empty Number Five, then Mrs. Gobblespud's, Mrs. Maizemunch's, Mrs. Grazegrass's, Mrs. Grubguzzle's. As the sows and litters ran out into the yard, he blundered across it to the store pens and fattening pens, throwing wide door after door till a hundred and fifty spotted shapes of all sizes were stampeding in the rushing flood. Only when he had opened the last door of all, the Squire's, did he allow himself one fearful glance over his shoulder. The wall of water was halfway across the last field in front of the buildings, and coming at the speed of a galloping horse.

The Pigman, like all his kind, knew that pigs are the most awkward animals in the world to drive, so he did the only thing he could. Handicapped though he was by his bulk and his boots and his long yellow oilskins and the sack of pignuts, he ran as hard as he

could toward the gate that led to Resthaven, shouting at the top of his voice the pigkeeper's universal
feeding call.

"PIG-pig-pig-pig-PIG-pig-pig-pig-PIG!" he yelled amid the noise of the rain and the renewed wind and the thundering of the watery threat behind them, and he pounded desperately toward the high ground at the top of the little triangular field.

And behind him rose two waves. One was white, spotted with black, and one was brown. One squealed with fear, and one roared with menace. One was moving as fast as it possibly could, but a pig cannot gallop half as speedily as a horse, and the other wave gained and gained on the first. As the last and slowest piglet struck the rising ground, the first and fastest wave of the flood was less than a sow's length from his curly little tail.

Then the flood turned before the hill and swept across the lower slopes of the field, smashing down the old oak tree from the place where it had stood for three hundred years and carrying it away like a matchstick. Twenty feet above Daggie's take-off place on the high bank went the oak, twisting and turning and thrashing its old arms in agony on its road to the windswept sea.

But the pigs were safe, not just all one hundred and fifty-one of them, but all one hundred and fifty-three. For the first thing the Pigman saw, when his pounding heart and bursting lungs had quieted a little, was a group of three figures standing at the very topmost point of Resthaven and staring at the great army of pigs covering the high slope. Old sow from Number Five's all right then, he thought. And that horrible little dag. Though Heaven knows what one of my ducks is doing with them.

There was noise all around them as they stood and panted on their hilltop refuge. The blustering shout of the wind competed with the menacing roar of the brook that had become a great river. On the waters of that river hissed the lash of the never-ending rain. At one moment Daggie imagined he heard, far out on the flood, an excited fluty whistle, as though someone were actually enjoying the storm. But suddenly, clear above the other noises, was heard a sharp cracking sound, and from the hill a hundred and fifty-five heads turned and three hundred and ten eyes looked back toward the homes they had left behind, to see the beginning of the first voyage of a strange craft.

The rats had been right to go, for the cracking noise proclaimed the launching of the Pigman's shed, as the flood lifted it bodily from its foundation. Past the drowned sties it came, over the submerged field gate, and out into the center of the great expanse of dark, sliding, eddying water that now stretched before the watchers. Its door hung open, as the pigman had left it when he ran to rescue them, and as the shed spun slowly in the current they

could see within it the great bins of barley meal and middlings and flaked corn and the piled sacks of pignuts, all sailing swiftly away to be food for the fish in the sea.

Another story came into the Pigman's slow mind from distant days in the village schoolroom. Looks like the Ark, he thought. Trouble is, we aren't on it. And all the food I have for them is this fifty-pound sack of nuts. Still, they won't be short of water to drink.

He went to the topmost point of Resthaven, and, opening the sack, threw the pignuts far and wide over the small triangle of field that was left high and dry. Within half a minute everything was eaten, and the multitude was squealing for more, while far in the distance the shed sailed on downriver.

The Pigman folded the empty sack, placed it on top of an ant heap, and sat carefully down on it. He sat motionless, his head in his hands, while the pigs jostled and grumbled below him. If there had been anyone on any of the other hilltops nearby, it would have seemed a strange sight: above, the bright yellow spot of the man's oilskins and rain hat; below that, the spotted throng; and below them, the chocolate-colored flood, darkening from milk to plain as the daylight faded. Mrs. Barleylove and Daggie and Felicity still stood together.

"Poor old Duckman," said Felicity. "He looks all in."

"Duckman?" said Daggie absently. "Oh, you mean Pigman. Yes, he does. Still, he's a good and faithful servant, you know. He did his duty." Felicity had also been thinking of the story of the Flood, as the Ark-like shed had drifted by, but, being better educated than the man, remembered more of it. She began to make the quot-quot-quotting noise, which Daggie now knew well was her way of giggling.

"What's the joke?" said Daggie.

"I was thinking of a story," said Felicity. "In a book. Called the Bible. About a man called Noah."

"Why?" said Daggie. "Is Pigman like Noah?"

"No," said Felicity. "More like one of his sons."

"What was he called?" asked Daggie.

"Ham," said Felicity happily.

12

Going for Help

In the early light of the following morning the scene was quite different. To begin with, the flood was not quite as high, for the burst pond was empty now and it had not rained in the night. The water had receded far enough to show the gaping hole where the old oak used to stand, but it was still running very wide and very strong, and there was no sign of the outline of the brook.

The other difference was one of color. The hilltops around showed brilliantly green in the light of the early morning sun, but what there was to see of Resthaven was black-brown, and milling on it were black-brown creatures. Pedigree Gloucester Old

Spots they might be, but no one would have known, for the herd had rooted and routed over every square inch, looking for something—anything—to eat, and they were plastered with dirt.

As the Pigman had said, there was no problem about drinking, for millions and millions of gallons of water flowed by them. It was food they were thinking about, and the first thing they had done was to graze off every blade of grass and gobble up every dock and nettle, even every thistle; every leaf and shoot they could reach through the boundary pig wire they had torn off, and where a hedgerow tree was close enough, they had chewed its bark. Then they had turned up the whole top triangle of the field and ferreted out the roots of every blade of grass, every patch of clover, every weed. Anything they came across went down them—worms, slugs, beetles, even some families of field mice, babies and all, and of all the hundreds of ant heaps that had dotted the upper slopes of Resthaven only one remained, and on it, yellow against the black-brown background, the Pigman still sat, head hanging, shoulders bowed, stomach rumbling with hunger.

Mrs. Barleylove and Daggie were just as black and filthy as the rest, for they, too, had been rooting everywhere for food. Only Felicity was spotlessly clean, not a black or a white feather out of place, for she, of course, had flown onto the flood for a thorough bath. She stood now on Mrs. Barleylove's broad back, to be out of the way of the pushing, shoving, squealing multitude of earth-covered pigs, and spoke into the big droopy ear, softly so as not to be overheard.

"Look, madam," she said. "We've got to do something—you know that as well as I do. This crowd's so hungry they're eating anything now. Let one little piglet get trodden on and they'll gobble him up. And then they'll start on one another. I'm right, don't you think?"

Mrs. Barleylove shuddered. She knew how every

pig worships food, and she was well aware, though she didn't know the word, that pigs are omnivorous, eating everything that is remotely edible. She remembered stories that her mother had told her of swill-feeding in the old days, when rats and sometimes cats would fall into the swill tubs and get cooked: the pigs would chomp them up quite happily, her mother had said.

" 'Course you're right, my dear," she said quietly. "We've got to get help. We've got to get food. But how? It doesn't look like the servant can swim or he'd have gone. And your going wouldn't do much good, if you'll excuse me; people wouldn't connect a Muscovy duck with a herd of pigs. The only one that can swim, after all, is . . ." She stopped, and her mouth fell open.

"Oh, no!" cried Mrs. Barleylove. "Oh, no! Not him!"

"It's got to be your Daggie," said Felicity. "If nobody goes, and no one comes to find you all, and the floods don't go down for a week, say, all hell will break loose here."

"But he may be drowned!" wailed Mrs. Barleylove.

"I don't think so," said Felicity, "though I admit it's a possibility. As against the probability," she said very slowly and clearly, "that if he stays here, he'll be . . . eaten."

There was a small silence between them, in the middle of the uproar of empty-bellied pigs.

"All right," grunted Mrs. Barleylove at last. "If he's willing, bless his little heart," and she blinked her white-lashed eyes very quickly. "But you'll go with him, dear, won't you? Please?"

"Of course," said Felicity. "Try not to worry, madam. I'm sure it'll all have a happy ending. If we can find some other servants like Duckman—er, Pigman, I mean—somewhere downstream, they'll see Daggie's spots and they'll know where he's from. After all, there's only this one herd of Gloucester Old Spots in the district, isn't there?"

"Far as I know," said Mrs. Barleylove.

"Well, then," said the duck, "they'll know something's wrong. And they'll get food here somehow, by boat or helicopter."

The sow had no notion what a helicopter was, but she had a lot of faith in Felicity, and she called loudly to her son.

Daggie came running. He was very hungry, for his mother's milk had dried up now, and he had been pushed and shoved away from anything that looked like food by his stronger brethren. But his eyes were bright and his courage was high, and as soon as he heard about the plan, he was wild to go.

Felicity flew down to the water's edge, and Mrs. Barleylove followed, barging her way through the press of pigs with Daggie at her heels. "Coming through! Coming through!" she shouted, and the other sows, hearing her voice, pushed forward to see what was happening.

They were all asking questions at once when sharp squeals from above made them look around. They saw the Squire come rolling down toward them, his tusks showing white in his muddy face as he tossed pig after pig out of his way.

"What's going on?" he asked in his deep voice when he reached the sows. "Mrs. Barleylove, dear lady, what's going on?"

"It's my son, Squire," replied Mrs. Barleylove proudly. "He's going for help. He's going to swim for help, to find someone to bring us food."

Those nearest to her heard her words, and as the news spread the herd fell silent, and every head was turned to listen.

"Your son?" said the Squire loudly. "Your son?"

"Our son, Squire," said Mrs. Barleylove softly, feeling her white parts turn pink, and thankful for the mud that hid them.

"That's better," said the Squire, and turning to the little piglet, he looked curiously at him. Little shrimp, he thought, he's not much bigger than a rat. And those front feet . . .

He spoke quietly now, so that the pigs at the edge of the crowd raised their heads to hear better as the great boar looked down at the little dag.

"So you're Daggie Dogfoot," said the Squire.

"Yes, sir," said Daggie politely.

"And you're going for help?"

"Yes, sir."

"Current's strong, you know. Water's deep. Understand you can—er—swim pretty well, but it'll be dangerous."

"Oh, I'll be all right," said Daggie. "Thank you, Father," he added daringly. The boar cleared his throat as though there were some kind of lump in it.

"Well, good luck, my son," he said in a loud, strained voice. "By Saint Anthony, I wish you the very best of good luck."

And the mob of pigs echoed him. "Good luck! Good luck!" they cried, and the Pigman got up off his ant heap at the noise and lumbered down to find out what it was all about.

He was just in time to see Daggie walk out into the shallows, the mud on him dissolving as the current began to wash him clean. Soon he was swimming, once again a white piglet with black spots, and then he was in midstream and the full force of the floodwater took him and whirled him away.

But every pig could see how beautifully he swam, and most of them could hear his farewell cry. One of them stood alone, belly-deep in the shallows, while a great tear ran down each of her fat cheeks and

plopped into the stream. Come back safely, my Daggie, said Mrs. Barleylove to herself.

Just then Felicity came flying back, low over the heads of the herd. The Pigman had taken off his hat, the better to scratch his head in his utter bewilderment at the sight of a swimming pig, and Felicity dived down, caught it in her clawed feet and tore it from him.

"I'll take this with me," she shouted to Mrs. Barleylove, as she wheeled to follow Daggie. "Maybe someone will know who this belongs to," and she flew rapidly away, the hat dangling below her, while the Pigman danced in anger.

"Dratyer!" he cried, and "Dangyer!" and "Blast-yer!" shaking his huge fist at the two fast-disappearing figures.

"Stupid, ignorant duck!" he shouted. "You and that horrible little dag, you make a fine pair. Never be no use to no one, not neither of you, nohow!"

And as the pigs ran to the topmost part of Rest-haven, they caught a final glimpse of Daggie Dog-foot, far down on the flood. They could see Felicity for a little longer as she flew low, directly above the swimmer. And then there was nothing to be seen but a great waste of waters.

13

Man on a Raft

Jumping around in anger had awakened the Pigman's brain from the daze of hopelessness into
which it had fallen, and he began to think what he
could do about the situation. It occurred to him, as it
had to the duck much earlier, that there would be
trouble with a capital T if the pigs remained unfed.
His shed, he knew, was gone, and help, if it ever
came, might be a long time arriving. After much
head scratching, a simple idea came to him. Resthaven, after all, was only one side of the little conical
hill on which they were marooned, so that there
must be grass and bushes and trees on the other
side. All he had to do was to take down the pig wire

that confined his herd, and then they could find something to keep them going.

To do this was not easy, since the fence had been well made in the first place, tightly stretched, and nailed to posts. Wire cutters would have done the job in a minute, but, of course, he had none with him. As he stood and looked at the fence, the Squire rolled up and stood beside him. They conversed in their separate languages.

"If only you had the brains, old fellow," said the Pigman, "you'd get your head under the wire and lift it up."

"If you had any sense at all, Pigman," said the Squire, "you'd use that branch that's lying there as a lever to get the bottom of this wire up far enough for me to put my head under it."

"If I had something for a lever," said the Pigman, "I might be able to lift the bottom of it a little. Then perhaps this old boar would see what I'm getting at."

"Man's a fool," said the Squire.

"Oh, there's a branch," said the Pigman. "That might do."

"At last," said the Squire with a sigh, as the Pigman slid the branch under the lowest-but-one strand of the pig wire, stuck the far end into the ground beyond, and began to heave upward. With great effort he managed to lift the bottom strand six inches above the ground.

"Ladies!" shouted the Squire. "I want you all on parade, please. Chop-chop!" And when the nine sows came galloping up, he said more quietly, "Spread out, please. Four on one side of me, five on the other. Snouts down. Wait for my word." And from the corner of his mouth he snarled at the servant, "Come on, Man!"

Almost as though he could understand, the Pigman redoubled his efforts. The bottom of the wire rose a fraction higher, the boar got his head under the lowest strand, then the sow on either side of him, and so on, until all ten heads were under and all ten great bodies tensed.

"Ready! Steady! Heave!" shouted the Squire, and with a twanging, tearing noise a twenty-foot stretch of pig wire rose up, up, up, till the retaining fence posts popped out of the ground.

"Forward!" bawled the Squire, and before the advancing weight of more than four thousand pounds of pig, the fence burst like a rotten tennis net, and the rest of the herd poured through. They went around the back of the hill, snatching at the fresh grass like mad things, and the Pigman was left alone.

The sight of his animals eating again reminded

him painfully of how empty his own stomach was. If only I had a boat, he thought, and he strained his little piggy eyes upstream as though wishing would make one appear. He did not see one, of course, but he did see something—two things, in fact. They were about ten feet apart, halfway between him and his drowned buildings, and he suddenly realized that they were the tops of the gateposts at the entrance to Resthaven.

Gateposts, he thought. Water must have gone down a little; couldn't see them before. Gateposts, he thought. There's a gate between 'em. Gate, he thought. Made of wood. Wood, he thought. Floats. Floats, he thought. Like a boat—well, like a raft.

He went down to the water's edge and began to wade back toward the gateposts. The current was strong, but the Pigman was powerful, and he fought his way along, deeper and deeper as he went down the slope. He was shoulder deep when at last he stood between the posts and, feeling underwater, found the gate.

Now was the moment of decision for the Pigman. As Mrs. Barleylove had guessed, he could not swim. Moreover, he was afraid of the water. As a child, he had once been taken to the beach on a school outing, but nothing would persuade him to go beyond the ripples. What he was doing now was, for him, an act of great bravery. But more was needed. In order to grip the heavy gate and clear it from the gatepost, he would need, at this depth, to put his head under the dreaded water!

And if he lifted it free, would it bear him? And if it bore him, where to? To food and shelter and help? Or out to the endless ocean? Desperate men do desperate things, and the Pigman closed his eyes, settled his feet firmly, and took a good grip and a deep, deep breath.

There followed a scene that would have seemed pure comedy if there had been a human watcher unaware of the underlying drama, but, for the Pigman, it could easily have been one of tragedy.

To begin with, the hinges were jammed on the gateposts, and it took three increasingly breathless dips below the surface before his utmost efforts could lift the gate free. And when it was free, the current immediately dragged it away, so that the Pigman had to make a wild, belly-flopping leap at it as it went. He caught the back end of it, whereupon it tipped up like a live thing, threatening to throw him off into deeper water. Somehow, gasping, spluttering, panic-stricken, he managed to scramble farther onto it, expecting all the time that it would submerge beneath him.

But it bore him, though the weight of the heavy man and his waterlogged clothes pushed it below the surface, so that he would have appeared, if there had been a watcher, to be floating motionless on the flood, like a bright yellow hippopotamus.

This was what he looked like to the first eyes that did see him. Most of the herd were on the reverse side of the hill, rooting and tearing at anything they could find, but the Squire and Mrs. Barleylove had not moved far from the break in the fence, and it was they who witnessed the Pigman's progress.

"By Saint Anthony!" the Squire burst out. "It's the servant! Seems to be lying on top of the water. Extraordinary! Fellow can't be as stupid as I thought."

Mrs. Barleylove watched as the current bore the Pigman steadily away. Daggie, she thought, where are you, darling?

"I'll be on the lookout," said the Squire, reading her thoughts, "when the level drops a bit more, so I can see the line of the hedges or fences. Should be easy to bust 'em."

"Easier with two, Squire," said Mrs. Barleylove.

Champion Imperial Challenger III of Ploughbarrow raised his heavy head and gazed at this wife of his with approval and affection. "Couldn't wish for a better partner," he said. "And try not to worry too much about the boy. We'll find him. You'll see."

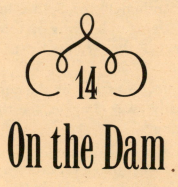

14

On the Dam

Not long after Daggie and Felicity had disappeared from the sight of the watching herd, the course of the flood took a turn in a new direction, and the course of their fortunes took a turn for the better. A mile or so from Resthaven the old brook had rounded the foot of a high spur, plunged, southwest and seawards, into quite a deep, steep valley and, though now swollen to many times its usual width, was nonetheless narrower at this point than the broad waters on which Daggie had begun his swim. Consequently the speed of the current increased dramatically, so that Felicity needed to fly at her fastest to keep up with the swimmer.

Daggie, of course, was too excited to be frightened. "Wheeeeeee!" he yelled as the racing water swept him along, but the Muscovy, ten feet above him, suddenly saw trouble ahead.

Something was blocking the way—a kind of rough dam, it seemed, though Felicity could not see what it was made of. But she could see that the rushing flood parted before it, swerved away to either side, and fell from sight in a boiling swirl. Felicity knew something about waterfalls and the terrible currents beneath them, and she instantly realized the awful danger Daggie would be in if he was swept over the falls.

Flying her hardest, she dropped low over the piglet, the strings of the yellow rain hat held tight in her claws, the rest of it hanging low.

"Grab it in your teeth, Daggie!" she shouted. "Quick! Don't argue!"

As soon as she felt his weight, she turned and faced upstream, beating her wings with all her strength. Try as she might, she could still feel herself being dragged backward, but at least she was cutting down Daggie's breakneck speed and keeping him dead center.

When a hasty glance over her shoulder told her the moment was ripe, she turned and dropped down onto a branch that stuck out at water level. She walked backward along the branch, pulled as hard as she could, and landed Daggie as an angler lands a fish. They were safe on the dam, and they could hear the thunder of falling water behind and below them.

Its purpose served, the yellow rain hat slipped over the falls on the start of a journey that was to bring help, for someone spotted it far downstream and fished it out, and inside it they could still make out the Pigman's name and address written in his horrible scrawl.

"Gosh, that thing tasted nasty," panted Daggie, wrinkling his snout. "What was that all about, Felicity?"

Felicity looked at him and made her quot-quot-quotting noise.

"Oh, nothing," she said. "I just thought we'd have a breather. Let's look around."

Curiously, perhaps because he was so breathless, sight was the last of Daggie's five senses to send messages to his brain. With the roar of the falls in his ears and the sour taste of oilskin in his mouth, the next thing he realized, through his sensitive forefeet, was that the bark of the big branch on which he was standing was familiarly rough, as though he had met, not just this *kind* of tree, but this *particular* tree before. Then suddenly, lifting his snout to the wind, he smelled food! And not just food, but pig food! And not just pig food somewhere miles away, but pig food near, very near, here, right on this jumble of objects in the middle of the stream! Then at last—and all this happened in a matter of seconds—he used his eyes. What he suddenly saw excited him so much that he nearly lost his perch and fell into the water again.

"Look, Felicity!" he shouted. "Look—behind you!"

And there, jammed among the branches, was the shed. It was still upright, its door still hung open,

and out of the door came the wonderful smells. Like shipwrecked mariners stumbling on treasure, they scrambled toward it.

Inside, the bins of barley meal and middlings and flaked corn still stood, their wooden lids tightly shut and far too heavy to be lifted by piglet or duck. But that did not matter, for on the floor were sacks of pignuts that had fallen as the shed had tossed on the flood. Some of these had broken open so that part of the floor was covered with a rich dark brown carpet of nuts, which Daggie pounced on. Some of this carpet had been wet into a beautiful mush by water seeping through the floorboards, so that Felicity could suck up a kind of delicious pignut porridge. For a long time there was nothing to be heard in the shed but the sounds of eating.

Felicity stopped eating first, because her crop was full. She went out to the edge of the dam for a drink. When her thirst was satisfied, she flew around to look at the far side of the obstruction. She found, as she had suspected, that the jam of timber had caused a wicked waterfall down which Daggie would surely have plunged to a horrible death.

When she came back into the shed, he was still eating. At last he staggered out and picked his way to the water and drank deeply. When he returned, he let out a huge belch, followed by a long sigh of contentment, flopped on his side on the floor, and fell fast asleep, his little spotted balloon of a tummy rising and falling. Not a bad idea, thought the Muscovy, closing her eyes.

An hour or so later Daggie woke suddenly with a shout of "Mommy!" A series of muddled dreams had turned into a nightmare, something to do with his babyhood, and sure enough, the very first thing he focused on was the hardwood club, still hanging on its rusty nail. Then he saw the kind face of his friend Felicity looking down at him from the top of a bin, and he remembered what had happened. Looking out the doorway, he saw a big branch that stuck up in the air, and on the branch were familiar crinkly-edged leaves, and among the leaves were some acorns.

"It's the oak, isn't it, Felicity?" he said. "It's the old oak from Resthaven."

"Yes," said the duck. "It jammed across this narrow place, against some rocks probably, and then caught everything else that came down, including, thank goodness, this shed."

"Gosh, yes," said Daggie. "What luck! What super grub. I feel like a new piglet."

"You look like a new piglet," said Felicity. "Your mother wouldn't recognize you."

Daggie's mood changed instantly. "Mommy!" he cried, jumping to his feet. "Oh, Mommy! Oh, how selfish I am! Here I am, making a pig of myself, and all the time Mommy's hungry, starving perhaps. And Father. And my aunts. And my brothers and sisters. And all the others. Oh, what a selfish pig I am!"

"Don't be silly," said Felicity shortly. "It's only sensible that as we've been lucky enough to find all this food, we should eat our fill. We must keep up our strength, you know. There's an awful lot to do."

"Yes, I suppose so," said Daggie, a little less miserably. "But what can we do? How can we get this food back to the others? We can't carry it."

"I don't know," said Felicity. "I honestly don't know. But I have a feeling that something will turn up." And she began to preen herself and to rearrange her feathers, while Daggie lay down again on his distended stomach and gazed out the doorway.

And as he gazed, something did turn up. At first Daggie could not see clearly what it was, for the sun was in his eyes. All he noticed was a yellowish lump in the distance, coming down toward them—a dead tree perhaps, he thought. But as it came nearer, he could see that it was not vegetable but animal, that it was not dead but alive, for it had a staring white face and wide flaring nostrils, and its teeth were bared in a grin of fear, while its tongue licked nervously over its thick lips. Its body, he could now see, was bright yellow, and it seemed to ride effortlessly on the water.

"Felicity!" yelled Daggie in an agony of terror. "A monster! A monster! He's coming straight at us!"

Felicity waddled to the door.

"I hope he is," she said. "We need him. It's Duckman."

15

Breakfast and Bed

The Pigman, low in the water, did not realize the danger ahead. Even if he had, it is doubtful that he could have done much about it, so paralyzed was he with terror. All he was concerned with was hanging onto his gate like grim death. This, in fact, was what saved him, for when the current took hold and whirled him off to one side of the dam and over the falls, he held tight; if he had let go then, he would probably have been sucked under by the down currents in the pool below, and drowned.

Felicity, flying toward the other side of the dam, saw the man and his raft plunge down beneath the boiling surface. But then the heavy wooden gate rose **again**, its rider still clinging to it, water cascading off the soaking yellow oilskins. Once he's clear of the pool down there and out in midstream again, he'll be gone, with nothing to stop him between here and the sea, thought Felicity. But at that moment a freakish current dragged the gate back toward the dam, toward a point where a strong branch of the old oak stuck out invitingly.

"If only he'd let go of the gate and grab that branch," shouted the Muscovy over the noise of the falls to Daggie, who was standing above, watching. "Otherwise he'll be gone in a minute."

Inspiration came to Daggie.

"Scratch his hands, Felicity," he yelled. "Fly down and scratch his hands. That'll make him let go!"

As the piglet looked on, Felicity flew down, pitched on the end of the gate, and deliberately dragged her sharp claws across the backs of the Pigman's tightly gripping hands. Then everything happened at once. The Pigman loosened his hold with a yell of pain and anger and grabbed frantically at the branch. The gate shot from under him, caught the force of the stream again, and sailed steadily away. The duck flew back onto the dam and perched beside Daggie.

Side by side, the friends watched anxiously as the

Pigman struggled to pull himself along the branch to safety. His clothes were soaked, his boots full of water, his tired limbs cramped, his hungry body chilled. But he was strong and he was desperate, and

at last, somehow, he scrambled onto the dam.

For a while he lay in the tangle of timber, gasping for breath. When at last he sat up and looked around, he saw the two watchers, and some color came back into his wet white face.

"Dratyer!" he cried, shaking his bleeding fists at them, and "Dangyer!" and "Blastyer!"

Then suddenly he lurched to his feet. His mouth, open from the last shout, gaped wider still, his piggy eyes glinted, and in a kind of mad blundering stumble he began to clamber over the mess of timber in the direction of the two animals.

Hurriedly the stupid, ignorant duck and the horrible little dag moved out of the way, but they soon realized the reason for the servant's excitement. Pigman had seen the back of the shed.

Above everything else, the Pigman was hungry, excruciatingly, ravenously hungry. For most of the thirty-odd hours that had passed since he ran from this shed in the face of the approaching flood, he had thought of food in general, and in particular of some sandwiches left in the pocket of his old apron (the very pocket that had once carried Daggie), which hung from a second rusty nail beside the hardwood club. They were ham sandwiches, his favorite, and the spittle ran down over his three chins as he fought his way to the door.

He clambered in, and there was the apron. He plunged his huge hand into the pocket, and there were the sandwiches. He tore off the paper in which they were wrapped and crammed them into his mouth. By the time Daggie and Felicity had summoned up courage to peep around the door, the sandwiches were gone, for there had been only two, meant for a mid-morning snack. As they watched, the Pigman broke open a sack of pignuts, picked out a handful, and began to chew them. A cautious look came over his face, then something like a smile, and then he sat down and began to stuff himself.

"Gosh, he must be full," said Daggie after a while. "What do you think he'll do next?"

"Don't know what to think," said Felicity. "First he comes floating down the river like a duck . . ."

". . . and then he makes a pig of himself!" laughed Daggie. "Extraordinary fellow, doncherknow!" he said in a passable imitation of his father, and they both giggled in a chorus of little grunts and quot-quot-quotting noises.

The Pigman had, in fact, decided what to do next. He had never had a deep thought in his whole life, but when certain simple ideas occurred to him, he acted on them without further ado.

At the moment his stomach was full, but the rest of his body was wet and cold and tired. His brain therefore received three messages. Get dry. Get warm. Get sleep.

The two heads looking around the door saw the Pigman move slowly into action. First he took off his yellow oilskins and hung them on a third rusty nail beside the apron and the hardwood club. Then he opened the three big wooden meal bins one after the other and looked into each long and earnestly, scratching his head like mad. At the last one, the flaked corn bin, he took off his rubber boots, emptied the water out of them onto the floor, and then solemnly filled them full of the crackly golden stuff.

Next he went to the middlings bin. He took off his trousers, his pullover, his shirt, and his socks, and carefully buried them all deep in the brown saw-dusty stuff.

Then the Pigman, clothed only in gray woolen underwear, went to the barley bin. Laboriously, with much grunting, he climbed into the bin and began to work himself down into the thick white powdery stuff like some giant lugworm burying itself in soft sand. When he was waist deep in it, he reached up to a shelf above for a bundle of old copies of *The Pig Breeder's Gazette*. He wriggled on down till he was shoulder deep. Then he slipped the maga-zines under his head, plunged his arms under the barley blanket, and lay back with a sigh.

"By Saint Anthony," said Daggie mischievously as the Pigman closed his eyes, "fellow's actually going to sleep," and they both burst into another fit of giggles.

16

Dreams

"Water's actually going down a bit," said the Squire. "Take a look at those young porkers over there, Mrs. Barleylove. They're grazing grass that was underwater a few hours ago."

By now the hungry herd had eaten everything growing on the little hill of which Resthaven formed a part so that the whole of it was now a black-brown hump. But at its edges a fresh green rim kept appearing as the flood level gradually dropped, and as fast as it appeared, the herd ate it. The vegetable matter kept them going, but such a diet was rather like humans living on nothing but soggy lettuce, and they longed for solid substantial food.

"Couldn't we try to get downstream now, Squire?" asked Mrs. Barleylove. Her belly ached for a square meal, and her heart ached for Daggie. The Squire heard the note of pleading in her voice and nodded his heavy head.

"Not long now, dear lady," he said. "I don't think much of either of us as swimmers, doncherknow, so we mustn't go beyond our depth. But you can see the line of the willows at the edge of the brook pretty clearly now. And the tops of some fences."

He thought for a moment. Then he gave his deep coughing grunt and shouted, "Ladies! This way, please. Chop-chop!"

When the other eight sows had joined Mrs. Barleylove and all were standing around him in a respectful circle, he addressed them thus:

"Listen carefully, please, ladies. Don't want to have to repeat myself. Now, it doesn't look as though help were coming. On the other trotter, water's dropping. Not enough yet to get the youngsters downstream, but Mrs. Barleylove and I are going to take a little stroll and see what we can find." He paused. "Any objections?" he barked, but the sows noticed the fierceness of his look and said nothing.

"All right then," said the Squire. "Look after the herd. And, ladies, one last thing. Do not attempt to follow us." And he waded off, breast-deep, Mrs. Barleylove in his wake.

Back at the shed, everyone was now asleep and dreaming. Felicity dreamed her usual simple happy kind of dream, all peace and warm sunlight and dancing water.

The Pigman's dream was more complex, and, like his waking thoughts, concerned food. A dream smell of roast suckling pig ran up his flaring nostrils, and he stirred restlessly in the barley meal bin, his white-lashed eyelids fluttering.

Daggie was having a nightmare. He lay in a pool of sunlight by the door, but in his mind he was back in Resthaven, before the flood, playing King of the Castle, jumping on Mommy's big stomach. Outside the shed the real sun disappeared behind a cloud bank, and the pool of sunlight was no more. And in his dream, too, the day turned gray, and his mommy vanished, and something horrible was coming toward him, something huge and fat and white.

The Pigman had settled so low in the barley meal that eventually he snored some of the floury stuff right up his nose. He woke up and rubbed his face with his mealy hands, so that he was white from top to toe. His brain received a message: I am thirsty. He lifted himself out of the bin.

Then everything happened at once. Daggie woke and squealed with terror as his nightmare became reality. Felicity woke, and thinking her friend to be in danger, flew at the Pigman's head. The Pigman put up his hands to ward her off, tripped as the piglet dashed between his legs, stubbed his toe in the doorway, caught his foot in a branch outside, and like a great tree falling, crashed into the water and sank below the surface.

As Daggie and Felicity watched, horrified, they saw on the far bank two great spotted figures galloping down toward the pool, and they heard in the distance a strange clattering noise.

The Pigman's head broke through the surface of the water. "Heeeelp!" he roared. "Heee-gurgle-glug!" and down he went again.

17

The Big Strange Bird

Back at Resthaven, things were looking up. To be more exact, pigs were looking up, at a big strange bird in the sky.

They had heard the bird before they had seen it, for it had a loud rattling voice, and they raised their heads and watched it appear over the eastern hills. It flew down the valley toward them, pausing over the mill with its ruined pond, and again over the farm buildings, now almost empty of water. Its glassy eyes twinkled in the bright sunlight, and its wings whirled above its body at great speed.

Suddenly it saw the herd in Resthaven, and it darted sideways toward the pigs and hovered above the little hill like some huge hawk, so low that they could feel the terrible wind of it. None of the pigs had ever seen a helicopter before, and they galloped around in panic. But the bird came no lower, so they gathered in a nervous huddle and watched as a hole appeared in its side and a brown object fell out of it.

"It's layin' eggs on us!" shouted Mrs. Grubguzzle in alarm, but before the words were out of her mouth, the brown object hit the ground and burst open. A familiar smell came wafting to the snouts of the herd, growing stronger by the minute as two, four, eight more sacks of pignuts were tipped from the door of the helicopter. Then it turned and slid away westward down the line of the brook.

When the helicopter reached the dam, the strangest scene met its glassy eyes. If it had really been a bird, it would have had the tallest of tall stories to tell to its children. As it was, of course, there were three men in it: the pilot, the observer, and the winchman. And in later years, when they had children of their own, old enough for storytelling, they all told the same tale to their goggle-eyed families.

It was during the Great Summer Flood, they said, when people and animals in that part of the country had been cut off from supplies. Alerted by the discovery of the yellow rain hat, they had been sent to an isolated pig farm and had found a herd of pigs and dropped food for them. Then—"And you'll never believe this," each said—they had come to a place where a big jumble of uprooted trees and other rubbish, including what looked like a shed, had dammed the stream and formed a big pool.

On one side of this pool stood two great spotted pigs. And flying above the pool was a black-and-white duck. And in the middle of the pool was a man—a huge fat man from what they could see of him—struggling madly in the water; they could hear nothing because of the noise of their helicopter, but they could see his mouth open in a shout for help before he went down again.

Then—"It's true, I promise you," each said—a little spotty piglet—"odd-looking thing with a head too big for its body and funny feet"—dived off the dam into the pool, swam—"yes, *swam*"—across it at tremendous speed, and seemed to say something to the two big pigs. They in turn put their heads down and tipped a piece of wood into the pool—"it was a fence post"—and the piglet lined it up so the sharp end was pointing at the struggling man —"Cross my heart." Then it swam around and pressed its snout to the blunt end—"Scout's honor." The duck landed on top of the stake and flapped its wings like mad—"Honest to goodness"—and the piglet swam like crazy, and the stake went whizzing across the pool like a torpedo, and they got to the man just as he was going down for the third time,

and he managed to grab the stake and hang onto it, and so the duck and the amazing swimming piglet saved his life.

"But is all that really true, Dad?" asked each of the families.

"Of course it is," said each father.

And, of course, it was.

"Saved my life, saved my life," babbled the Pigman as he lay on the floor of the clattering helicopter. "And to think I called 'em stupid and ignorant and horrible! And now see what they've done for me. I'll make it up to 'em, I'll make it up to 'em. You see if I don't."

"Yes, yes, old man," said the helicopter pilot

soothingly. "Just you relax and don't worry. We'll get you to the hospital right away."

"Hospital?" said the Pigman loudly, struggling to his wet feet. "I don't want to go to no hospital. You get me back to the farm. I've got a job to do. I've got to get everything ready for 'em. When they come home."

18

Missing

By evening the herd was comfortably full of food and the Pigman once again ragingly hungry. He stood beside the helicopter, which had landed in the yard, and stared at the concrete foundation where the shed had stood. He was shocked and soaked, and his sluggish brain was hardly working at all. What thoughts he had were all of eating. But not pig meat, not ever again, he said slowly to himself. Not ever again. Nor duck. Not after what they did for me. Not nohow.

And almost as though he were a mind reader, the helicopter pilot said, "You must be pretty hungry, old buddy. I mean, we had a good breakfast of bacon and eggs"—the Pigman shuddered—"but you probably haven't eaten for days. Have my sandwiches. They're Spam."

"I couldn't," said the Pigman in a low voice, and, thinking that he was too embarrassed to accept their hospitality, the observer said in a friendly tone, "Well, I can offer you something better than Spam, old buddy. Have mine. They're duck paste."

"Oh, I couldn't," said the Pigman, more miserable than ever.

"You're welcome to mine," said the winchman, holding out some large foil-wrapped sandwiches, "but they're nothing special."

"What are they?" asked the Pigman in a tremulous voice.

"Peanut butter," said the winchman, and then drew back in surprise as, with a great grunt of delight, the Pigman snatched the sandwiches from his hands, tore off the wrapping, and stuffed the whole wad in his mouth.

The helicopter crew watched silently as the Pigman chomped and chewed with his strong yellow tusks, his big nostrils flaring, his little eyes shut tight in ecstasy.

No wonder he's fat as a pig, thought the pilot.

Talk about greedy as a pig, thought the observer.

He sure looks like a pig, thought the winchman, as with a last snort of pleasure the Pigman finished the sandwiches and ran his tongue over his lips in search of crumbs.

And almost as though he were reading the crew's thoughts, the Pigman suddenly shouted, "Pigs!"

"What do you mean?" cried the pilot as all three of them jumped back nervously.

"Pigs. My pigs. Out there." The Pigman gestured toward Resthaven. "They must be starved. Got to get grub to 'em. Got to get my shed back somehow."

They explained to him that they had dropped some food. And then the pilot said, "That hut thing we sighted—where we pulled you out of the water —is that your shed?"

"That's her," said the Pigman.

"How did it get there?"

"She floated."

"Well," said the pilot, "how about our towing the thing back for you? If it floated down, it might float back. It's no use to you down there."

So they left the Pigman with dry clothing and lifted away downstream. On their way to the dam, they passed the black-and-white duck flying toward the farm.

Felicity landed on her perch in the alder tree and looked around. In the distance she could see the herd in Resthaven. They were lying in the sunshine, apparently contented. Beyond them, she could just make out the figures of the Squire and Mrs. Barleylove splashing homeward. The Pigman was hard at work sweeping the last of the water from the sties and bringing dry bedding straw from the top of the barn, where the flood had not reached it. He was a picture in navy blue overalls and boots. Everything's returning to normal, Felicity thought to herself. Except for the shed, but that's asking a bit much.

But it wasn't, for before long she heard the rattly voice of the big strange bird, and there beneath and behind it was the shed, stately as a galleon, coming slowly upstream on the end of a long towrope.

At the dam both winchman and observer had gone down the cable while the pilot hovered, and had fastened a rope under the shed as though tying a giant parcel. Now, close by Felicity's alder tree, the winchman released the towrope, refastened the cable to the top of the parcel, and raised his hand.

Gradually the shed rose out of the stream, timbers creaking, door swinging, sailed over the buildings, and was lowered, gently, exactly, onto its foundation. The rope was released and drawn up, and once again the helicopter dropped down into the yard.

"O.K.?" shouted the pilot to the Pigman. "All right now? All your pigs back?"

"I'll just check," yelled the Pigman, and he walked out into Resthaven.

Five minutes later he was running back, his big

face white and his fat cheeks wobbling.

"My dag! My little dag!" he shouted. "He hasn't come home!"

"Dag?" cried the pilot.

"Yes! The one who saved my life!" roared the Pigman, and tears came out of his piggy eyes and ran down his cheeks and over the hills and valleys of his three chins.

"Oh, is that what he's called?" yelled the pilot. "Well, don't worry, old man. We'll fly back and see where he is. He's probably swimming home." And away they went downstream again.

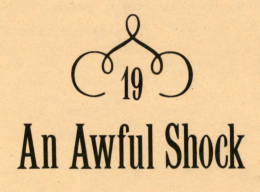

An Awful Shock

When the Squire and Mrs. Barleylove had started home from the dam, they had given Daggie permission to go on ahead of them. They did not believe he could come to any harm on the fast-drying bank. He's a big boy now, and sensible, they said to each other.

But like any adventurous youngster, Daggie decided to do not what he had been told but something much more exciting instead.

"Let them go home by land," he said loudly as soon as he was out of earshot. "I'm a swimming pig, and I'm going to swim home."

He hid himself until he saw the shed sailing by,

and until his mother and father had passed him and disappeared. Then he slipped into the water.

The current was still fairly strong, but he was confident he could swim against it. Still, he thought he would start in a quiet place, a deep inlet that was out of the main run of water. He glided out from the bank, but instead of going straight into his usual racing crawl, he decided to splash and play. He put his head under and found himself staring into a pair of cold, hard eyes, set behind narrow wolf jaws, and backed by a long barred body.

Before he could move, there was an explosion in the depths beneath him. He felt a violent blow that almost lifted him out of the water, and the pike clamped its jaws on the end of his snout.

In an agony of fear Daggie pulled back with all his strength, thrashing and flailing in the water as he tried to get free. But the pike was bigger than he, and stronger than he, and its cruel teeth were tight in his tender nose, and he could not breathe. Gradually he grew weaker, and gradually the fierce fish pulled him deeper, and his mind began to spin, and a whole series of faces flashed across it, all in a split second: his mommy's face, and the faces of his father the Squire, and his kind aunts, and the servant, and Felicity. And before his whirling senses became a blank, black emptiness, there sounded in his ear a thin, hard cry.

"I-zaak!" it seemed to say. "I-zaak!"

When Daggie Dogfoot came to, there was still a face in front of him,. But this time it was a real face, a live face, a round whiskery face wearing a look of deep anxiety. And out of it came a worried voice.

"Old pig! Old pig!" the voice said. "You're all right, aren't you? You're all right? Now don't say you're not, 'cause you are."

Daggie looked around him and found that he was lying in the grass on the bank of the brook. He spit out a lot of water and lay panting, his whole body shaking with shock.

"Ike!" he croaked. "Oh, Ike! What happened? What was it? Oh, my nose! And the back of my neck!"

"What happened, old pig," said Ike, "was that you came pretty close to being drowned and eaten, and don't say you didn't, 'cause you did. Your nose is sore because you've had a couple of dozen razor-sharp teeth stuck in it, and your neck's sore because I had to haul you out by the scruff."

"But what was it, Ike? What was that dreadful fish?"

"Pike," said Ike. "That was a pike, old pig."

"But it was so big," said Daggie. "I never knew they were as big as that. Felicity never warned me."

"She never knew either, old pig," said Ike. "That's the biggest one ever. Lived in the millpond and got washed out when the sluice gates burst. I've been dying to meet him, and now that I have, *he's* dying!" The otter threw back his head and shook with silent laughter.

Daggie staggered to his feet and looked down into the water. Floating there on its side was the long barred shape of the monster pike of the millpond, the wolf jaws split wide in the gape of agony caused by the otter's death bite. Between the dorsal fin and the tail was a terrible scooped-out gash.

"I broke his back, old pig," said Ike, standing beside the gazing piglet. "And don't say I didn't, 'cause I did. Now I'll pull him out and we'll eat the best of him. I'll be laughing all the way to the bank!"

20

"Not MIGHT, But CAN!"

Daggie was very, very full. He was also, suddenly, very tired, from the strain of all his adventures, and particularly from the shock of the last one. He flopped down on the bank and rolled over into a slight hollow, so that he lay on his back, all four legs stuck up in the air. Immediately he fell into the deepest of deep sleeps.

Minutes passed, and in the bright sunshine bees buzzed and a big fat bluebottle landed neatly on the staring eye of the dead pike.

Suddenly there came a wailing, mewing noise from the blue sky above, and Ike, looking up from the bushes where he was dozing, saw a solitary buzzard circling on wide wings over the sleeping piglet. It had come down from the hills, feeding on the carcasses of drowned sheep.

The otter knew that buzzards were carrion-eating cowards, and he had no fears for Daggie's safety. If his friend did not wake, he thought, he would give it a sudden awful shock. He grinned happily.

The buzzard dropped lower. It could see below what appeared to be a very dead animal, whose belly was blown up like a drum and whose legs stuck out stiffly. Moreover, its nose was caked with dried blood.

The scavenger prepared to land, but at that moment it heard a loud noise in the distance, and a big strange bird with twinkling glassy eyes and wings that whirled above its body came clattering downstream. The buzzard flew away with a cry of alarm, and even the bold Ike slid out of the bushes and into the water, where he lay with only his mask showing and watched. The helicopter checked and the crew peered down.

"There he is!" shouted the observer. "But dead as a doornail by the look of him. Something got the poor little thing. Look at the blood on his snout."

"We'd better pick him up," the pilot said.

"Death of a hero," said the winchman.

"Tell you what," said the pilot. "We can fly him

home in state. After all, he was the one and only swimming pig. Let's give him the grandest possible return to his last resting place."

"On the end of the rescue cable?" said the observer. "So that the mourning multitudes can pay their respects?"

"That's it," said the pilot. "Remember the old saying—'pigs might fly!'" The three young men grinned at each other.

"Well, let's make a good job of it," said the winchman. "I'll go down and strap him on—I can adjust the harness—and then I'll wait here and you can pick me up later when you've delivered him home."

So down went the cable with the winchman, and he fitted the straps around the small spotty body, thinking as he did so that the piglet could not have been dead long; he was so warm. He raised his hand, and the helicopter lifted gently away with Daggie Dogfoot dangling thirty feet below it.

Until that moment—and only Saint Anthony knows how—Daggie had remained in his deepest of sleeps. Through the cries of the buzzard and the rattling of the helicopter and even the harnessing of his body, he had slept on relentlessly. Indeed he had just begun to dream his old dream, of flying with his mother and father through a warm and milky sky, when the tightening of the straps and the rush of air at last wakened him to reality.

Twisting in the harness so that his little legs hung down, he saw below him, fast growing smaller, a man on the ground and an otter in the water, staring up at him. His ears flapped and his tail whirled, and in terrified surprise he kicked like mad with all four legs, his mouth wide open as he squealed with horror. The watchers, two above him, two below, could, of course, not hear his squeal, but they could see that the gallant hero was very much alive. Three of them grinned their relief and pleasure, and the fourth one laughed so much and rocked about so wildly that eventually he sank below the water and swallowed some mouthfuls.

But once he had come to his senses and understood that he was safely anchored to the great bird above, Daggie stopped feeling so panic-stricken and began to look around. Below him, as they gained height for the homeward run, the river became a stream and the stream a trickle. Great trees shrank to the size of thistles, and far below him the swallows flew in ignorance of the miracle above. He opened his mouth wide again, but this time the unheard squeal was of excitement, of happiness, of triumph!

"Pigs might fly!" shouted Daggie. "That's what

Auntie Gobblespud said. Not *might*, but *can*! This pig is flying! So look out, Auntie, look out, Father, look out, Mommy! WHEEEEEEEEEEEEEEE! Here I come!"

21

Home and Dry

Meanwhile, back at the farm, they were indeed looking out, every one of them. The Squire had brought the herd down into the yard and called the roll, and now everyone knew that Daggie was missing, Daggie, who had somehow saved them all by going for help, summoning the great clattering bird, bringing back the servant and his shed. They did not doubt that it was he who had now caused the waters to go down. Probably he could not only swim in them, but could walk on them, too. But would he? Would they ever see him again?

At the distant sound of the approaching helicopter, every head raised. At first they could make out

only the machine itself, coming up the line of the brook, a black dot in the eye of the westering sun. But as it drew nearer, they could see below it a small figure and knew themselves to be looking at still another miracle.

And now what rejoicing broke out among the Ploughbarrow herd! How the weaners waltzed and the store pigs sported and the fatteners frolicked!

"We love him!" shouted the eight aunts, shaking their floppy ears. "Isn't he the cleverest ever!"

"Oh, Squire!" cried Mrs. Barleylove. "What's happening? Surely Daggie can't really be flying?"

The great boar looked at her and then up at this amazing son of theirs kicking and flapping and twirling above them.

"By Saint Anthony!" bawled the Squire. "He's doing better than that, my dear. Must be something wrong with that thing, and the boy's towing it in, butchered if he isn't!"

Once above the buildings, the pilot made the helicopter describe a couple of tight circles so that Daggie was whirled around in much larger circles. Felicity flew up to greet him, but he was traveling so fast that she could only catch his squeals of excitement each time he flashed by her on this most marvelous of merry-go-rounds.

Now the helicopter was hovering, directly above the yard, directly above the figure of the Pigman in his new navy overalls, waiting anxiously below. Gradually Daggie's circles grew smaller and slower until at last he hung still. Gently, very gently, the pilot lowered the piglet. Gently, very gently, the piglet touched down. Gently, very gently, the Pigman came forward to release the straps of the harness. To do so, he had to kneel down, and the herd, of course, was duly impressed that at long last the servant was showing a proper degree of respect.

"Hey, you, Pigman. Scratch my back," said Daggie Dogfoot. And the servant, of course, obeyed.

Above them all, the pilot and the observer waved their final farewells before clattering away into the sunset to pick up the winchman and return to their base. And as their racket died away, a shrill, clear whistle pierced the evening air, and a long, low creature with a grinning whiskery face and a battery of sharp white teeth hauled out of the water near Felicity's alder and came to join the pigs.

Now everybody looked at the returned adventurer. And everybody saw his bloody nose, which only one of them knew the reason for. And everybody saw his curious puppy-like forefeet, which some of them knew about. But what everybody saw and everybody knew was that here in front of them was a brave hero, the only dag ever to be taken away and yet come back, who had risked his life on the swollen waters to swim for help. And that help had come, precious food from out of the skies, manna from heaven. Thanks to Daggie Dogfoot, they were all home and dry.

Then the herd turned and moved contentedly away to the familiar comfort of their sties and pens and the pleasant anticipation of a good supper to come. The otter slipped back into the brook and the duck followed him. Only Mrs. Barleylove and the servant still stood by the hero. The Pigman brushed a great hand across his face and sniffed a bit.

"Drat me!" he said softly, and "Dang me!" and "Blast me!" And he, too, turned away and went to prepare the meal.

"Happy, baby?" asked Mrs. Barleylove gently.

"Oh, yes," said Daggie, "but, Mommy, there's just one thing I'd like to do before bedtime. Can I have a swim?"

"Of course," said his mother, and together they walked down through Resthaven to the old pool below the high bank, where the water was almost back to its usual level. The kingfisher sat once again on his perching root, brilliant in the last light of the setting sun, and the rails murmured happily in the reeds. Two bathers were already in the pool.

"Coming in, Daggie?" called Felicity as she twirled and splashed in a shower of golden drops, but he was already gone, running to the top of the slope to prepare for the downhill take-off. "What about you, madam?" the duck asked mischievously. "Going to try it?"

"That'd be a sight to see," said Ike, "and don't say it wouldn't, 'cause it would!" and he opened his mouth very wide and rocked to and fro.

But Mrs. Barleylove wasn't listening. She gave an absentminded grunt and moved up the hill to the spot where the old oak had stood, her eyes on her son.

Daggie Dogfoot turned and began to run downhill at great speed, faster, faster, faster, till at last he leaped out over the high bank of the stream and disappeared from her sight. What clever things her brilliant baby was doing in his favorite element she could not see, but she could hear the joyful squeals and the fluty whistles and the soft quot-quot-quotting noises as he dived and splashed and raced with his friends.

And high above she could hear the cries of the homecoming crows as they circled in the warm air and marveled at the miraculous skills of the amazing swimming pig.

"Caw!" they shouted to one another in awestruck admiration. "Caw! Caw! Caw!"

About the Author

Dick King-Smith loves reading, writing, and, of course, pigs. Born in South Gloucestershire, England, he attended Marlborough College, then served with the Grenadier Guards. *Pigs Might Fly* is drawn from his 20 years of farming experience. He now teaches young children in a village primary school.

He and his wife have three grown children, four grandchildren, and live in a small cottage in Avon, England.

About the Illustrator

Mary Rayner has a weekend cottage in Daggie Dogfoot's countryside—Wiltshire, England. Born in Burma, she moved to England when she was eleven years old. She attended St. Andrews University and Chelsea School of Art. She has written and illustrated many children's stories, including several about pigs. Her drawings for *Pigs Might Fly* are based on the Gloucester Old Spot pigs in the children's corner of the London Zoo. She now lives in Surrey, England.